Political Ecologies of Cattle Ranching in Northern Mexico

Society, Environment, and Place

Series Editors: Andrew Kirby and Janice Monk

Political Ecologies of Cattle Ranching in Northern Mexico

Private Revolutions

Eric P. Perramond

The University of Arizona Press   Tucson

The University of Arizona Press
© 2010 The Arizona Board of Regents

www.uapress.arizona.edu

Library of Congress Cataloging-in-Publication Data

Perramond, Eric.
  Political ecologies of cattle ranching in northern Mexico : private revolutions /
Eric P. Perramond.
    p. cm.—(Society, environment, and place)
  Includes bibliographical references and index.
  ISBN 978-0-8165-2721-2 (hard cover)
    1. Farm management—Mexico—Sonora (State)   2. Ranching—Mexico—
Sonora (State)   3. Ranches—Management—Mexico—Sonora (State)   I. Title.
  S562.M6P47 2010
  338.1'76213097217—dc22   2009044276

Publication of this book is made possible in part by a grant from The Social
Science Executive Committee at The Colorado College.

15   14   13   12   11   10   6   5   4   3   2   1

This work is dedicated to the living, Brenda Corrales Corrales and Aurora Loera, and to the departed, Ricardo Loera (d. 1995), Orlando Loera (d. 2007), and Alejandra Corrales (d. 1996), *perlas del Río Sonora.*

Contents

Figures

Unless otherwise noted, all photographs are by the author.

Tables

Preface

Make everything as simple as possible, but not simpler.
—Albert Einstein

This book is a study of contemporary private ranches and ranchers in the state of Sonora, Mexico. It is based on long-term fieldwork, the bulk of which occurred between the years 1995 and 1997, with two return visits in 2002 and 2003 and archival work during the summers of 2006 and 2007. I keep in touch with a handful of ranchers, all of them profiled in this book, to get periodic updates about the Río Sonora and ranches in this valley of Mexico. Telephones and e-mail were helpful when ranches have passed on to the next generation. Observation, ethnography, field measurements, and informal conversations are the basis of this work. It is not a book I could have written ten or even five years ago, given that I was trying to understand a lifestyle and form of land use that has continually changed. It is not a work of history, in spite of my visits to several archives over the last ten years, because my interest is in land and water management decisions, actions, and contemporary ranching ecologies.

I neither defend nor condemn this livelihood and form of land use; a ranch owner, Miguel, pointed out the futility of such actions when he acknowledged that although previous family members had made mistakes, as he had, he was interested in doing better for his property. The question he put to me was simple: "What are we doing well and what are we doing wrong?" What I hope to have done is highlight the geographies, politics, and ecologies of private ranches while comparing and contrasting these with the other land management institutions of Mexico. The kinds of management decisions, actions, and daily tactics for herding have changed little over time and space. The numbers, economics, cattle breeds, and land-use strategies have changed. I hope this work comes close to answering Miguel's honest question.

I have written this book as much for students as for my colleagues in geography, environmental sciences, area studies, history, sociology, and anthropology. Clarity of expression and explanation is the emphasis, and I can only hope that ranchers and policy makers who might stumble upon this work will find a set of clear messages. Private ranchers are not a monolithic class of people; they act in wildly different ways, compete against each other, and simply think in contrasting ways. Traditionally, land tenure in Mexico has been reduced to a picture of communal versus private landownership. The binary has worked insofar as past writers have created a false dichotomy for explaining rural Mexico. But it does little to honor and explain the continuum of landholding arrangements in Mexico. Grasslands and rangelands are, of course, of concern to a wider pool of specialists and general interest. There is an extensive literature in "range science," largely using experimental methods, but little of it touches on the human dimensions of ranch management. In Mexico, range specialists spent a great deal of time on the specifics and applied knowledge for improving rangelands, yet paid little attention to the ranches or ranchers themselves. This attitude is slow to change. Ranchers across the Americas share much in common. I hope this book addresses some of the traditional shortcomings in scholarship on ranching without succumbing to, or repeating, past conventional wisdom.

Acknowledgments

First, thanks go to Bill Doolittle in the Geography Department at the University of Texas at Austin, who served as chair of my studies and dissertation, and who continues to serve as adviser and mentor long after my exodus from Austin. Second, I am grateful to the committee members who critiqued and carefully appraised a much older version: the late Terry Jordan, Francisco Pérez, and the late Robert C. West. Terry consistently asked, "When is this thing going to be a book?" and I only wish, in hindsight, that I had heeded his words earlier and before his untimely passing. Third, my fellow cohort of graduate students at the time was invaluable to my approach and perspective. This extended family has also kept the fires burning since graduate school. Andrew Miles and Rachel Waldinger provided an air-conditioned respite from Austin's heat during the summer of 2006, as I moldered in the welcome stacks of the Benson Library at the University of Texas at Austin; Taco XPress ensured that none of us forgot what was important.

Much of this work has been presented in a variety of forms at the annual meetings of the Association of American Geographers (AAG) and at the Conference of Latin Americanist Geographers (CLAG), with the latter group serving more constructive purposes in refining the perspectives and findings you will read in these pages. *¡Saludos a mis amigos CLAGistas!* Incidentally or not, several postgraduate school colleagues were crucial to the development of this work: Peter Klepeis, Paul Robbins, Eric Keys, and Rinku Roy Chowdhury.

Access to and from Sonora was greatly aided by a few folks, namely Diana Liverman and Bob Meredith, who generously allowed my pit stops with patience and great humor. Diana's input, suggestions, and critical probing pushed me to examine further some of the economic and structural constraints that play so heavily in the decision making of ranchers.

Institutional support during my extended stay of 1996–1997 was provided by the Centro de Investigación en Alimentación y Dessarollo, A.C., and especially by Ernesto Camou-Healy, Emma Paulina Pérez López, and Shooko Doode. I thank them all for their very generous help and hospitality during my days in Hermosillo.

My work has been funded by a variety of agencies, none of whom necessarily agree with, or should be held responsible for, my positions or statements: the Institute of International Education Fulbright-García Robles, the National Security Education Program Fellowship, the Tinker Foundation, the Institute of Latin American Studies, and the Center for Mexican Studies at the University of Texas at Austin.

Further funding for recent visits and work were obtained from the College of Arts and Sciences at Stetson University (2002–2003). But my current institution, Colorado College, has provided generous funding, from the Social Sciences Executive Committee in 2006 and 2008 to a generous Mrachek Fellowship during the summer of 2006. A mini-sabbatical during the winter of 2007–2008 provided time for the eventual transformation, and total rewriting, of this volume. Christine Szuter first courted the idea of this volume at the University of Arizona Press. But it needed some contemplative updating and another editor, Allyson Carter, to pry it from me. She bravely read through three complete versions of the manuscript in your hands. Two blind reviews on the first version of this manuscript and the valuable comments and suggestions of those reviewers have improved the quality of the work. Shortcomings and oversights that remain are my own doing. Jan Monk and Nathan Sayre were vital in providing early comments, feedback, and context for the work and audience I had in mind: students at a liberal arts college. Pat Cattani, the copy-editor extraordinaire, helped me avoid textual and graphical embarrassment during final production of this manuscript.

My new home base at Colorado College (CC) comes with a clutch of valuable colleagues who have shared their thoughts and critiques about my work. I am also back in the West, where such questions about landownership, land use, and range ecology actually matter to most folks. Anne Hyde has been unfailing in her collegial support and encouragement, maneuvering my schedule to allow for writing time and providing critical feedback on my first chapter. Anne, Mike Taber, and Sally Meyer made my teaching loads manageable and arranged it so that CC students in the environmental science program also got a first, if scrambled, preview of this work in progress during a seminar presentation in early 2006. The Hulbert Center for Southwestern Studies at Colorado College has been a cozy place to work; Kathy Kaylan, Suzi Nishida, and Maria Varela have all helped in one way or another, and they have my gratitude. David and Christina Torres-Rouff, Brian Rommel-Ruiz, and John Williams also made valuable comments as part of our writing cabal during 2007–2008.

I want to thank the many students at Colorado College and Stetson who read portions of this book or earlier versions: This book was written with them in mind and secondarily for colleagues. Both students and faculty colleagues urged me to make this work more comparative, and a summer institute on the environmental history of the Borderlands in 2009 has widened my perspective significantly. Working in this comparative context has helped me with teaching an often controversial form of land use, at least for some observers, without resorting to romantic or pessimistic notions of its future. The first two offerings of my Human Ecologies of the Southwest course at Colorado College led to several important changes and a sudden realization of who would most likely read this work. An informal presentation to the environmental science program at Colorado College also highlighted several missed opportunities in the previous version of this work. The students' questions and feedback exposed the weak logic and overreliance on jargon in past versions, and students are still my most dogged and valued commentators. Therefore, I hope that they will gain some insight and inspiration to continue work in the rich tradition of place-based human-environment research, regardless of their current majors.

Most important, I want to thank those people with whom I spent so much time, the panoply of Sonoran cattle ranchers, land managers, *ejidatarios*, ranch laborers, *chiltepín* pepper pickers, mescal makers, and Río Sonoran inhabitants: I can only hope that this work comes remotely close in describing their generosity and explaining the complexity of their lives. Although I have systematically used pseudonyms for all of the ranch owners, cowboys, laborers, and spouses in this book, there are exceptions. Two families helped me find my place in Baviácora, Sonora. The Loeras were the first to receive me and the last to see me off at every stay.

The generosity of the late Ricardo Loera formed the first connections to my stay in Sonora, and Aurora Loera, his widow, has maintained that first friendship. The relations of the Loeras, the Corrales, also provided me with my first true ranch experience in Sonora, one that did not end with my first visit in 1995. Brenda, Efraín, and Jesús Corrales Corrales guided the ways of an ignorant *gringo* for several months, gesticulating and playing neo-charades with me and my barbaric version of Spanish, before I was able to be largely self-sufficient in making introductions and gaining entry to other private ranches.

To Ann, who has lived through and helped with the thinking, writing, editing, and revisions, you have my love, my thanks, and my deepest respect. My parents, Daniel and Mary, and my brother Marc have always humored me with intellectual questions and maintained their patience in the darkest of personal times, here and abroad.

Political Ecologies of
Cattle Ranching in
Northern Mexico

1 The Secret Geographies of Mexican Cattle Ranching

We saw Don Benito just in time. He was making his way out of the Tecate shack as we drove by. I slowed and Miguel Sarella, in the passenger seat, called out to him.

"Hey, haven't you recovered yet from last night?" teased Miguel, a big grin on his face.

"God, I was so drunk last night I drove past town and was halfway to Sinoquipe!" shot back Benito.

Señor Benito is an infrequent visitor to Banámichi, as he prefers the company of his girlfriend in Hermosillo to that of the few remaining beasts on his ranch west of town. The years had cumulatively ruined the quality of his cattle herd, so Benito made the drastic decision to sell most of his herd to the first buyer he encountered in Hermosillo. So we were lucky to find him in town and away from the state capital that day. It gave us the chance to catch up, to see how he was doing and how his ranch was faring, even if he was eager to get home.

"My cows now have plastic and stickers surrounding them," he joked, referring to their probable fate in the supermarkets of Hermosillo.

Like many of his neighbors, Señor Benito viewed the years of drought in the early to mid-1990s in boom-and-bust terms, so that herds would return only if rainfall and the price of calves increased in the following years. He said he was storing his capital in a savings account and added, "until times get better, like they used to be for us. It hasn't been the same since . . . oh, maybe since Echevarría was president, when was that? I guess it was the late [19]70s, but prices just seem to get lower on the animals and everything else just keeps going up. Maybe we should just adopt the dollar as our money!"

His statement was one of my first introductions to cattle ranchers along the Río Sonora Valley, in the state of Sonora, Mexico (see fig. 1.1).

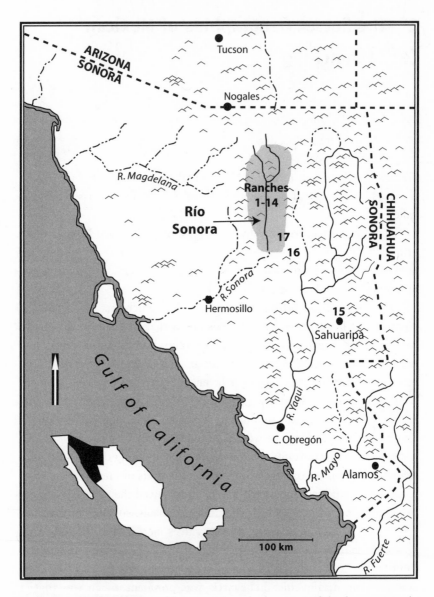

Figure 1.1 Regional map of Sonora. Note the location of the fourteen study ranches in the Río Sonora watershed, as well as the three additional ones outside it. (Cartography by Andrew Nelson; adapted from Perramond 1999)

My first reaction was to think, "great, I crossed a border to find that ranchers are also selling off their herds here, too." Don Benito, however, was largely an exception at the time. The valley is still cattle country, a semi-arid valley that presumes to support temperate-climate animal breeds, and cattlemen dominate the local economy and local politics. How they survived the era of agrarian reforms, when they fought back with their own measures, and what the future may hold for ranchers are the stuff of this work.

Ranching's Private Revolutions

To accurately render and explain a portrait of private cattle ranching in northern Mexico, the content of this book is both thematic and regional. Readers will note certain humanistic, ecological, and political-economic undertones throughout the volume. I never intended to write a case study, so I hope my audience will understand what is important to this book and what is not. I am neither a booster nor an opponent to ranching in general. The industry of cattle ranching was never about efficiently using land or water resources, until such rhetoric developed in the twentieth century. Ranching is, at least for rural elites, rather about power and possession of the landscape, and reflects the long history of unsettled territoriality in northern Mexico (Truett 2006). Yet it remains only one form of a long and rich historical tradition of using domesticated livestock for human livelihoods. While ranching retains some of the features inherited from the longer experience of pastoral nomads, such as the movement of livestock, ranching is a practice, a lifestyle, and an industry firmly rooted in particular places and regions. Arguably, it has reached its apogee in the Americas.

Accommodation, conflict, and revolutions have all wrought a fractured landscape in this part of the Americas. Ranches are both agro-pastoral and industrial sites of activity. And ranchers play to both contexts, referring to past nostalgic and bucolic imagery (when advantageous) and to the role of cattle in "productive, industrial" development in the state of Sonora. Grazing lands with livestock is a way to turn a profit from photosynthesis in a region that offers little in the way of economic employment.

The well-known Mexican Revolution of 1910–1917 is the foundational example used in many works about Mexican society. However, the private revolutions of landowners—their reactions to land reforms sparked by the larger Mexican Revolution—are poorly documented. As the opening snippet hints, ranching is also a difficult way to make a living in Mexico; the challenges to ranchers are legion. Add aridity, an unpredictable climate, and shifting economic winds, and the Río Sonora Valley, centrally located in the state of Sonora, is a sensitive template and product of human occupation and natural processes. This Sonoran river valley has been converted into an ecological life-support system for temperate-climate improved cattle breeds, with most field agriculture dedicated to the intensive planting of improved feed crops for these animals.

Cattle dominate the Sonoran landscape like no other occupation, industry, or animal, as is common in most semi-arid zones that have some measure of grassland. No wonder so much strange, rural lore involves cow abductions by aliens; extraterrestrial visitors might be tempted to think cattle are the dominant species on the planet given the amount of space they occupy. While sheep are present in the state, they are by far in the minority; this is cow country, even if the obsession with fine, local, fast horses reaches sometimes epic proportions. Ranching's legacy is visible in the dry stubble-clumps found intermittently between various species of cacti. Ranching mythology is also ripe in the mind of Sonorans, Mexicans, and their American neighbors to the north. And since the 1940s, these desert rangelands have been increasingly fenced and demarcated as ranchers and landowners enclosed the open range. The dilemma of contemporary ranchers, increasingly squeezed between the demand for low meat prices and regional climates that are often fickle at best, is well known throughout North America (Bennett 1969). But what do we truly know about these private ranches? Perhaps more important, what is the future for this industry, for these families, and for this way of life?

Intent and Motives

This book has three major purposes, with notable aspects that distinguish it from past studies. First, I will explain how private ranching in northern Mexico has evolved from a method of land control and controlling territory, to an industry, and finally to become part of the bucolic fabric of Mexico with its own nostalgic capital. The caricature of ranchers with "black hats" in Mexico is a familiar one to social scientists who have so often used private landowners as the bad guys, literally, in narrative strategies. But there is no single kind of ranch or rancher in Mexico, or in North America for that matter, and not all of them are men. I hope to explain that the range, or continuum, of ranches as spaces and of ranchers as people is far more complex than some past work would have it.

Second, I will detail the management and labors expended on different private ranches, and explain why land and resource management vary so sharply. Ranchers do not think alike and take vastly different approaches to managing land, water, and cattle. There is an assumed and presumed advantage for large ranch owners: somehow they have figured out a "better" way to manage their properties, and this belief is echoed in the narratives of local private ranchers and their communal counterparts who graze the marginal commons, known as *ejido* lands, close to town. Why is this belief so strong? Does it have any merit? The empirical chapters of this work treat the management, economic and ecological, of these ranches to see if this conventional wisdom passes muster or is yet another example of rancher mythology. The complicating factor, in this case, is that many ranchers do not directly manage their land and water. Instead, they have local labor, cowboys and ranch hands who are directly charged with the physical responsibilities for herd management, fence repair, and road maintenance. Small ranch owners rarely have this luxury and are more directly involved with ranch tasks.

The third and final thrust of the volume is aimed at adding complexity to the literature on human uses of natural resources and the presumed, supposed, or clear struggles that occur because of them. As a geographer, I hope to clarify the spatial connections, complexities, and common themes of cattle ranching. With few exceptions, we have generally ignored the topic and the time-space dimensions of this livelihood, this industry, and the people who manage and own these private ranches. Analyzing resource struggle and use through the lens of political economics is now much more common in anthropology, geography, and political science, though most of the work is more focused on the political. Most contemporary studies about the access, rights, and struggles over resources are, strictly speaking, about the political economy of natural resource access and use. Little ecological explanation or complexity enters the calculus, and even less work treats ecology as a serious notion to be engaged with a larger body of human-environmental scholarship (Turner 1997; Zimmerer 2000).

In other words, in the cast of characters, nature is rarely a protagonist or central player. Most likely, this omission is caused by two factors: First, most scholars of natural resource struggle were highly influenced, educated, and in some cases inculcated in the peasant studies and Marxist literature of the 1960s and 1970s. Second, this strain of political economy analysis has been enriched by post-structural analyses and continental theories. Unfortunately, this work has occasionally lurched to the point where many of my colleagues and writers speak of either the "death of Nature" or at least the sublimation of it in new and awkward hybrid forms (Whatmore 2002). As a global perspective, and on a theoretical level, I find much that is compelling about this kind of work. It does argue against simple binaries and false dichotomies of culture/nature, us/them, and black/white, thus avoiding the "Manichean logic" that has also been prevalent in the literature on ranching (Starrs 2002, 4). On the ground, in a specific place, I find it leaves much to be desired. It can also be impenetrable as a literary style.

Readers will thus find a mix of cultural lore, individual stories, as well as the larger political and economic explanations that have to be recounted to make sense of ranching as an industry and a way of life that is important to people who practice it. And unlike some of these studies, this study will illustrate that struggles involving natural resources are cursed and riddled with a variety of prepositional conflicts: conflicts about resource use, conflicts about access, arguments over the nature of the resource itself, and the worldview conflicts and negotiations between so-called local versus so-called expert knowledge systems (following Kull 2004). Simply put, the plurality of conflicts and concessions and the continuum of land-tenure diversity cannot be simplistically reduced to binaries of "either/or" or "communal versus private" owners. And it certainly is not just about conflicts over access to resources. Language, rhetoric, and everyday ideology matter not only for explanation, but also to those who practice specific ways of framing their challenges. Ranchers employ their own lexicon for this, as do local farmers, and so do local politicians.

I have thus used the plural "political ecologies" in the title because there is no single "political ecology" for ranching anywhere, as if it were a single "ecology" in movement, flow, or outcome.[1] Each ranch has its own distinctive political ecology, caught in a larger cultural landscape of neighboring ranches and regional decision making. I have not abandoned generalizations, conclusions, or comparative findings that may be useful elsewhere. Few ranchers are able to make a healthy living from ranching alone, and the evolution of this livelihood has developed along similar lines common to other regions of the Americas. Fewer still ranch for wealth; indeed, much of what remains today is a pale comparison to the lifestyle ranching afforded decades ago. Starting a ranch from scratch as a new owner or merely continuing to ranch a long-held family property is a profoundly personal, political, and cultural statement. This view does not imply economic ignorance or naïveté. Economic diversification, worshipped and reified on Wall Street, is also the name of the game in Mexican ranching today. But this complexity in diversification is rarely found in existing scholarship.

I give specific attention to landscape change, the changing dynamics of local knowledge about ranches and ranching, and the local contexts within the regional network of agricultural connections. Landscapes are a central concern for most geographers, anthropologists, and archaeologists because of the observations we make on the ground (Olwig 1996, 2002). They also must be taken as serious, material reflections and products of what humans do in particular places, even if the scale of analysis is occasionally problematic for ecological research (Allen 1998; Sayre 2005a). Even if the scale or level of landscape analysis matters little to ecology and environmental processes, which is debatable, it is important precisely because it is an anthropocentric concept.[2] Humans not only produce landscape change materially, they produce it conceptually as a mental construct because it is our scale of existence, vision, and movement (Sluyter 2002; Robbins 2004).

The focus of this work is to explain and convey the impacts of private land managers, state officials and policies, ecology, and economics on cattle ranching in Sonora, Mexico. I examined small, medium, and large ranches during the course of my research, which began in 1995, resumed in September 1996, and continued through November 1997, with return visits in 2002 and 2003. A more explicit description of the various research methods employed in this book are given in appendix B. My approaches were both quantitative and qualitative: the former were needed to understand the micro-dynamics of ranches, decision making, and labor; but the latter were necessary to explain much of the behavior and action witnessed and described. The lack of qualitative studies in range science, in fact, has been one of the primary stumbling blocks in understanding how management can vary among private ranchers and what their motivations are in making different decisions and following variable courses of action (Sayre 2004).

My intention with this book is to make the case for seemingly straight-forward arguments that articulate three concerns. The first is that ranchers are not a homogenous, monolithic class of landowners who think and act alike. They are much maligned yet poorly understood by schol-ars working in the social and natural science realms, cast as either socio-economic oppressors or environmental predators. In the social science literature, particularly the work based in Latin America, ranchers are depicted as working in concert against communal forms of land tenure. They have typically been cast in this role, in either straw person argu-ments or as the other side of simplistic binary arrangements and argu-ments. In complementary fashion, ranchers in ecological science papers are cast as the primary agents of deforestation and soil erosion, and increasingly, as the purveyors of exotic grasses in the Americas. One would think that academic disciplines most closely associated with cattle ranching would have a better understanding and gauge on the industry, but this is rarely the case. In range science, for example, the conventional wisdom has been that private producers will choose the best practices available, as perfectly rational human beings trying to maximize profit (Sayre 2004, 668). We now know this assumption is not the case, after decades of studies. Yet the dominant strands of research within range science have focused on such minutiae that most findings are of little import or interest to the field practitioners, the ranchers themselves. In Mexico, scholars of the ejido system have largely reflected the commu-nal bias or perspective at the cost of private ownership, even as state agencies and extension agents have played on the myth of the perfectly rational rancher.

Social scientists and, to a lesser extent, natural scientists have largely focused their research efforts on the communal forms of landownership in Mexico: the *comunidad* and the ejido. While a comunidad is recognized as a village or community that pre-dates the Mexican Revolution (1910–1917), the ejido is a product of that revolution, a communally distributed grant of land made by the Mexican government. Specific to Mexico, the ejido has held the imagination of generations of scholars. What amounted to one of the first, truly successful, redistributive land and resource programs in Latin America endured for decades, only tapering off in the 1970s. Much less attention has been paid to elite landscapes, more specifically the effects of rural elites in shaping past and current relationships in Mexico, excepting some works in the field of history.[3]

The pseudo-socialist noblesse oblige of the Mexican government went into a coma during the 1980s and was shelved in the early 1990s, as President Salinas de Gortari, in concert with a whole host of previous reforms and measures such as the North American Free Trade Agreement (NAFTA) and the General Agreement on Tariffs and Trade (GATT), effectively signed the "death sentence" of the ejido system. At least, that description was the conventional, academic wisdom of the ejido's fate. The assumption was that the ejido would be lost, privatized, sold off in bits and pieces to private landowners. As affairs in the state of Chiapas, Mexico, have shown, the struggle between communal and private concepts of ownership is slow to disappear. Following the January 1994 micro-revolution in Chiapas, a new wave of private land invasions, with subsequent communalization efforts on these areas, occurred in the wake of rural violence as neo-Zapatistas once again claimed a high ground for agrarian reform (Harvey 1998; Collier and Quaratillo 2005). Among the landowners who lost terrain and territory in Chiapas were cattle-ranch operators (Bobrow-Strain 2007).

Private ranchers as a whole, alternately threatened or protected by the various administrations in Mexican history, fared comparatively well in the twentieth and into the twenty-first centuries. While it is surely true that a small percentage of the Mexican population controls the majority of land and water resources, it is just as true that the majority of private landowners do not live the lavish lifestyles of the true, landed elite in Mexico. It is difficult to remember that class, as a concept, is always relative to the context of the society. Our conventional wisdom and scholarship thus poorly capture the processes and realities of landownership in Mexico. Few have written convincingly about *ejidatarios* becoming private landowners, much less private ranch owners, despite this being a common occurrence. Few have treated with any depth the practice of joint ownership (*condueñazgo*), or extended family owners, that begin to muddy the dichotomous waters of "private" versus "communal." Joint ownership has been ignored, perhaps, because it does not fit the neat categories of the literature. Indeed, as I hope to make clear, land tenure is a continuum, not the binary function of private versus communal so apparently enforced in our popular and even academic conceptions of landownership in Mexico.

Picking a Ranching Space

This study could have been completed in any region of Mexico. If there are distinctions to be made for an "arid lands" approach to this research, Sonora then becomes a logical choice, and the state shares much in common with the struggles and tribulations of ranchers in other semi-arid climates. Private ranches in Sonora have long been influenced, shaped, and occasionally powered by affairs bleeding across the national border. They face the same kinds of risks as ranches in Arizona, or Texas, or New Mexico. At the local level, ranching is a form of livelihood that is envied, and in Mexico the contrasts between qualities of life can be striking. Communal farmers and ranchers express jealousy and resentment about the resources held or enjoyed by the private owners who do, typically, own more animals and have direct control over their titled lands. The history of social relations in the Río Sonora Valley has largely been driven by the complex set of relationships among landowners, the landless, comuneros, ejidatarios, miners, American prospectors, and capitalists—all have sporadically dipped into this dry land for livelihoods that have been, and remain, profoundly unequal (Hart 2002). In contrast to other parts of Mexico with a more recent history of land or agrarian conflict, however, Sonora has been remarkably peaceful for decades. Ironically, little overt violence is visible in this state that fomented much of the early activity leading to the Mexican Revolution.

That private ranches survived the era of Mexican revolutionary land redistribution projects is remarkable to some, and Sonoran ranchers fared especially well, given the special dispensations accorded to them because of the semi-arid climate and sparse vegetation (Bantjes 1998). The power variously flexed by the militant land reformers and the landless, sometimes collectively referred to as *agraristas,* and the private landowners determined most of the Río Sonora Valley's dilemmas in the latter half of the twentieth century. Again, ranchers defended their large landholdings, and only foreign-owned estates and ranches were affected disproportionately by agrarian reforms and land redistribution. Yet while biophysical landscapes and livelihoods are frequently mapped and spatially explained by geographers, power rarely is, and this last element is crucial to understanding and explaining private ranching in Mexico.

For example, for the first few months of fieldwork, I was struck by how different the arrangements of land tenure in Mexico were from those typical in the United States. In contrast to U.S. private ranchers who must ask for public lands grazing permits, their Mexican counterparts have long enjoyed a greater measure of autonomy in decision making, as Mexican ranchers enjoy outright title ownership. Courtney White (2006, 20), an American conservationist, director, and co-founder of the Quivira Coalition in New Mexico, has termed the U.S. system a "federal commons." In much of Mexico, there is no "federal commons" component to private grazing; communal lands are held by specific individuals with specific access rights and obligations under federal ownership rules and understandings. Private ranchers in the United States are subject to federal regulation because of the permit structure. In Mexico, while the communal farmers and ranchers are subject to the federal ejido structure, private ranchers successfully fended off much of the federal interference that could have resulted from the Mexican Revolution.

Arguably, Mexico's institution of the ejido is a federal commons, as land that was owned or expropriated by the federal government and redistributed during land reforms in the early twentieth century. But this program did not apply to all private landowners at the time. A minority of landowners were affected by federal expropriation of private lands. At the same time, as Mexico's agrarian reforms were placing new resources in the hands of poor residents, they also made important concessions for small private enterprise. The term *small* was open to interpretation, and some large, landed estates survived the post-revolutionary land distribution reforms in Mexico. Today, however, private ranchers in Mexico have no analogue to U.S. ranchers in dealing with "the state" for grazing access, even if many of them have long viewed the ejido as an enemy to private property or resources. So the issue of "private power" and "public access" or the wider common good is completely different in Mexico and requires some distinctive explanations. Instead, the local conventional wisdom voiced in Sonora centers on the assumed superiority of private ranches. In many ways, this opinion is shared across the many ranching cultures of the Americas.

The Cultural Context of Ranching

If you travel around the western United States, you will likely find that almost everyone has an opinion about cattle ranching, whether they know anything about it or not. These views are typically strong, polarized, and rarely calm or reasonable. Most of my peers either like ranches as places or hate "ranching" as a practice, depending on their worldview. This attitude is a product peculiarly "American" in nature, in that the long-standing conflict between ranchers and public lands agencies in the United States has shaped or distorted public knowledge, even if the relationship is completely misunderstood (Merrill 2002). This conflict is, frankly, one of the main reasons I chose not to do this study in, say, Texas or New Mexico. The possible difficulties in doing so were brought home during some tentative ranch visits in the mid-1990s, just as I was starting to think about this larger project. During an early visit to a ranch outside of Austin, Texas, one ranch hand looked at me after about fifteen minutes of polite conversation and asked: "So, do you like beef, or are you some kind of Austin vegetarian that hates ranching?" Indeed, chicken and pickles are frequently on the "vegetarian" menu in many a Texan barbeque joint.

The binaries of carnivore/vegetarian, us/them, and public/private have been difficult to work through in many rangeland communities. Working in Mexico was no less difficult and no less conflicted, but it was clear the "private ranches versus public lands" debate could be largely avoided. If

Sonoran ranchers were suspicious of my presence, it was not because of dietary preferences, but because of my national origin and the purpose of my long visits. As anyone with a long-term field experience can attest, it took several months of living within the community before questions of the Central Intelligence Agency (CIA), Federal Bureau of Investigation (FBI), or Drug Enforcement Agency (DEA) were settled to local satisfaction. Even then, some local folks were never quite sure why a gringo academic would bother to study a struggling ranching industry in the middle of a desert.

It would be disingenuous to say that no progress has been made in the debate on U.S. public lands grazing; witness, for example, the Quivira Coalition in New Mexico, an organization founded on a new vision for cooperative forms of ranching. Several authors have also argued against the past, simplistic assumptions inherent within the ranching debate, notably Paul Starrs (1998, 2002) and several colleagues based at land-grant institutions that typically work with rural producers (e.g., Knight, Gilbert, and Marston 2002). For them, and rightly so, it is about reforming institutions and the larger structure of federal rules and regulations. Thus, there is no shortage of views on ranching, especially cattle ranching, in both academic and popular press circles. Ranching is a complex industry embroiled in academic and societal dispute. Folklorists, ranchers, and local historians view this livelihood as a rich vein of regional and national culture and identity, while ecologists and environmentalists typically view cattle ranching as a rogue land-use practice (see Fleischner 1994 and Wuerthner and Matteson 2002, for example). Ranching has been blamed for soil erosion, tropical deforestation, rural inequalities in land tenure, and the unethical treatment of animals for industrial purposes.

But ranching, as a cultural lifestyle, has also been praised for its emphasis on individuality and for preserving large, open tracts of grasslands in countries that are increasingly losing farm and grazing lands. And there is no lack of appreciation by those who view ranchers as one of the heritage "folk," a valued subculture in many countries of the Americas (Jordan 1993). What is the Argentine Pampas without the *gaucho*? What is the western United States without the image of the cowboy? The thought of rural Mexico without the ubiquitous *vaquero* seems at odds with the bucolic landscapes and folklore that surround this livelihood and lifestyle.

Russell (1993) has described this mind-set as a "battle of mythologies" as the new American West faces new forms of conflict over the character of Western natures. So ranching (and ranchers) is both politically charged and culturally valued; it is not a matter of choosing "whether" culture or politics explains everything because both are needed for understanding how the cultural lifestyle and the economic livelihood fit into the larger landscape.

Ranching has endured and evolved, both as an industry and as a way of life, for millions of Latin Americans. Regions of the Americas have supported domesticated livestock for centuries. Northern Mexico is one such region, where ranching occupies the greatest land base of any industry and where it has a long history. Most of this land, in turn, is held in a variety of small to large private ranches. Sonora was itself one of the hotbeds of revolutionary fervor in the beginning of the twentieth century. What distinguished the region, and the state specifically, was that much of this early "revolutionary" foment was generated from upper-middle-class landowners. For multiple and complex reasons, these northern Mexican patriarchs, many of them ranchers, were as eager as their southern counterparts to get rid of long-time dictator Porfirio Díaz, who ruled Mexico largely uninterrupted between 1876 and 1911. The reasons for doing so, again, were different. Northern Mexicans were far more conservative in their conception of what might follow the overthrow of Díaz. Ranches and ranch owners did host a large number of revolutionaries and revolutionary activities during the unsettled early twentieth century.

In Mexico, private ranches have survived and indeed prospered through the country's multiple revolutions. From the Mexican Revolution of 1910–1917, and during the era of agrarian reform, private landowners found new ways to hide property and resources. During and after the Green Revolution of the 1950s–1970s, ranchers benefited from the new injection of capital and technology inputs, and many found themselves ahead of their communal brethren. The more subtle, if not hidden, Brown Revolution slowly emerged as a real consequence of the Green Revolution: this Brown Revolution, also known in Mexico as "cattleization" (*ganaderización*), converted food-producing areas to livestock-feed producing areas. The more recent, ambivalent, neo-liberal revolution has been slowly turning back or privatizing the past efforts of Mexico's land reforms. Each of these transition or eruptive epochs yielded increasingly subtle changes to Mexico's rural countryside, and Sonora did not escape them.

From brute, physical violence and rural near anarchy during the Mexican Revolution to the slow, steady erosion of agricultural commodity price supports in the latest neo-liberal era, private ranching has survived. But this livelihood is struggling, as ranchers attempt to cope with market demand and fluctuations, with climate uncertainty, and with the lingering resentment toward Mexico's enforced structural adjustments that have touched far-flung locations for the past twenty-five years. So while private ranches and their owners have warded off the majority of land reforms in semi-arid Sonora, the lack of meaningful analysis as to their past and current resource management is a striking lacuna in a literature otherwise replete with a range of polarized findings and opinions (Sayre 2004).

While animal science and range science are well-established literatures in both English and Spanish, the majority of the research pursued is logically reductionist and quantitative, focused on limited sets of specific questions. By reductionist, I mean that countless range science studies will take two or three "factors" and try to correlate or test these against each other, such as soil erosion and its relationship with a particular grazing regimen. Controversial or insightful correlations then breed another dozen or so studies, all testing that relationship, without much attention to other factors that may affect the actual correlation. This research is valuable from a basic science perspective, although little of the findings are scaled up or useful to producers and other scholars of rangelands. In many ways, then, these fields reflect the obsession to understand the natural resources that aid or obstruct range and animal science goals, rather than an attempt to understand how human behavior and the link between humans and livestock movements may determine the response of those natural resources. For too long, the land sciences have been closely influenced by the field of economics, with little influence from the fields of anthropology, geography, or history.

Geographic and human-ecological components are sorely lacking in the range science literature. As a result, a constellation of land-use and -management practices has been virtually ignored, despite the fact that most landscapes are devoted to grazing livestock (Sayre 2004). Anthropologists have paid some attention to the grazing practices, movements, and institutions of nomadic pastoralists in semi-arid locations (e.g., Barfield 1993), but have had less interest in the industrial version of the pastoralist: ranching. There are notable exceptions to this general rule (cf., Ingold 1980; Sheridan 1988, 2007; Sayre 1999, 2002). To call modern-day cattle ranching a form of sedentary pastoralism seems, at best, wishful. At worst, it ignores the reality of the livelihood; it is one of the strangest forms of rural industry. Unlike pastoral brethren more dependent on long-distance mobility, ranching and its fixity were more concordant and agreeable to most forms of nation-state governance: ranchers could be located, taxed, and pinned on a map. Even in the twentieth century, developing countries yearned to fix the boundaries of traditional, pastoral-nomadic cultures using livestock. Encouraging the establishment of "ranches," understood to be fixed enterprises easily located on a map, was one of those efforts underwritten by development agencies as well (Taylor 2005, 108). As ranching still occupies the vast majority of remaining grasslands throughout the Americas, its presence remains formidable, and yet the diversity of its practitioners should not be underestimated.

In a study of the former Buenos Aires Ranch in southern Arizona, Nathan Sayre (2002) has demonstrated the effects and transitions of cattle ranching, as the Borderlands region in general is witness to an historical shift of landscape values, away from extraction and toward conservation values. These same processes, while distinctive to the U.S. side of the border, are slowly gaining traction in Mexico, as nongovernmental organizations begin to exert influence on the aesthetics of landscape in Sonora. One of the largest nature preserves in Sonora is the Ajos-Bavispe National Forest and Wildlife Refuge area located near the U.S.–Mexico border, a partnership between a Sonoran nongovernmental organization and the Nature Conservancy. It is still unclear whether the appeal of conservation in Mexico will reach the proportions discussed in Sayre's work, but there are clear indications that what people "value" in a landscape are changing. The environmental perceptions of Sonorans, of course, vary tremendously and have always changed in accordance with the historical flow of information, ideas, and values. How they perceive these changes in the land, climate, and plants is complex but roughly conditioned or influenced by both material and conceptual ideas of nature.

What is clearer is how they hope, with every ranching generation, to reproduce the ranch lifestyle in this region of northern Mexico.

Producing Rangelands in the Greater Borderlands

The Río Sonora region has no extensive, speculative housing frontier, unlike other places draped along the international borders of the Greater Borderlands; there is no competition here between cows and condos (Sheridan 2001). What has occurred is the first step toward a revaluation of the ranching and distinctively Sonoran landscape, as some private ranches convert themselves from the calf-cattle market to one serving the interests of hunters. Urban-dwelling hunting enthusiasts have been rare in northern Mexico, but are increasingly common, with a majority crossing the border from the United States in search of their prize trophy. Bird-watching as a form of rural recreation has also been rare in Mexico, and yet here too, a steadily increasing stream of visitors to Sonora is bringing a new form of landscape and wildlife aesthetic to the functional, agrarian landscape values that still dominate. These new facets to ranching are not without controversy, even in Mexico.

Sayre (2002) has thus referred to the mixed forms of valuing old and new landscape uses in his discussion of the "species of capital." This conceptual device can be read both ways: that new species are competing with the old ones for new forms of speculative "capital," and also that the very forms of capital change over time, from agrarian to industrial to post-industrial conceptualizations. The Río Sonora region has yet to capture the interest of most global conservation organizations. But the aesthetic-symbolic constructions of a Sonoran "ecosystem" are beginning to impinge, in a way that will make conservation-development questions in this part of the Borderlands thorny and contentious in the future, similar to the debates occurring elsewhere in Latin America (Zimmerer 2006). So I use this region as a regional coda to compare and highlight the similarities and differences in ranching, and to examine how this livelihood has fared in national and transnational discussions. The "state," whether federal or state-level, still matters, of course. But ranchers in Sonora share remarkably similar concerns with their counterparts in Arizona, California, and New Mexico, logically, as ranchers on both sides of the border have flexibly coped with climate, revolutions, and changes in land tenure.

Ranching in Sonora

Extractive industries, such as mining, forestry, and livestock grazing have long been at the heart of livelihoods in Sonora. This is still true in modern Sonora, even as the blossoming coastal cities of Hermosillo, Ciudad Obregón, and Guaymas have added commercial, industrial, and service industries. As a component of the economy, the extractive industries are a steadily shrinking percentage, and in particular, field agriculture and livestock now form a miniscule portion of the state's economic products. However, ranching still occupies large portions of Sonora's space, with little labor and little so-called added value to the economy. Ranching's legacy is also visible in the landscape, local and regional, and reflects the long historical geography of human impacts in the region. The lack of clean, continuous historical sources makes it difficult to assess the long-term ecological impacts of grazing (alone), yet Sonora's experience with cattle ranching is similar to that of Arizona's (Bahre 1991). The lack of water resources and arable lands certainly made cattle ranching one of the few options for inhabitants of the Sonoran Desert and the foothill regions of the Sierra Madres, known as La Serrana (West 1993). Residents do, of course, supplement traditional agrarian occupations with wild collection of plants and mescal-making (Nabhan 1985; Burwell 1995).

But why focus on Sonora? The state is among the top five producers of livestock in Mexico. It has an arid to semi-arid climate, a trait shared with the other extensive cattle-raising areas of the world. In terms of climate and vegetation, the state is in no way exceptional; it shares features with states both within northern Mexico and those that share the common border in the United States. Culturally, there is great similarity on both sides of the border (Griffith 1995).Thus, in this case and indeed along the other border states of Mexico, geography matters. The longtime dictator of Mexico, Porfirio Díaz, once wryly commented on "poor Mexico," in that it was so far from God and so close to the United States. That proximity made it one of the first trial areas for the so-called improved cattle breeds imported during the mid-twentieth century as the livestock version of the so-called Green Revolution took root in Mexico. Because of the proximity, Sonora has also actively linked their regional cattlemen's association with its counterparts in Arizona as a way to encourage interaction and technology exchange. These changes have been swift and sudden. Although barbed wire was being used as early as the 1900s on some private ranches, most pastures within private ranches were unfenced until the late 1970s. This trend was common not only in Sonora but throughout northern Mexico as ranchers first prioritized separation from communal grazing areas, and only later considered separate grazing spaces within their own estates. Even during my long-term study period, private pastures were still being divided and devised for rotational grazing, reflecting the ongoing decision making and spread of this simple but influential technology. Simply put, Sonora's ranches were still in the midst of transformation, whereas most U.S. ranches underwent this process decades ago. No "stages of ranching culture" statement is being made here, no implicit assumption that these ranch outfits are somehow lost in time or stuck in the colonial period; rather, the challenges are simply different for Sonoran ranches, cowhands, and the owners of these spreads.

The Study Area

The Río Sonora Valley is like many of the regional watersheds in central and eastern Sonora, with its north–south drainage and transverse mountain ranges separating the thin, green ribbons of irrigated land and riparian vegetation found only along the major surface waters of the state (see fig. 1.2). In this work, I chose seventeen study ranches, and their owners and laborers were intensively studied and monitored. Most of the attention was squarely on this valley with a few exceptions: three ranches that were outside of the Río Sonora drainage. Two of these were just due east in the intersecting range between the Sonora and the Moctezuma rivers. The other was farther distant, found in the town of Sahuaripa (see fig. 1.1), and yet provided real contrast because of its location and special set of challenges.

The Río Sonora Valley has characteristics that were appropriate in a study of private ranches. Five of the top 25 *municipios,* or townships,

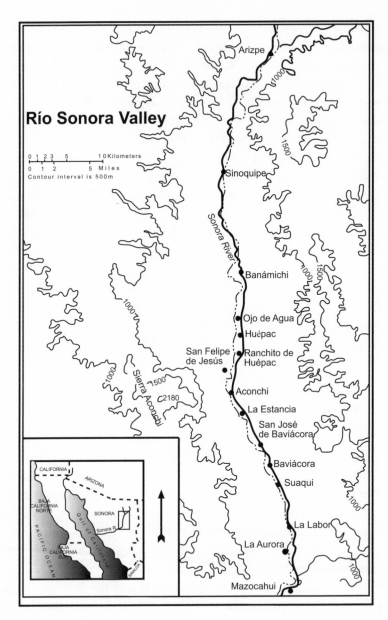

Figure 1.2 The Río Sonora Valley. The solid line is the main paved road. The thinner line, occasionally dotted, is the mighty Río Sonora, which is ephemeral and seasonal during the spring and summer. (Cartography by Andrew Nelson; adapted from Perramond 1999, 2005)

that are the "most privately owned" are located in the valley (Instituto Nacional de Estadística Geográfica e Informática [INEGI] 1994b). Private ranches dominate 80–90 percent of the land base in the five municipios studied along the Río Sonora Valley. The municipios included in the Río Sonora Valley include, from south to north, Baviácora, Aconchi, San Felipe, Huépac, Banámichi, and the largest by area, Arizpe, which was the old provincial capital for decades. These small towns, for which the municipios are named, are located on Pleistocene terraces overlooking the river and its floodplain. Most of these settlements were preexisting villages of the indigenous Opata peoples, overlaid by Jesuit missions founded in the 1640s and resettled along the river's elevated terraces. This pre-Columbian pattern, reinforced during the Spanish Colonial period, still shapes the basic human geography of the watershed today. Unlike the image of Mexico as a booming demographic phenomenon, these towns have also lost population during the last twenty to thirty years. Their population levels are small and fluctuate seasonally because of labor migration in the summer (Secretaría de Economía, Gobierno del Estado de Sonora 2008):

Aconchi	2,452
Arizpe	2,959
Banámichi	1,464
Baviácora	3,404
Huépac	1,032

The private ranches are located east and west of the central towns and hamlets, on the pediments and elevated plateaus extending into the mountain ranges. The floodplains are irrigated for some food crops, but increasingly for livestock feed, a truly "hybrid landscape" support system for the livestock industry of the state.

Wander the fields around these towns and it is apparent that wheat, corn, soy, sorghum, and alfalfa are ubiquitous crops along the Río Sonora watershed even as the shift from food to feed progresses. The region experienced several mining booms throughout the colonial period, largely small operations, and a mid-twentieth-century cotton expansion now largely forgotten. A visitor can still occasionally find an old volunteer cotton plant along ignored portions of the fluvial floodplain. Since the decline of cotton in the 1950s, an increasing number and concentration of fodder crops has dominated the riparian agriculture of the region, with alfalfa, ryegrass, and oats especially prominent. Farmers and ranchers have also eagerly tried new feed hybrids from the United States in an effort to create a local cash crop or simply to supplement the lack of rich forage grasses on their ranches. Again because of proximity to the border, European cattle introduced via the United States and grasses from Texas A&M, based on hybrids blended from African and Indian grasses such as buffelgrass, were early arrivals in the region.

Sonora is also a marginal environment, both for agriculture and livestock, because of climate and increasingly because of economic and political policies (Liverman 1990; Camou-Healy 1998). Sonorans were active in the more recent PROCEDE program of certifying and titling of ejido lands, effectively finished in Sonora by the end of 2004, either in parcels for arable land transactions or for retaining and titling communal grazing lands.[4] Home to some of the earliest and most populist land reform redistributions in Mexico, Sonora's communal institutions are now actively seeking greater autonomy and flexibility, a seeming contradiction for people who were so vital to the Mexican Revolution's success (Sanderson 1981). Ejido and comunidad members, however, are more precisely smallholders, and few describe themselves as revolutionaries, much less as socialists. These arid land ejidos face difficult prospects in surviving as a form of institution (Whiteford et al. 1998).

Men and Women in Black (Hats)

Every story, academic ones too, needs a villain or a villainous class of people. In rural Mexico, the landed elite are usually a convenient and understandably persuasive target for narrative constructions of a nemesis. And so, private ranchers in Mexico have long served this purpose, sometimes with good reason, but in all cases the portrait is one of caricature and does not reflect the continuum of land-tenure arrangements, conflicts, and realities in Mexico. Nor does this treatment pay much attention to gender at all, in the sense that the "bad guys" are, in the caricature, bad guys (fig. 1.3). There has been precious little room or role for women in ranching stories especially in regard to land or resource management, yet

Figure 1.3 Men in Black Hats? Here, at a workshop on pesticides, private ranchers are learning about how to deal with a thorn scrub invasion of their pastures.

they are a presence here, either as ranchers or somehow pivotal to ranching households (but see Moynihan, Armitage, and Dichamp 1990). Cattle ranchers in the United States have also been branded with a generic stigma as ecological villains, especially by a limited set of environmental groups, even if these relationships are now changing (Sayre 2005b). A final mistake sometimes assumed, occasionally ignored, is that all private ranches in Mexico today are direct products of past landed estates or haciendas handed down from generation to generation. There are few such estates anywhere in contemporary Mexico; the fits and starts of ranching in Sonora—punctuated by Apache raids, rural instability and violence, cyclical drought, and the boom-and-bust mining operations of northern Mexico—have never allowed for such continuity in ranch ownership. Private landowners in the state have had to cobble, defend, and articulate their properties in a piecemeal way, as they have elsewhere in Mexico (Perramond 2002; Bobrow-Strain 2007).

An additional set of concerns is squarely centered on the aspects
of land and resource management. Contrary to some bucolic pastoral
ideal, not all ranchers are equal, not all ranches are equal, and the decision makers and spaces reflect this imbalance, this unequal geography
of landscape, resources, and power. Some ranchers have blessedly flat,
grassy tracts to manage, a landscape that is much prized and not often
found in Sonora. A choice few owners have a wide variety of resources
at their fingers, natural and economic alike, with which to make difficult
decisions. These fortunate few also can exert some degree of local or
regional power, not uncontested, as they maneuver agencies, neighbors,
and laborers in strategic ways. So if the focus here is on the Río Sonora
and adjoining ranches, scores of other ranches and ranchers were visited, consulted, and used for this study as well, for comparative purposes.
A study of the powerful, rural, landed elite makes sense only if the context is clear. In the following list of the seventeen study ranches and of
informants, ranch names with an asterisk and all personal names are
pseudonyms.

Small ranches (300–1,000 hectares)

Torredo brothers	480 ha
El Chuto*	750 ha

Medium-sized ranches (1,000–3,000 hectares)

Pedro/Miguela Sarella	1,000 ha
El Aguaje*	1,450 ha
Eduardo Ortiz	1,600 ha
Poncho	1,800 ha
El Guero	2,600 ha
Chevita	3,000 ha

Large Ranches (3,000–6,500 hectares)

Ana Dellot	3,300 ha
El Cartucho	3,500 ha
El Lobo	4,000 ha
Ernesto Sevillano	4,200 ha
Don Benito	5,200 ha
Adolfo Dariel	6,408 ha

Mega-ranches (more than 10,000 hectares)

Victor Saguado	13,000 ha
El Morro*	16,000 ha
La Pamplona*	20,000 ha

Other interviews

Vaqueros on other ranches	42
Additional ranchers in the region	20
Laborers working on ranches	37
Mescaleros on ranches	6
Chiltepineros on ranches (including 8 women)	41
Women interviewed	30

Conceptually, power is not simply out there waiting to be found; it is not a thing. It is a condition of human relationships, extant because of intimate and distant contacts, whether in handshakes about personal debts, or economies of scale that structure overall relations in a community. Power is also expressed in the written word, in documents, in studies that purport to represent or portray communities in place and space. As an author, I am also implicated in these relationships of power and have no illusions about totalizing objectivity. This fact was certainly clear enough when members of the local ejido expressed to me their concern that I was colluding with the wealthier, private landowners, despite my objections to their characterizations. By design, most of my time was spent on private ranches, studying their properties and their management's decisions. Partial mollification of ejidatario concerns was possible through attending their meetings, listening carefully, and responding honestly to their questions about my work. Once it was clear to any individual ejido member what my goal was, a common yet surprising response was, "Well, they do a better job ranching anyway."

This explicit and implicit conventional wisdom about private landowners in the region, that they manage resources better or more efficiently than the communal landowners, was of course utilized by private ranchers. But this hegemony of common opinion is voiced by communal landowners as well. The daily, lived experiences with this aspect of consensus power are more subtle, the balance between coercion and consensus remaining tenuous, and the scale of this quotidian dimension is difficult to capture in more structural arguments dealing with power (Marston 2000). In fact, very few authors have addressed this beyond simply asserting that the "hegemony" of landowners exists, even if it is never complete or they face difficulties in defending their presumptive rights (see Bobrow-Strain 2007).

The uneven ecological distribution of natural resources, along with socio-economic scarcity, must be accounted for in any regional portrait and study of ranching. Landowners in the Río Sonora Valley use their animals to generate a livelihood for their families, for market returns, and as a way to maintain their land base. These are landscapes of intent, even if the consequences of decisions are occasionally unintended or unanticipated. Each private rancher manages his or her ranch quite differently; most do so directly although many do so indirectly, letting the decisions fall to assigned ranch managers, work bosses (*mayordomos*), or occasionally to trusted vaqueros. Through a combination of quantitative and qualitative methods, it became clear that some important management practices varied by the size of the ranch. It was also during the course of follow-up visits, additional discussions with ranchers and ranch families, workers, and spouses that I came to appreciate how culturally motivated some management decisions are for private owners. They do not represent *homo economicus,* perfectly rational economic human beings, even if a percentage of their logic resembles that of an economist; most have a wider appreciation for the subtleties and complexities of landscapes, wildlife, and aesthetics. They are just as happy discussing their cell phone as they are discussing cuts of meat for a perfect meal.

My third and final body of arguments relates to the issue of how we write about, explain, and understand societal struggles with natural resources. In geography, anthropology, and increasingly in history, these struggles either resemble portraits in failure or, more commonly, are invoked as political economies of resource conflicts and struggles. Under various guises, environmental or resource conflict has been a subject for study for decades, and the latest subdiscipline that encapsulates this approach is known as political ecology. Across these disciplines, and increasingly in political science and area studies programs, political ecology has gained traction. With varying degrees of focus or emphasis on the "political" or "ecological" side of explanation, the thrust has generally been to critique underexplained notions of conservation and development in a variety of contexts.

However, the society/nature separation and dichotomy implicit in the name of this subdiscipline is unhelpful in some ways because it does not reflect the wide range of challenges, the successes, or the panoply of choices faced by resource managers. It is rare that the studies entitled "a political ecology of (fill in the blank)" reflect the role that nonhuman nature may play in these ecologies (Robbins 2004). Cattle drink, graze, and browse directly, even if humans manage them rather indirectly. Contemporary Sonoran landscapes reflect the long-standing interaction between these exotic, domesticated species and the natural and imported vegetation, even if shaped and guided by the human hand of policies, historical events and accidents, and unintended consequences. Too much structural analysis or political economy can also dehumanize the context of this livelihood, rendering human agency as another simple cog in the capitalist machine. The people discussed in this book are not caricatures or characters in a play. As one cowboy noted when I asked about his working conditions, "Sure, it's lonely out here and I sometimes hate my boss, but he's also my second cousin and I can't ignore that." The close kinship ties can complicate a too-structural focus on social relations of production yet few studies using political ecology are willing to disclose this. By the end, I hope, this work will demonstrate that these are as much cultural relations as they are social.

Narrative Trails

Chapter 2 provides an historical-geographic introduction to cattle ranching in general and to the Río Sonora region specifically. This introduction provides the context for the field-based empirical chapters (3–6), dealing with the private ranches and ranchers in chapter 3, and the ecological dimensions of the same in chapter 4. Chapter 5 delves into the fundamental aspect of gendered livelihoods in the ranching landscapes of northern Mexico, a dimension to this lifestyle that remains both understudied and undervalued. While the presumption that ranching entails the geography of masculinity is true, a more nuanced set of gender-based portraits reveal the remarkable variety in livelihoods and the critical articulation of households in a ranching economy. In chapter 6, I provide a context for understanding the contemporary landscapes of ranching in Mexico and the U.S.–Mexico Borderlands, and connections to natural resource policies shaped at the local and regional level. The final discussion in chapter 7 is focused on providing a larger context for these arguments and how ranching has fared, or will fare, across North America and the Americas in general. Many colleagues and friends have sounded the clarion for geographers to interact with public and natural resource policies, and where possible, I present the findings and policy suggestions in the conclusion as an earnest attempt to be useful. It was, in the first case, the ranchers profiled here who pushed me for some general findings that they could apply to their own daily life and with which they could compare their efforts to those across the U.S.–Mexico border.

The utility of any policy recommendation, however, should be kept in context. To wit, the understandings of "public" and "private" in Mexico are quite different from those principles as practiced on the U.S. side of the border, as American ranchers squabble with public land agencies for grazing permits, negotiating fees and access in a way that most Mexican ranchers would never understand. For readers interested in the ranching and regional literature, including prior work in and around the Río Sonora, I refer you to appendix A for a brief essay. In appendix B, I have provided a general outline and description of the research methods used in this study.

Coda for Comparison

Those familiar with ranching controversies and challenges in the U.S. context will find some remarkable parallels and contrasts. What Sonoran and Mexican ranchers have experienced in the twentieth and early twenty-first centuries is similar to the prospects remaining for any culture using livestock husbandry as their primary way of life. Ranching was never fully sedentary until the twentieth century, still depending on long travel to regional markets and transhumance (seasonal herd movements), and in some cases ranchers never felt settled until barbed wire stretched across pastures and a paved road intersected the ranch roads crisscrossing the dry arroyos of their rangelands. Like barbed wire, paved roads reaching the area in the 1970s facilitated access to new markets and control over certain resources hotly contested as cattle gained value. It is certainly a more sedentary lifestyle currently, with some ranchers visiting their outfits only once or twice a year, and no guarantee that the owner will actually live within easy reach of the ranch itself.

Absentee landownership, while common in sixteenth-century Iberia, is now a fact for the largest of these properties. Yet cattle remain vital to the regional identity, economy, and cultural discourse of the regional inhabitants, the so-called Serranos (Burckhalter, Nabhan, and Sheridan 1998). The ritual consumption of meat, largely tied to personal and familial events such as wakes, *quinceañeras* (a girl's fifteenth birthday, a notable event), and weddings, remains in place. The expectation that ranchers share or at least sell some meat locally is still intact. And in countless villages, a common hot topic for debate is who exactly provides the best base for the holy grail of local cuisine, *carne asada*. To translate this term simply as "steak tacos" is both an insult and near blasphemy. While these cultural aspects may seem mundane for those wanting instant or easy policy advice on "what to do" in the great debate over cattle ranching, they are vital to the ranchers and residents from these valleys. "Without the lore," as one rancher put it, "we would simply be working for a living." The living and working dynamics of ranching, in a strongly interlinked and global economy, are also constantly changing.

Mexico's latest reforms to liberalize communal management may, in fact, draw private and communal land-tenure systems closer together. Private ranchers may now directly and legally lease, rent, or purchase formerly communal lands. I know many ranchers based in the United States who are jealous of the tenure structure in Mexico, where public lands are few and field-based park bureaucrats even fewer. Of course there are "range experts" in Mexico, though few are assigned in field stations accessible to most land managers. For all the difficulties faced by Mexican ranchers, they have remarkable autonomy and flexibility in shaping their own ranch management policies as they see fit and, unlike their American counterparts on public lands, do not need permit systems to graze animals. Yet if land tenure in Mexico has been complicated and contentious in the past, it shows no signs of becoming simpler anytime soon, as the country struggles with its own revolutionary land-tenure system born in the twentieth century, layered with legacies from the colonial era, and now intermingled with globalizing economic policies that are slowly or suddenly intruding into the ranch landscape.

There has never been a clear historical trajectory for ranching, or for Mexico for that matter, and readers should not assume that neat sequences dominate. There is no endgame or goal that is preordained for this form of land use and industry. The cultural and social relations within ranching communities remain strewn with a fascinating and complex blend of colonial ethnic ideals, modernist conceptions of economics, and altered gendered behaviors shaped by both lifestyle and livelihoods.

2 The Development of Cattle Ranching in Sonora, Mexico

Since their introduction to Mexico in 1521, domesticated livestock have successfully expanded into new, unfamiliar ecosystems. By the late sixteenth century, the presence of livestock was ubiquitous in the eastern lowlands of Mexico and, to a lesser extent, on the Pacific side of Mexico by the end of the seventeenth century. Historian Alfred Crosby (1986) discussed this inundation of livestock as part of the larger biological conquest by Europeans, or in his phrasing, as "ecological imperialism." In temperate regions of the Americas, the domination of the landscape was as much human as it was livestock driven; the environmental and historical record of impacts was mixed (Hernández 2001). In northern Mexico, where the arid frontier limited the growth of Spanish settlement, livestock and mining formed a conjoined and transformative landscape complex (Sheridan 1992). The movement of lay settlers and livestock northward into Sonora, after the establishment of Jesuit missions, followed the coastal Pacific route of earlier Spanish explorers. The origins of the Pacific extension of cattle ranching are generally treated as originating from the Guadalajara region, where the cultural phenomena of *charrería* (a style of rodeo) and *mariachi* music may have also taken root. Indeed, these last two attributes of the region have become stereotypical of Guadalajara and immortalized in Mexican song and dance. Horse and cattle culture, the seeming essence of rural and rustic Mexico, spread easily along the Pacific route into Sonora.

The first cattle in northwestern New Spain arrived with the Vázquez de Coronado expedition of 1540, which traced the Pacific coast of Mexico on way to Fray Marcos de Niza's cities of Cíbola, bringing some 150 head of livestock to maintain the soldiers during the voyage. Some animals apparently escaped near Culiacán (in present-day Sinaloa), and these few rogue livestock had multiplied into thousands of untamed cattle by the time Francisco de Ibarra arrived in the same region 25 years later (Wagoner 1952). To be sure, however, the foundations for the cattle industry in Sonora were transplanted by the Jesuit missions that arrived via the Pacific Coast (Jordan 1993). At the time of mission establishment along the Río Sonora Valley, in the mid-1640s, the balance of sheep and cattle was roughly equal and would stay so until more private ranches were established in the region (Radding 1997). Until cattle became king in the region, the pastoral systems in place were closer to what might have been found in central Mexico, with a balance of cattle and sheep in the landscape. Sheep were especially valued in missions, whether Franciscan or Jesuit, because of their relative docility and their size.

Cattle herding, since the first years of Spanish colonization, also had a peculiarly cultural meaning: Spaniards did not look down upon ranching as they did upon field agriculture (Chevalier 1952, 110–25; Prem 1992). This preference for herding was strongly linked to the contemporary cultural geography. Menial field tasks were delegated to Mexico's natives and a growing black population, while *caballeros,* or gentlemen, rode horses. This tendency of ethnic-spatial division of agricultural labor roles survives in many aspects today. Cattlemen in Sonora have more prestige than farmers, even if the "gentleman" horseman mythology broke down on the far-flung frontiers of the Spanish Empire. Mestizo and mulatto vaqueros became the norm, not the exception, in these peripheral regions of the Americas (Iber 2000). This is a crucial point of distinction for the spatial nature of ranching, as conflicts between farmers and ranchers have been multifaceted, not just based on "ethnicity" crudely understood as they are in other world regions. Unlike pastoral societies in Africa, for example, the spatial fixity of ranching versus the dispersed nature of nomadic pastoralism has created clear distinctions in how cultivators and herders interact (Bassett 1988; Barfield 1993). What distinguished extensive cattle and sheep raising in the New World was the immediate contrast to anything preexisting on the new continent, and it became the mark of difference, a cultural "brand" for Spaniards to use as a marker of status, class, and ethnic relations.

Domesticated livestock, especially sheep and cattle, occupied a particularly favorable cultural and ecological niche in Mexico. They expanded due to Spanish efforts to supplant native agriculture and culture, at the expense of both native population numbers and New World ecosystems (Crosby 1986; Sluyter 1996). Continued and rapid colonization served not only imperial or personal goals for the Spanish explorers, but also relieved the bottlenecks of animal populations in already conquered regions of New Spain (Chevalier 1952; Butzer 1992). Native protests of animal intrusions into agricultural fields were swift, as were de jure regulations implemented by the viceroy, and growing discontent related to livestock led to the establishment of a New World version of the Spanish institution of the *mesta*, a livestock management institution (Dusenberry 1963). Still, native populations were adept at using the new livestock, especially sheep, in their long-term livelihood strategies. They were smaller, more easily herded, and offered wool for textiles and clothing. Cattle rarely assumed the same level of importance for indigenous populations in the New World until the nineteenth and early twentieth centuries (Iverson 1994).

The root of livestock-based conflicts was founded on the Spanish belief in the right to graze "unused" lands or those in fallow, though abuses included attempts at excluding all natives from using "rangelands" or forested areas (Chevalier 1952, 115–22). Attempts to resolve increasingly intense conflicts over grazing rights resulted in a royal order in 1550, declaring it necessary to locate all private ranches (*estancias*) far from native villages and agricultural lands (Orozco 1974, 41). New estancias were to have a buffer zone of one league, about 2.5 miles or 4 kilometers (although even these distances could vary in Mexico) from the closest native settlement, and the custom of branding livestock was enforced to ease identification of owner and hence responsibility for loose livestock (Chevalier 1952). Cattle continued to be prolific in numbers, and by 1542, the price of livestock in Mexico was seven to eight times cheaper than it was in Andalucía (Chevalier 1952; Camou-Healy 1994, 68). As Aguilar-Robledo (1998, 2003) has clarified, however, the distinctions between or within the concepts of estancias and haciendas were muddied and multiple; in his case study of the Huasteca in San Luis Potosi, Aguilar-Robledo noted the prevalence of estancias as pasture properties to be assembled into larger haciendas, in which a single estancia was home to the main house of the *hacendado*. So estancias could be contiguous, or discontinuous, separated from the other estancia pastures that made up

Figure 2.1 Ranching has been viewed as a way to control territory, and barbed wire has helped in the effort.

the larger hacienda. Confounding this tenure diversity, the term *hacienda* could also mean the livestock herd, adding additional complexity to colonial land-tenure concepts and terminology.

In spite of this bewildering variation in land-tenure and ownership concepts, we have a better understanding of the pre-revolutionary landholdings such as haciendas (Chevalier 1952; Harris 1975) than we do of the contemporary practices of private ranches. But what is, exactly, a private ranch? Is it a *latifundio,* or are those gone? Is it part or whole of a former hacienda? The complexity of land tenure in Mexico is legendary and has never held firm footing, even in historiography. Terms for land tenure or practices, adopted or modified from their Iberian or indigenous contexts, have changed in almost every century. Even regional comparisons are difficult in Mexico, where terms from Sonora rarely mean the same as they do in the Yucatán. Yet the enduring image of the private rancher is one of a despotic land-hoarder, perhaps still reflecting a modified Black Legend view of past hacienda and estancia owners in their treatment of indigenous peoples and New World landscapes. These ranches, although largely ignored in both the social and natural science literatures, are usually depicted as mechanisms of landed elite territoriality (fig. 2.1). To be sure, some individual "case" ranches have been examined, but generally in isolation, treated in anecdotal or nearly mythological terms, with qualitative results rarely framed in a larger, regional, comparative analysis even in the historical literature (Van Young 1983). Cattle have also wrought ecological changes, intended or ignored, since their arrival: livestock were fundamental to the Spanish and Portuguese displacement of indigenous tribes, as were the diseases of the Old World (Crosby 1972; Sluyter 1996).

The Roots of Ranching

Ranching is a distinctly different and modern form of pastoralism, and refers to a pattern of fixed settlement, with little migration of peoples involved from region to region during the course of a year. As such, it differs from more traditional forms of agro-pastoralism, especially given the focus on cattle as the primary form of livestock raised (Barfield 1993; Salzman 2004). Today's private ranches are far less integrated into field agriculture than they once were, when large multipurpose landed estates mixed livestock with sugar cane and food crops in the rural hinterlands of the state and in northern Mexico in general. Ranching's distinction vis-à-vis other forms of agro-pastoralism, despite its spatial fixity, did not preclude local and regional transhumance, a practice common in Sonora until the 1950s. This seasonal movement of livestock has its roots in the pan-Mediterranean practice of herding animals according to climate and grazing conditions. These movements could involve large, seasonal herd movements over hundreds of kilometers or take place on a more local scale where lowland-highland rotation was practiced.

What remains today of transhumance pales to the distances once covered by animals and herders alike, although there is still a notable connection between upland and valley locations, to make use of field stubble after crop harvests. Paradoxically, as globalization and its related processes have taken hold in rural Mexico, even highly capitalized industrial livelihoods such as cattle ranching have become more spatially rooted to place. Movements between valleys, ranches, and towns are now much more localized and more compressed in time and space than previously, even if the animals end up hundreds of miles away in a U.S. feedlot. Many of the ecological problems visible in the cattle industry or on rangelands in general stem from this paradox. If capitalism thrives on capital mobility, the subjects of that capital must remain spatially fixed, a point long emphasized by David Harvey (1981). Ranching as a form of industrial capital investment has worked to decrease animal mobility in nearly all grazed environments. This outcome is as true in Africa and parts of Asia as it is in contemporary Latin America.

Existing scholarship in geography and history has detailed the origins and development of this particular pastoral complex as it was transferred from Old World to New. The British Isles, the Iberian Peninsula, and Africa are typically singled out among these studies as important sources for practices and animals found in the New World. All three land areas have lent their practices to cattle ranching, although in Mexico, the Iberian tradition of pastoralism was predominate. An underappreciated, and largely unheralded, process of livestock diffusion, innovations, and technological exchange in the Americas did take place beginning in the late nineteenth century. This spread or diffusion of new animals and associated innovations was not always a one-way street, from Old World to New. For Mexico, one of the notable arrivals from Africa through Brazil was the South Asian zebu cattle breed, present by 1884 although only important in Sonora from the 1950s (Rouse 1977).

When François Chevalier's (1952) work on the great estates of Mexico first appeared, his conclusions did not shake historical scholarship or conventional wisdom; indeed his findings confirmed what was known all along: that haciendas were great land-extensive enterprises, often using a debt peonage labor system (Simpson 1963). His more specific contribution was a detailed depiction and regionalization of these estates—their inherent diversity in form and function. These assumptions were troublesome for Gibson's (1964) later work in the Valley of Mexico, where Chevalier's apparently monolithic haciendas varied in size and were clearly agricultural in emphasis. Instead of an extensive grazing strategy, landowners were intensifying agricultural production through a mixed system of livestock and wheat farms, with a parallel trend of elaborating existing irrigation systems. Studies that followed concurred with Gibson: closer to the densely settled areas of New Spain, the average size of the great estates decreased (Harris 1975; Brading 1978; Murphy 1986).

These findings coincide with two of geography's basic assumptions about location and land use. First, the early nineteenth-century German economist von Thünen demonstrated that land prices affect the zonation of agricultural land use: the most labor-intensive zones are closer to the "city," and land-extensive ones, like ranching, are out on the periphery of his model of concentric rings (Chisholm 1979). Second, population growth can also lead to more intensive forms of land use, but it took Boserup's (1965) thesis on agricultural intensification to convince geographers of this general pattern. Chevalier's characterizations of the landed estates did hold true, in general, for the northern expanses of New Spain where market demand was weaker and the scarcity of water encouraged the growth of massive landholdings that were rarely contested (see also Harris 1975). Nevertheless, subsequent scholarship about these land institutions (such as haciendas, *encomiendas*) came under closer scrutiny. González-Sánchez (1969) illustrated the flexibility of the term *hacienda* in her analysis of estates in Tlaxcala, wherein she demonstrated that even 600- to 800-acre landholdings were still denoted as haciendas, despite their relatively dwarfed size when compared to estates on the northern frontier. The term *hacienda* has also never been static as Aguilar-Robledo (2003) made clear using examples from the Huasteca of lowland Mexico. Encomiendas were awards of land and associated native labor given to military officers or minor nobility, and were not typical in Sonora. Another parallel to the spatial-analytical findings of these historians and geographers is that the landlords' "hegemony," their ability and power to dominate, also decreased with increasing population density; that is, labor was not as tightly regulated and there was more variation in land-use decisions and practices.

These conclusions accord well with those of other geographers. Ewald (1977) posited that a von Thünen–model explanation for agricultural land use in colonial Mexico was valid, at least in regions having adequate historical records available for analysis. The Bajío of central Mexico is one such area where available documentation made it possible to assess changes in land-use history (Brading 1978). The geographer Murphy (1986) found that during the early 1630s, agricultural intensification was occurring in this region of Mexico due to market demands and a growing population, and labor-intensive irrigation networks were installed (or extended) in areas where wheat cultivation was feasible. For cattle ranchers, this meant a general displacement of animal grazing to more removed locations at higher elevations. A general economic recession gripped most of New Spain until the 1720s, when silver strikes spurred economic growth, and intensification of agricultural production ensued, resulting in livestock being pushed further out of Mexico's core agricultural regions such as the Bajío (Butzer 1992; Butzer and Butzer 1995). But it is difficult to call these old colonial-era estancias and haciendas true "ranches," since today's cattle ranches feature a spatial fixity that was not characteristic of these landholdings in the Spanish colonial era.

These agricultural changes, however, were following larger societal shocks, including the depopulation of the Americas and the arrival of Euro-American cultures. Later historical and geographic theories of overseas expansion sought to place these events in a larger context. Borrowing the ideas of the historian Louis Hartz (1964), geographer R. Cole Harris (1977) proposed that European cultures and traditions, including agriculture, were simplified as they moved overseas. The concept of the "simplification of Europe" in geography is not too different from the historian's view of the "devolution of European society" on new continents. But was this the case for ranching? Certainly confronting new lands and peoples had their shock value on European perceptions and traditional practices (of land use in this case). At least parts of the argument still hold true for ranching, however, as those Iberian land-use institutions did not fully travel across the Atlantic. This statement does not imply that ranching itself was simpler, because the practice as we know it today did not exist at the time, but rather that many of the proscriptive rules about grazing domesticated livestock were never enforced, discussed, or of concern to most missions and lay settlers in New Spain. This colony was not a land "without history," of course, to borrow Eric Wolf's (1982) phrase. Indigenous peoples did complain and file suits in New Spain when livestock trampled or ate their crops. But livestock institutions or restrictions were, at best, an ad hoc affair in most of northern Mexico. Extensive cattle ranching, a rarity in Spain, became the norm throughout the Americas, if not by intentional practice then certainly by default.

At least three important facets of Old World agriculture were abandoned or dropped in the implantation and adaptation of new livelihoods in the New World. First, much of the complexity associated with animal agriculture in the Mediterranean, especially its complementarities vis-à-vis field agriculture, faded in many parts of New Spain. As many documents and authors have made clear, field agriculture or being a land-tied smallholder was not the first goal of either conquistadores or decommissioned officers and soldiers in the New World. The logical extension to this was that they expected to be noble horsemen, to dominate and use native labor as their early land grants provided, and never to toil in open fields under the hot sun. This mentality, of the horse-bound hidalgo supervising his peones in the fields, survived for at least two centuries, well beyond the actual span of legalized land grants that incorporated native labor into the first *mercedes*, or royal land grants. The system in New Spain also stands in contrast to other cattle-ranching regions of the Americas, in that labor was provided not by slaves but by indigenous populations, although Gulf Coast ranching labor complexes shared much in common with lowland South American cattle ranches (Butzer 1988; Jordan 1993; Bell 1998).

Even when lay settlers did finally arrive in important numbers during the late seventeenth and early eighteenth centuries, the assumption that nearby native populations would aid in cultivation agriculture was foremost on early pioneer minds. The cultural and spatial dissociation between field agriculture and livestock was difficult to mend because of the ethnic assumptions and images related to each pursuit. In northern Mexico, and certainly for the Río Sonora Valley, the added dimension of settlement geography profoundly influenced these earlier tendencies. As the Jesuit and later Franciscan missions were established along the Río Sonora in close proximity to native settlements, field agriculture was the main pursuit even if complemented by keeping herds of livestock. Lay Spanish settlement consisted of larger, private estates on the outskirts of mission lands and extensive grazing across the foothills of the Sierra Madres.

Second, Spaniards encountered environments in which rainfall patterns were either seasonally reversed from their usual Mediterranean regional system or more sparsely scattered than they were accustomed to; indeed, we should keep in mind the relative scarcity of so-called Mediterranean climates globally, in that European colonists were arriving from a climate and region that was the exception, and not the rule. Even if settlers were from regions of Spain that compared evenly with Sonora in terms of annual average rainfall, the pattern and seasonality of this rain was the complete opposite: Mediterranean peoples were used to their rain arriving in the winter, not the summer, as is the case in Sonora. So it cannot be viewed as a small irony that the traditional start of the rainy season in Sonora is on June 24, the feast day of Saint John the Baptist. And the fickle, unpredictable nature of precipitation in this region of Mexico has made both agriculture and cattle ranching subject to the wildly varying whims of seasonal and annual rainfall.

Third, and as mentioned earlier, many of the localized or regional institutions of Spain did not transfer to the New World. The diversity of local land-use practices, designated land-cover descriptions, and juridical language of sixteenth-century Castile was never universally transferred to the New World (Vassburg 1984). Of course, there were some rough analogues to what Spaniards might have called the *ejido* in central Mexico, such as the Aztec *calpulli*, but they were more different than they were similar in their nature. Even the later organization of the Mexican mesta, roughly modeled on its Old World predecessor for managing regional livestock movements and transhumance, did not have the same legal complexity or clout. So what may have worked in Spain and in the Mediterranean Basin generally had emerged gradually, over centuries, with local practices adjusted and accommodating larger, regional institutions of transhumance or grazing associations. No such structure was in place in the New World, and in Sonora no similar institution evolved until well into the twentieth century. Efforts to colonize the northern frontier, however, would be led by the missions. In what would later become Sonora, these activities were led by the Jesuits.

Colonial Missions and Private Ranching

The most detailed, hence the most useful, accounts of Sonora's past peoples and environments come from the missionaries present between 1630 and 1767. The vast majority of the critical and well-known documents derive from the Jesuit period of dominion in Sonora. The missionary domination of livestock ownership and land use in Sonora is perhaps unique to Mexico: most future, private enterprises at least initially depended on

Figure 2.2   An old Catholic Church in Baviácora, Sonora. The church and plaza are still the heart of social life in the small towns of Sonora.

the missions for seed animals. The fact that these missions also focused on communal management and allocation of resources greatly influenced future patterns of livelihood. Livestock herding techniques were part of the missionary instruction to indigenous peoples; for missions, a mix of sheep and cattle was popular. In a sense, indigenous and missionary communalism became fused into one assemblage, regionally variable but remarkably integrated (Radding 1997, 2005). Indeed, most of the villages located along the Río Sonora Valley study area claimed communal use of a large area adjoining towns in post-revolutionary Mexico (Baroni 1991). So even if the ethnic self-references along the Río Sonora are nearly all mestizo, the settlement geography and patterns of land use were largely in place during the colonial period: communal, agricultural towns with extensive grazing and fuel wood collection in the surrounding foothills (fig. 2.2).

   The shift from missions to secular towns included a demographic change; the number of natives decreased, while the number of Spanish *vecinos* increased (Jones 1979). The impacts of Old World diseases, now known to have produced some dramatic population nadirs in the New World, were also serious for the native Sonoran population (Denevan 1976, 1992; Reff 1991). In fact, the earliest accounts of illness among the indigenous populations of Sonora come from Cabeza de Vaca (1962, 119), on his expedition in 1535, when he noted that among the inhabitants of northern Sonora, "all the people, *sick* and well, came to us in an attitude of urgency to be touched and blessed [emphasis added]." While this quotation does not indicate the types of diseases, much less the origins or vectors, it does suggest the possibility that Old World diseases were already taking their toll on native populations from afar. The decline of Opata inhabitants in the study region mimics that of other New World indigenous populations. The estimates for New World indigenous declines by Denevan (1992), up to 90 percent in many cases, are matched by those of Gerhard (1982, 190, 285) for the Sonoran province.

Although mission districts were disparately integrated, some mission regions were more burdensome financially to the Jesuit order. Of the three important mission districts under consideration here, only one was reported to be in debt during the years of 1741–1744: the mission of Banámichi. Within the confines of particular mission districts, such as Aconchi (which also included Baviácora), the numbers of livestock by type (cattle/sheep) were fairly balanced. In 1749, for example, the mission of Aconchi reported 4,043 head of livestock, of which 36 percent were cattle. Another 40 percent were sheep, and the balance was a mixture of horses and mules (Radding 1997, 77).

The peak period of mission population and success, for the Río Sonora at least, was between 1700 and 1740. After this period, yields of grain declined, and increasing competition from secular colonists began to disintegrate what little control the missionaries once enjoyed. Radding (1997, 96–97) argued that the mission control was so tenuous that indigenous populations under a missionary were already selling their labor, land, and other assets to colonizers well before the Jesuit expulsion of 1767. The competition for control over resources also led to tremendous ethnic mobility, and many indigenous groups began to make treks across the province as rural merchants (*rescatadores*), in many instances underpricing both missionary and secular colonists alike. Most likely, this early form of migrating merchants was the precursor to what later were termed *falluqueros* or *fayuqueros*. Though declining in importance, these rural merchants were important in bringing external, manufactured goods to remotely located Sonoran villages. The effect of this privatization was the creation of a large, mobile workforce available for exploitation on private ranches and in mines.

Private Haciendas and Ranchos

Considerable confusion and regional variability exist in the use of terms such as *hacienda*, *estancia*, and *rancho*, as these terms do not necessarily mean the same thing to all people. In the historical literature for Sonora, however, the use of these terms has a clear progression. Early records refer to "estancias," then later to "haciendas," and finally to "ranchos" in the more recent past (Romero 1995). This progression may also be indicative of the decline in relative size of operations. The institution of the hacienda, at least in Sonora and other isolated regions of northern New Spain, was never as common as the more modest ranchos during the colonial period (Jones 1979, 238). More recently, however, ranchos are defined by Sonoran social scientists as the truly large ranches. This terminology is problematic because it does not hint at the proportional differences between ranches.

The vast, centralized yet diversified estates of central Mexico known as haciendas were prevalent on the northern frontier. Northern varieties of the hacienda, however, typically emphasized livestock production rather than the more diversified approach common in central and southern Mexico. This emphasis is perhaps not surprising, given the lack of markets on the remote periphery of New Spain, the climatic aridity, and the quite tenuous control over labor exerted by lay Spaniards during the colonial period. It is perhaps ironic that the literature on past private landholdings is far greater than the sum of present-day research on private ranches. For Sonora, historical data on private ranches are yet sparser, due to the lack of quantitative information through time. In fact, Velasco (1985, 19) himself noted this problem in 1860: "puede asegurarse sin equivocación, que si en algún estado de los que se numeran en la República Mexicana es difícil la formación de una estadística exacta, es sin duda en el de Sonora."[1]

The legacy of privately held livestock operations is rooted in the early exploration of the state of Sonora. Pedro de Perea Ibarra, the son of Sonora's colonizer (Captain Pedro de Perea), is said to have established the first private holding in 1640 amid the grassy plains of the Bacanuchi Valley, to the northwest of the eventual capital of Arizpe. Inhabitants of present-day Bacanuchi, many of whom claim to be descendants of the Perea/Ibarra legacy, swear that a small remaining set of rubble is the old hacienda of 1640 (A. Lopez, interview by the author, December 3, 1997, Arizpe, MX). By 1685, another five ranches were established in the Bacanuchi watershed, four more in the valley of Teuricache, one near the mission of Opodepe in the San Miguel Valley, another along the Río Sonora, and nine in the mountains close to the mining site of San Miguel Arcángel (West 1993, 58–59). Unfortunately, no sizes were recorded for these ranches. Despite the paucity of private ranches, there is evidence that the numbers of domesticated livestock were already high, for during the 1660s they practically had no value (West 1993, 59). These early, private operations were largely untitled and were run as temporary homesteads. An example of this pattern of unregulated land tenure appears in a report of ranch, mine, and mission activities in Sonora conducted in 1717, during the official visit of a presidio captain. Among the twenty-three recognized ranches, only a quarter had official title, while the vast majority consisted of simple households with a few herds. More mobile operations were located in the dry foothills adjacent to the irrigated mission lands in the river valleys of Sonora (Garate 1993).

It was the latter form of private interests that created conflict between secular Spaniards and the early Jesuit missions, with bitter reports by missionaries appearing as early as 1713. In the mission district of Oposura, today called Moctezuma, a miner from Nacozari was accused by the Jesuits of running thousands of cattle in the irrigated lands of the mission. A decade later (1723), missionaries filed complaints against six ranchers for running some twelve thousand head between the Moctezuma and Sonora River Valleys, as well as on the Llano de Tepache east of the mission of Oposura. Material cultural evidence of such early activity in this same area can be found today. In two locations close to the floodplain of the Río Moctezuma, which was the irrigated domain of mission lands near Oposura (now the town of Moctezuma), there are

Figure 2.3 An early rock corral near Moctezuma. These are well-known features in the watershed east of the Río Sonora. One possible explanation is that they are old droving corrals for livestock.

clear remnants of early cattle corrals (fig. 2.3). The following discussion concerns historical archaeological remains first noticed by W. E. Doolittle in 1977. I revisited these features in June 1997 and recorded the locations of these corrals using a global positioning system (GPS) receiver. A follow-up visit in September 1997 resulted in more precise measurements and dimensions of the corrals discussed.

The physical location of the remains above the floodplain is suggestive of a corral mechanism. Additional characteristics hint at their past uses. The first of these corrals is more closed and compact than the second corral, with multiple cell divisions within the high walls. The large, volcanic rocks are a natural feature of the Llano de Tepache to the east, located above the eastern edge of the Moctezuma River floodplain. In addition to petroglyphs that resemble early cattle brands, multiple bedrock mortars provide strong evidence that the Opata previously used this site as some form of settlement. The second corral, further south along the eastern edge of the plateau that overlooks the floodplain of the Río Moctezuma, is larger than the first corral feature. Spatially, it is both expansive and less divided by rock walls than the first corral. While it is difficult to interpret whether private or missionary herders used these corrals, the spatial arrangements suggest that each corral probably served a different purpose.

I propose that the first corral was an extraction pen for cattle coming out of the irrigated lands after having grazed field stubble, a practice that continues to this day, and the division of herds was facilitated by the inner walls of the first corral. This arrangement probably aided herders in dividing, branding, and inspecting the individual animals. The second corral, which featured no definite outer wall to the east, seems to have been the herding pen for cattle moving into the irrigated lands for stubble grazing. I based this tentative hypothesis on the similar general arrangement of current fencing materials along river floodplains in Sonora, and most ranchers that I discussed the remains with generally agreed with the explanation. This rock arrangement was the only one of its kind that I saw in Sonora during my stay, though I heard of several other similar features in the higher elevations of the adjoining state of Chihuahua. Their position high above the floodplain and their excellent view of the flat volcanic badlands to the east would have made excellent defensive positions as well. They may also have been used by the previous, native inhabitants as rock shelters, strategic posts to thwart nomadic Amerindian attacks.

Things were not peaceful by any means for the lay Spaniard settlers practicing livestock farming in Sonora. Escalating raids by nomadic indigenes such as the Apache and later Seri and Yaqui raids depopulated the more remote ranches and settlements. In fact, by 1764, only twenty-four localities were occupied permanently, out of approximately two hundred. Of these twenty-four inhabited sites, only two were "inhabited estancias and ranches" (West 1993). The growth of private ranching operations can be generally traced, with some degree of consistency, with general figures for total numbers. In 1764, there were apparently only two functioning entities. Three years later, the Jesuits were expelled and the Franciscan order was asked to lead the missions in the Río Sonora Valley. A 1783 report by the presidio captain, Teodoro de Croix, recorded nine haciendas and sixty-seven ranchos (Jones 1979, 180). By 1810, there was a total of 45 estancias-haciendas, most of which were considered haciendas. By 1910, that number had grown to 310 occupied estates, most between one thousand and ten thousand hectares in size. The number of ranchers was listed as 356 in 1810 and 1,286 in 1910, figures that are consistent with records from the so-called Reforma years, when land allotments from 1877–1893 dissected the communal landholdings of Sonoran towns, creating 4,501 individual titles. Privatization of the irrigated districts, or irrigable tracts, was a clear priority over concerns for rangeland distribution and tenure (Jackson 1997).

Romero's (1995) thesis is the only attempt at determining the pace of privatization in Sonora during and following the Franciscan mission period. His data were analyzed chronologically, though he divided the state into "districts," providing some spatial perspective to the process. Under Romero's regional classification, my study area falls into the "Ures district," excepting Arizpe. In regional terms, private properties awarded during the epoch of 1740–1860 in the study area varied by time period, but were not as large as coastal claims in the districts of Guaymas, Hermosillo, and Magdalena. Most of the private grants were given in the measurements of a *sitio*, which is generally accepted to be equivalent to 1,747 hectares of grazing land for *ganado mayor*[2] (Simpson 1952). Romero (1995, 38), however, gives the figure 2,075 hectares per *sitio de ganado mayor*. It is entirely possible that changes in the size of sitios occurred in colonial Mexico. Contemporary ranch sizes, however, suggest that the original grants were closer to the 1,747-hectare figure given by Simpson (1952). For a detailed explanation of property size, see Romero's (1995) introduction. In original documentation of the study ranches, the titles of ranches provided the size of a sitio as between 1,740 and 1,750 hectares. Romero's (1995, 46) size classification system was useful in understanding the dimensions of these colonial land-grant practices.

Colonial property variation was due to imprecisions in measurement. Remarkably, the consistency in the land surface granted to ranchers endured into the Bourbon rule of colonial Mexico and into the era of independence. One of the better summaries on Mexican agrarian law has fixed the number at 1,775 hectares for a sitio (for large livestock) with smaller breeding ranches pegged at 438 hectares, or about a quarter of the size of a major sitio (Lemus Garcia 1987, 87). The vast majority of private land grants in Sonora between 1740 and 1860 were of modest dimensions. Current statistics kept by the Sonoran government suggest that the average size of the "typical" ranch is about 1,900 hectares in size (E. Carranza, interview by the author, October 30, 1996, Hermosillo, MX). Most of the ranches included in this study are larger than this statistical average.

Ranching in the Río Sonora Valley

Bezarra Nieto, during his 1717 visit of missions, recorded the first two ranches in the Río Sonora Valley. Although listed as haciendas in the report, both were associated with small silver-mining operations. It is unclear if these operations were near each other or somehow related, though their names were different. A brand registered in the study region under Estevan de Peralta in 1718 was located in a hacienda named San José de Basochuca, which was eventually processed as a land grant. It is clear that this ranch was associated with the mining operations of Basochuca. The current ranch named Basochuca, however, is located further north than the current abandoned mine, which suggests that Peralta had extensive holdings related to the support of his mining operations. Local historians in Arizpe strongly associate the old mine with the current ranch toponym.

By 1722, Spanish ranchers and miners had established fourteen cattle ranches, eleven farms, and eight smelters in the areas associated with the mission lands of Banámichi, Aconchi, Huépac, and Baviácora (West 1993, 68). The distribution of these operations, from north to south, was largely tied to the geography of small mining facilities between Motepore (south of Arizpe) and Concepción (just east of Mazocahui). This pattern continues to this day, the geography of land use having changed very little, as cattle ranches are located in satellite locations to the main towns (which were once *cabeceras* or *visitas*). Early haciendas and cattle ranches were inherited, divided, and sold. The names of the owners changed, but their general location did not and even most of the early ranch names have survived. This scenario is remarkable, given the widespread abandonment of ranches and mines reported in the early eighteenth century. Nevertheless, the population consisting of *gente de razón* (Spanish and mixed blood descendents) in 1767 amounted to 40 percent of the Río Sonora population. The pattern of secularization, decline in both indigenous numbers and cultural persistence, and land privatization dramatically increased after 1767. The number of titles distributed during the Bourbon, viceroyal, and early Mexican national periods supports this argument. Of all titles given to private ranches between 1760 and 1840, 96 percent of these were given during the Bourbon Reforms and the early Mexican national eras (Romero 1995, 213). Land titles were a slow process, then, until the strictures of the colonial era were lifted.

By the end of the nineteenth century, privatization of both irrigated lands and rangelands was nearly complete, and only portions of communal lands adjacent to the old mission sites were hotly contested (Baroni 1991). Certainly between the passage of the infamous Ley Lerdo that targeted ecclesiastical communal properties for dissolution, and the aggressive privatization during the Reforma and early Porfiriato, between the years 1856 and 1890, the bulk of communal lands not assigned to human settlements fell into private hands (Holden 1994; Boyer 2003). What is more troubling and perhaps contradictory is that the wholesale dissection of mission communal lands was driven by both nineteenth-century liberal ideas on nationalism and by the more conservative and authoritarian Díaz regime. Craib (2004) has written about Mexico's peculiar obsession to know itself spatially in the late nineteenth century, as the state attempted to pin down and fix Mexico's so-called fugitive landscapes— the complex mosaic of land use, ownership, and usufruct rights held in seemingly infinite varieties at the time of the liberal reform laws. What these changes wrought over Sonora, as they did across Mexico generally, was a profusion of new, privately owned ranchos. The outcome was, in essence, the birth of Sonora's middle-class ranching sector, as well as the creation of a larger landless base of peasants, who would wait several decades before finding some small degree of land-tenure justice following the Mexican Revolution of 1910–1917.

In the upper and middle Río Sonora Valley, the pattern of rancho dominance is clear in net numbers. The number of haciendas, however, does increase to the south.[3] A nineteenth-century list of haciendas and ranchos in the municipios under study was produced by Velasco (1985 [1860–1865]). It should be noted that the term *rancho* was not always indicative of a cattle ranch, but rather was a general term used for small peasant households in rural areas.[4] In Sonora, however, the bulk of these ranchos survived by ranching cattle. Serrano (2000) found a similar pattern in Aguascalientes, as the ratio of ranchos to haciendas went from 5.6 in 1792 to 23.2 in 1906, clearly emphasizing that smaller units were distributed following independence and during the early stages of the Porfiriato. Ironically, too, it was these more modest holdings that prospered after the Mexican Revolution, as land redistribution by the federal government targeted the larger hacienda estates along irrigated valley bottoms and spared the smaller ranches from expropriation during the land reforms of the twentieth century.

Communal Resources Institutionalized: Ejidos and Comunidades

As anthropologist Daniel T. Reff (1991) demonstrated, much of the success that the Sonoran Jesuit missions enjoyed was due to the similar social and economic organizational strategy that existed in the river valleys prior to their arrival. Communal labor and a community-based system of rule and religion were already in place among the Opata in the Río Sonora culture area. This form of social capital, then, was the crux of the Jesuit system until it was "deconstructed" in the late eighteenth century. The disappearance of the Jesuit institutions only aided in the process of land privatization, as regional parcels of Church wealth were expropriated and in most cases distributed to lay settlers (Bazant 1971). Although the Franciscan successors attempted to hold the mission systems to some semblance of the past, the most successful years had long since passed. The growing influence of work options for the Opata, as wage laborers in the mines, cattle ranches, and estates of lay Spaniards or as paid soldiers in the Spanish presidios, undermined the communal system once integral to the mission towns.

The ideology of Mexican revolutionaries in the early nineteenth century, although well intentioned, was not always favorable in reinstating communal systems of property. Even Molina Enríquez, the progenitor of the idea of collective *ejidos* in Mexico, had certain notions of evolutionary stages in peasantry and land tenure. Molina clearly believed in the utopian possibilities of rural, collective communities and logically reasoned in this fashion to produce village-based land reforms in revolutionary Mexico, in many ways to reverse the Díaz privatization efforts in the late nineteenth century (Kourí 2002). In northern Mexico, where the revolution began, it was a side note to regional and local battles between largely elite families. Land redistribution (or outright distribution) was not guaranteed, but was certainly part of the revolutionary rhetoric (Sanderson 1986). The ambivalence of Mexico's political leadership in regard to communal resources and management led to a fractured geography of communal institutions. Phases of populist land redistribution have been countered or subverted by private interests, or reversed, during presidencies that favored single-party ownership (Sheridan 1988).

The new geographies of communal resources in Mexico established after the Mexican Revolution were a matrix of both old and new ideas. On the one hand, the populist-socialist element influenced the creation of the "new" ejido program that would become the cornerstone of land reform efforts in twentieth-century Mexico. On the other, the extant indigenous communities could reclaim communal ownership through the formation of *comunidades* (alternatively called *bienes comunales*, depending on the context). The distinctions between these communal "agrarian nuclei" seem minor on the surface, but the institutional cultures of each are quite different, and each created a patchwork of contrasting rules, customs, and smallholder practices for communal management. As Robert Netting (1993) has demonstrated convincingly, smallholders are much more concerned about specific title, control, and ownership over arable land. Mexico's land reform efforts following the Mexican Revolution held true to this general pattern, and the results were remarkable compared to most other Latin American agrarian reforms (Dorner 1992).

The ejidos of the study region along the Río Sonora were among the very first in the state of Sonora following the Mexican Revolution. Most of the preliminary reforms and land grants to the community were performed in the middle of the 1930s. Still devastated from the conflicts of the revolution, towns like Huépac nevertheless benefited from these early land reforms (Hewes 1935). Before the end of the 1930s, in fact, new agrarian nuclei in Baviácora, Aconchi, Banámichi, and Arizpe had all received ejido lands, redistributed from privately held irrigated cropland and arid rangelands (Baroni 1991). Another arrangement was that of the comunidad, which harkened back to an "indigenous" past in the legislative rules governing this form of land ownership system. Unlike the ejido, the comunidad was not a "state-supported" redistribution. Those filing under the comunidad laws were then distinguished from the ejido. Both comuneros and the federal agencies that served the ejidos generally recognized that it paid to be part of the ejido system, which was simply more plugged into the political process of land redistribution. In addition, once the boundaries of the comunidad are set by law, they cannot, in theory, be increased in the future. Conversely, ejidos in the past could file for expansion and increased redistribution of private lands (Sheridan 1988). In a twist that may exaggerate the difference between comunidades and ejidos, the 1992 reforms to Article 27 of the Mexican Constitution specifically spelled out that only ejidos would be allowed to gain full, private rights and land titles (see chapter 6). These latest reforms did not apply to indigenous comunidades, since the comunidad could decide to approve or not approve individual titles for comuneros. To take part in the PROCEDE process, a comunidad would have assembled as a community to publicly decide whether or not to go through the certification process before any such distribution to individuals could occur.

Private Revolutions, 1937–2007

The post–World War II boom of cattle ranching in Mexico is well known and well documented (Chauvet 1999). For the first time, scrawny, bony, free-range cattle acquired an international price as targets for international trade and development efforts. Unlike southern Mexico, northern Mexico had long been home to an extensive cattle-ranching industry, historically tied to mining (West 1949). Yet the seeds for private ranching's survival were, ironically, planted in the Cárdenas administration: a 1937 decree that any property having five hundred or less head of livestock was a "small property" and thus not subject to redistribution as Mexico underwent its largest and most aggressive phase of agrarian reforms. This short-term measure was later amplified as local cattlemen's associations began aggressively pursuing an extension to the previously temporary reform freeze. The "private revolutions," a slow but steady consolidation of private ownership not prone to land redistribution, are still in effect. In Sonora, and throughout northern Mexico, ranchers persuasively argued for large tracts of open rangeland to support the theoretical five hundred livestock. Cleverly hiding these five hundred was sometimes a challenge for local ranchers, who would deed or gift several hundred head to a wife or child, or simply move them to a neighbor's land if any agrarian official came to call at the ranch. But these practices make it clear that property as a concept is a contentious right, not a thing, and has been continually contested between individuals and the state (Merrill 2002, 5).

The study ranches along the Río Sonora Valley, all fourteen, and the other three lying outside the watershed, have survived the era of land redistribution—though many owners still begrudge the loss of irrigated *milpa* (irrigated field) resources and find the ejido's presence cumbersome or illogical given the number of cattle now found on communal property. All of the Río Sonora study ranches received certificates that would stymie future efforts for communal property expansion in the region; these were all received in the early 1940s, with one arriving as early as 1938. The three ranches located outside of the Río Sonora Valley have also survived intact, with practically no loss of resources, due to their distance from populated villages and their political heft with local authorities. As Bantjes (1998, 225) has summarily stated for Sonora, "The continuity of the Sonoran economic elites is marked: neither the revolution nor Cardenista reform replaced this group with a new revolutionary bourgeoisie." Pushing further in this vein, one of the overlooked elements to Mexico's revolutionary agrarian reforms is the built-in accommodation for private property; it was never just about communal lands. Yet new agrarian communal nuclei and previously land-poor households did benefit from the reforms.

One eighty-year-old ejidatario, however, had a different take on the creation of corporate, ejido lands. He remembers that when the ejido programs began to include a fight for more grazing lands in the 1950s and 1960s, private ranchers in the municipio of Baviácora immediately invested in barbed wire fencing, fenced off as much land as possible, and defended their "new" lands zealously. The legitimacy of this move is still questioned and one of the great local "games" to this day is to move fencing back and forth between private and communal ranches and even between private ranch spaces. Lands that before the ejido programs were commonly grazed by dozens of owners without much thought or coordinated control were now in private hands for the first time. And the boundaries between the false binary of "private" and "communal" have begun to ossify into something profoundly influential on the social relations of local communities, even if, in rural Mexico, local practice and continuing assumptions about joint ownership remain.

The era of free-range cattle grazing was closing quickly in the latter half of the twentieth century, although in areas where ejidatarios could not afford fencing, it survived sporadically in a patchwork mosaic well into the 1980s (Pennington 1980, 240). The changes meant that communal cattle ranchers had to tread more carefully and on smaller grounds than before, seriously increasing the number of animals per area in the corporate grazing lands. In no small way, then, the "tragedy of the commons" was created not by a free-rider problem of selfish cattle owners, as Hardin (1968) would have it. Rather, it was the conjoined technological diffusion and adoption of fencing and the success of private ranchers in rhetorically and legally arguing for the small property that could support five hundred head of livestock. In the first case, fencing off enough of the previously open range and the lack of land became a tragedy for those hoping to increase their herd numbers; they were simply confined to a smaller space for grazing, with the same consequences for native grass cover as happened in southeastern Arizona (Bahre 1991). In the second case, the rhetoric of the "small property owner" in Mexico became difficult to counter; private ranchers successfully defended any communal thrust into rangelands for decades, with only limited expansion success in the 1960s confined to the dryer western side of the river valley.

As ranchers successfully and spatially ringed the communal town areas of the Río Sonora with private properties, ejidos and comunidades were physically constrained. That spatial fixity of the communal lands was exaggerated in the late twentieth century, as the ejido's herd grew with no physical "room" to grow. Some forty-two hundred animals now graze only thirteen thousand hectares in the municipio of Baviácora, a very high grazing pressure for what is essentially desert vegetation (INEGI 1986). Small bribes to local police enforced the new de facto if not quite de jure boundaries of private ranches. These private ranches within the Río Sonora Valley expanded during the twentieth century.

Location and Context of Study Ranches

The fourteen study ranches in the Río Sonora region, along with the three larger estates located outside the study region, reveal the similarities of geography in ranch locations and distributions throughout the state of Sonora. Most private estates remain away from the river valleys, in the foothills of the Sierra Madre Occidental and in the mountainous regions of La Serrana. The distributions of these ranches first evolved in association with nearby mines during the Spanish viceregal era and now appear loosely clustered as satellites to nearby towns that are the social focal points. Although some ranchers may travel hundreds of kilometers, as in the case of absentee landowners living in Hermosillo or any other large Sonoran city, most of the ranchers reside ten to fifty kilometers away from the ranch. Of the fourteen study ranches, all but three were affected by land reform efforts stemming from the revolution. The three ranches that were unaffected by the redistribution of resources were all located outside the region. Their locations far from nearby towns decreased the political pressure felt by officials at the time and ensured the survival of these enormous landholdings. In fact, it can easily be argued that the latest wave of ejido reforms enacted by then-president Salinas in 1992–1993 may have consolidated this reactionary evolution of land tenure.

The Mexican Revolution and its aftermath were more centered on the unbalanced distribution of arable land and cultivated earth, not on the semi-arid grazing lands that served as the extensive areas of the large estates. Ranches along the more arid coastal plain also escaped the effects of communal land reforms, though many ranchers who owned irrigated pastures in the large watered districts, east and west of Hermosillo and along the Río Yaqui, did have substantial amounts of cropland taken during the 1970s. The landed estates closer to the American border, however, were much more open to redistribution. Many of these had been American owned and were thus appropriate "political" targets for redistributions. The few American-owned ranches in central Sonora, along the Río Sonora and Río Moctezuma, also suffered this fate. While the owners of these ranchers had largely left the region by the end of the revolution, many of their relatives (*parientes*) and associates remained behind. For example, "Frisby" is a common family name in the Río Moctezuma

Table 2.1 Land resource ownership in the Río Sonora Valley: Ejido, communal, and private property, by percentage and hectares

Municipio	Ejido (%)	Communal (%)	Private (%)	Combined (ha)
Arizpe	0.6	–	99.4	254,781
Aconchi	1.3	–	98.6	11,630
Banámichi	1.6	–	97.4	62,562
Huépac	1.6	1.2	97.2	12,699
Baviácora	4.1	1.0	94.8	35,632
Rest of state	20.9	1.2	72.6	7,519,245

Source: INEGI 1994b.

Valley, near Cumpas, because an American family intermarried with the surrounding community, a common occurrence prior to the Mexican Revolution (Truett 2006).

Landownership patterns in the municipios of the Río Sonora Valley reflect the successful retention by private owners of the majority of the land base. Table 2.1 clearly illustrates the dominance of private properties in the valley.

But while private ranches have always held many common features, these ranches are quite different from one another, in terms of biophysical characteristics and of management tactics and strategies employed by the owners. Ranching has always relied on proxy labor, second-hand human agency, and features of these estates and small ranches diverge at the level of the organism. The original *criollo* breeds and herds are disappearing, interbred and slowly dissipating as newer, European strains of cattle are folded into the mix. Animal scientists in the livestock industry refer to this interbreeding as "herd improvement," with little attention given to the external costs of genetic changes on ranches. Indeed, in the twenty years between 1970 and 1990, the categories of "fine" and "crossed" livestock (those considered "improved") grew by 585 percent (INEGI 1994b). What are the unintended consequences of these genetic improvements? Who can afford them, and how do they benefit ranchers, if at all? First, we turn to the land managers and owners in chapter 3, and then we discuss the ecological dimensions of these changes in the following chapter.

3   Land, Labor, and Resource Management on Private Ranches

The private ranchers of Sonora, including those in the study area of this book, have successfully defended much of their landed estates, despite the early twentieth-century land reforms. Their role in the defense of private property has been likened to a passive-aggressive nature, and while hired guns are not uncommon, they are less common today than during the height of land and water conflicts (Bobrow-Strain 2007). The tactics and strategies pursued by private owners reflect those pursued elsewhere in Mexico, as they flexibly accommodated or fought certain provisions of land redistribution along the valley. The lack of large, irrigated, private estates along the Río Sonora meant that little of the privately owned milpa land was affected by land reforms. Unfortunately for ejidatarios and comuneros, the national provisions for dividing large estates were not customized for local conditions, and along the Río Sonora and other narrow, semi-arid valleys of northern Mexico, much of the most valuable arable land was excluded from expropriation by the state. In fact, the early grants along the Río Sonora to communal owners consisted of a mix of rain-fed (called *temporal*) and irrigated lands, and not the prime green irrigated areas so coveted by landless cultivators. The land-tenure revolution, however, did little to change range management in northern Mexico. Barbed wire, changing labor relations, and the influx of new capital did play significant roles in how contemporary ranches are managed.

As private owners with outright title to their properties, ranchers make both direct and indirect decisions for land and resource management. Small and modestly sized properties depend on the ranch owner primarily, although family and hired labor certainly add to the mix and variability of decision making. Without family participation, the smaller properties are never financially viable; few owners can afford nonfamily labor for their ranch spreads. The larger properties have a form of management by proxy: indirect by the owner, more direct by the laborers or mayordomos (work bosses) who essentially make the decisions on a daily basis. Complementing the range of decisions handled by ranchers and their labor crews, mayordomos must also handle the relationships between ranchers and ranch workers. The human resources, then, of ranches are just as important as the biophysical natural resources that most range scientists focus on. For some, however, the ranch remains not only the economic base for their living, but their identity.

Management by private ranchers entails both decision making and the manipulation of natural resources on the ranch. By *management* I simply refer to the control of production and reproduction of the ranch unit. While the overtly functionalist nature of the word is difficult to sidestep, these land managers also care deeply about aesthetic and seemingly nonfunctional aspects of their daily tasks. One rancher, for example, was absolutely compelled to move rocks to the borders of footpaths. When asked if that was to protect the hooves of calves using these paths, he simply responded, "Well, sure, but I also like the way it looks and it helps me find my way around." So while many of these daily routines and habits have some *function* to them, they may not be as overtly functionalist as observers might interpret them to be. By *resource,* I mean any biophysical feature that is either important in caloric yield per unit or culturally identified as important or useful. What may be a resource for one person may not be viewed as valuable or needed by another, underlining the importance of perception in the definition of a *natural resource.*

Ranch management occurs on two levels, not scales per se (Sayre 2005a). The ranchers (or owners) themselves are the ultimate decision makers who set overall ranch policy. Their employees, the mayordomos or vaqueros who reside much of the time on the ranch, are responsible for decisions involving day-to-day operations. The scale of management can be understood at the micro-level, where the herder or vaquero is vital, or at the macro-level, where the ranch owner or mayordomo makes the larger decisions based on market prices, shipping costs, and balancing the inputs and outputs of the ranch itself in the context of competitors and regional prices. Perhaps not surprisingly, the degree of involvement of the private rancher is inversely correlated with ranch size: the larger the ranch, the less the owner is involved with daily management operations. This rule holds true in the ecological management of the ranch, yet the rancher is the central figure in the economic management of the property.

Ranch labor, then, is incorporated in the production process at the most basic level: primary extraction from natural resources. The extraction of surplus value for the rancher operates between his *base* primary economy of nature and labor, and the eventual value of animals as they exit the ranch. As the private ranches in this study vary widely, a distinction must be drawn between the land base and the resource base available to each rancher. This distinction is central to my arguments: the ranchers with a variety of economic options generally do not place the ranch as the central concern in their long-term economic strategies. Those ranchers more closely tied to their land base as the primary, or sole, source of income place greater emphasis on both the economic and ecological management of the ranch. The importance of the ranch to these ranching households decreases with size along a continuum of size and land resource reliance. This difference between land base and resource base is especially apparent, and important, for the larger ranches, which are discussed later in this chapter.

Land Base versus Resource Base

All things being equal, the larger the ranch, the wealthier the rancher: perhaps easy statements for an economist, but unfortunately, not all things are equal or stay equal. In fact, let us dispense with the expression "all things being equal," as they have never been. It must be emphasized that ranchers are not homogenous in nature as a social class. They should not be treated as one pole of a binary opposition to communal or ejido ranchers (see Vásquez-León and Liverman 2004 for one example). This diversity of class roles is as true for Sonoran ranchers as it is for livestock owners everywhere. Class differences certainly cannot be ignored or discounted, but they are not the only fulcrum point in understanding rural conflict based on or about resources.

As much conflict occurs between private ranchers as occurs between private ranchers and communal farmer-herders (ejidatarios). Only when the question of debate is pitched at a larger-than-ranch scale, such as in arguments over the expansion of communal lands or rights, do private ranchers collude or agree to cooperate as a loose conglomerate. Then, and only then, some form of livelihood identity takes shape as so-called stakeholders begin to see commonalities or threats to their perceived well-being. Socio-economic history, inheritance, and variety are much more critical in understanding the geography of ranches both large and small. Private ranchers do, of course, collectively stick together when faced with communal annexation or unclear governmental intervention. Any inkling of collective bond, however, is strongly shaped by how vital the ranch is to a household; for some, it is a minor part of their livelihood strategy. Bonds between ranchers are also shaped by the local, political culture, and conflict or disagreement between private ranchers can be accentuated in an election year. Such was the case between two ranchers in the town of Banámichi.

El Cartucho turned off his computer and came out to meet me late one night in Banámichi. We spoke for a few hours, and then headed to the local hamburger joint to discuss the details of a visit to one of his two ranches. On our way over, I waved to Señor Sarella, whose ranch I visited a few weeks before. Cartucho waved but did not turn to look at his neighbor.

"So you know Eduardo?" he asked me.

I told him that I was there two weeks ago. He grunted an acknowledgment and then continued.

"So did he talk about politics the whole time?"

Unsure how to respond to this question, I answered him that we kept the discussion to his ranch and his family's history in Banámichi. Cartucho nodded slowly.

"Good," he continued, nodding.

I was unsure why he said it, but I didn't press the matter. It was only a few days later, in the same hamburger joint, when the owner of the establishment explained to me what was going on in the town.

"You see, we're tired of how things are done here. We want the PRI [*Partido Revolucionario Institucional* (Institutional Revolutionary Party)] out of the town hall; we want change, not so much corruption." No matter how I attempted to escape the issue or change the subject, it always came back to local politics, as 1997 was an election year. It was also a conflictive time for the valley's ranchers, and many were involved on opposite sides of the political fence, for the first time in their lives. El Cartucho is cousin to the family that for the better part of twenty-five years has been in charge of local politics in the municipio of Banámichi—and they are all supporters of Mexico's official party, the PRI.

"These people [PANistas—supporters of the generally right-wing opposition *Partido Acción Nacional* (National Action Party)] are all talking about 'change' like it means something—as if the PAN is going to change everything. Of course it's not, and the point is that if we vote for the PAN, we will lose a lot of the benefits from the governor, from the state." Like many ranchers, Señor Cartucho was emotionally wrapped up in the political scene that election year (1997), and it had led to some conflicts that he knew people would regret.

"The other night at the quinceañera of my cousin's daughter, a fight broke out between some people wearing some PAN paraphernalia, and the security at the ballroom door. The local police refused to let them in because they were wearing political decorations, you see, and that's not the place or time for that sort of thing."

The election of 1997 came and went, and Banámichi stayed with the PRI but only by a narrow margin of votes. Despite a few problems on his ranch, Cartucho was pleased for several weeks and eager to forget the neighborly animosity of several months.

Many small ranch owners have a far greater variety of resources, in the form of businesses, irrigated land, or farm machinery, than the size of their ranch would suggest. In contrast, many large ranchers are limited by the lack of other capital resources, even if the land base of the ranch is tremendous. So the amount of external capital that can be used on ranch properties swings across a wild spectrum: ranchers depend on family, on friends, and less frequently on formal bank loans or government programs for resource improvements.

These other resources, then, may be viewed as economic options: sources of income in times of rancher need. This concept harkens back to that of the "range of choice." Pre-dating Blaikie and Brookfield's emphasis on the "land manager," the "range of choice" in land management reflects the use of resources and the options faced by any given land manager (Wescoat 1987; Kull 2004) and serves as an important distinction for understanding the human ecology of how ranch management occurs. Adaptation is not a preoccupation for ranchers, as short-term decisions are the major concern; thus the tactics adopted by individual ranchers or vaqueros are more strategic in nature rather than reflective of an "adaptive strategy" that goes beyond the immediate needs of the ranch or rancher (Perramond 2007). For those few ranchers who still derive the majority of their income from their ranches, ranching is not a lucrative venture, but the value placed on that lifestyle is such that economic arguments rarely matter.[1] The analysis of ranch sizes makes distinctions easier, as one moves progressively from smallholding ranchers to the truly landed estates, here termed *mega-ranches*.

Private Ranch Management: Labor, Allocations, and Decisions

Before considering a quantitative approach to management approaches on the various ranches included in this study, some critical qualitative aspects of traditional ranch management need to be understood and explained. Most of these practices have been documented in previous studies, but never as a whole body of knowledge that could be called "traditional ranch management." And yet, similar to traditional crop farmers in Latin America (see Wilken 1987), homegrown Sonoran ranchers have a variety of activities that shape and direct the landscapes of their own ranches. Many of these categorized activities, of course, melt into other facets of ranch management: maintaining ranch infrastructure such as a road can help stave off further slope erosion that can cut off ranch access in the rainy season. These are not, then, separate mental categories reflecting their approach to ranch management. These are almost purely observed behaviors, a way of understanding the different facets and aspects to private ranch management. But they add a further dimension to this analysis of private ranches, a flavor for the diversity of challenges and lifestyles of these cattlemen and cattlewomen. Such activities are important to understand since many studies on ranching fail to include even basic management decisions in the landscape context. Range science and agricultural economics are less concerned, in other words, with landscape change than they are with the micro-level decision making or broader economic context and impacts of cattle ranching. The study ranches are then compared in quantitative terms.

Herd Management

Cattle ranchers, to varying degrees, actively manage their herds. They are able to actively shape and influence ecological processes through the movement of animals. Yet the simple term of *herding* belies the complexity of decision making and possibilities involved. Herding, or the movement and rotation of animals from pasture to pasture, can take shape in multiple ways. Some ranchers are able to seasonally rotate their animals by pasture, especially if a ranch has substantial elevation differences across grazing areas, although this is more typical of larger ranches. Small ranch owners must typically make do with four to six pastures, separated only across horizontal space, with less topography to work with over the course of a year. When, where, and how often these pastures are used are the critical decisions to make for the herding operations. Pasture rotation of animals is also, not surprisingly, where ranchers differ from each other both by opinion and by actual herding practices.

One small ranch owner I spoke with, not part of the seventeen case ranches intensively followed in this work, claimed that spreading all his cattle across his entire 800 hectares minimized damage throughout the year. It also allowed him, he claimed, to minimize labor expenses since the cattle were not actively herded on a daily or weekly basis. He simply kept bulls, calves, and heifers separated in the various pens as he shifted them once every month or so. His concern was for cost and less for the condition of the ranch, even if it simply allowed him to excuse his own lack of active herding. The ranch's location near floodplain fields, rich with alfalfa, close to Arizpe, certainly made it easier to supplement his animals with feed crops during drought. When I recounted this herding decision to another rancher living outside Alamos, to the south of the Río Sonora, he called this "madness." Instead, he managed his 1720 hectares according to strict precipitation and vegetation conditions. "Look, if you don't take advantage of what God provides or ignore rain patterns, you're screwed. If I let my cattle stay in the same place for longer than two weeks, my ranch would be ruined and the animals dead." In fact, most ranchers do practice some form of rotational grazing, however hap-hazard the system may seem.

Herding practices and beliefs provoke intense discussions at gatherings of ranchers and emphatically highlight the different approaches taken by individual owners and by the cowboys they employ. Small ranch own-ers rarely have the means, if the ranch is their primary livelihood and source of income, to invest more time and labor in herding strategies that may reflect the state of the art in range science. By comparison, some larger ranch owners are justifiably proud of their ability to keep up with "modern advice," as one cowboy put it. Sonoran ranchers with a larger resource base share much in common with private ranchers across the border in southern Arizona, as they attempt to track weather fronts and stay current with market-price triggers in the livestock trade, a point that has been made in comparative studies of ranchers (Vásquez-León, West, and Finan 2003). These efforts are a key factor in running any kind of ranch operation, and over the course of the last ten years, prices paid have fluctuated seasonally but have slowly declined in real value. In 1997, the average price in the calf export market was US$1.52/pound; by 2007, this price was hovering at US$1.50/pound (Unión Ganadera Regional de Chihuahua [UGRC] 2007). But while small-time ranchers may not be able to track this kind of information carefully, it does not mean they spend less time on management.

The size of the ranch is a good proxy for the amount of active "rancher" involvement, in that large ranch owners have several laborers on their property, and small ranch owners almost never have the luxury of a hired hand. While herd management does center on labor, access to labor, and the skills of a herder, it also intersects with what is being managed. The *corriente,* or criollo, cattle so common prior to the arrival of improved breeds are still visible in Sonoran herds. While some look like they just got off Hernán Cortés's boat at Veracruz, most are now intermingled hybrid species, with some additions from the western U.S. and European breeds now common throughout northern Mexico. The type, number, and individual vagaries of animals all have a strong role in how the herd is managed, when it is done, and how often cattle are moved or rotated between pastures.

Rangeland Slope Management

Most Sonoran ranchers are not worried about what resource managers, scientists, and bureaucrats term *soil erosion*. As one owner of a small ranch put it best, "I'd worry about that if I had good soils, but look around you, it's a desert. I'm lucky anything grows here. It all depends on the rain." Ranchers and vaqueros will use the term *erosion* in Spanish when they see it on a roadside or a hilltop, but it is generally not an important consideration when managing a large property such as a semi-arid ranch. All of the ranchers in this study, however, did recognize the importance of soil slope maintenance and management. Their concern is less with soil than it is with animal access, pasture maintenance, and their own ease in moving about their property.

For animals, especially those with a high percentage of improved breeds, the gentler slopes enable easier access to fall and winter pastures. Broken terrain, gullies and soil pedestals, and canyons do not make for easy access. The longer-horned corriente cattle can scramble up and down steep soil faces at an alarming rate and are of less concern for ranchers. But owners of prized breeds are especially cautious and conservative about allowing Brangus or Charolais bulls to roam at will or go beyond eyesight in broken topography. In this aspect of management, only four of the study ranches allocated any labor to maintaining slope integrity and trails for cattle. In every case, the concern was for expressed "trail maintenance," so that animals could navigate and negotiate the difficult terrain to and from pastures at lower or higher elevations. This took the form of lining trails with rocks, bracing eroding or slump slopes to maintain access, or in the case of one owner, sowing steep slopes with collected grass seed. Nonetheless, these are minor forms of land manager intervention as most ranchers are far more concerned with their water resources and manipulating ranch environments or with low-tech solutions to provide for their cattle.

Water Management

Private ranchers in Sonora have always considered water sources an important asset to their operations, whether these are the more common ephemeral dry washes that course through their properties or a more permanent spring. Even on the large ranches, water resources are scarce and troublesome to manage, but they are the most precious commodity given the dependency of large livestock on fresh water. Add to this challenge a large range of water needs, according to cattle breed, and it quickly becomes clear why land managers and cowboys are anxious about water.

Various settings, distributed unevenly throughout the region, provide water resources. And while efforts in range science and conservation groups are bringing new attention to low-cost options for managing rangeland water resources (see Sayre 2001), most ranchers in this region remain highly skeptical of these new low-tech derivatives given their past experiences with the range science "development" experts. Beyond the local cattlemen's association in any major town, ranchers are frequently reluctant to engage in work that seems bureaucratic. The state-level institution for networking and doling out "expert" advice, PATROCIPES (Patronato del Centro de Investigaciones Pecuarias del Estado de Sonora, A.C.), still occasionally struggles in its efforts to create "progress in the ranching industry," one of its stated goals.

Natural Springs. Five out of the seventeen study ranchers have natural fresh springs on their properties (fig. 3.1). In the geological setting of the Río Sonora, these are more common on the eastern side of the mountain ranges, where small limestone fissures interspersed among the older rock formations provide an escape for artesian springs and perched seeps, especially above eight hundred meters in elevation. Unlike some areas on the western side of the valley, these are rarely geothermal and contain little of the noxious sodium content that could prove harmful to cattle in a dry environment. While the springs vary from a small, pathetic trickle putting out perhaps a liter per minute to a large water source pumping out a hectoliter per minute, their use by ranch managers is key to the survival of livestock. Two of the ranches featured fresh springs so minor they sustained only a minor drinking pool for cattle. Yet the owners viewed them as critical for the survival of their animals, given the broken and uneven terrain of their properties. The other three ranches had substantial springs, used not only for livestock but also for ranch manipulations.

Figure 3.1 A rancher at his natural spring. These water sources, while frequently small, are critical to the success of the ranch.

The latter can resemble crude irrigation devices used to spread water across semi-arid rangeland in order to promote vegetation growth.

Pseudo-irrigation Strategies. For ranchers lucky enough to have a surface spring or seep with enough flow, a type of pseudo-irrigation is possible. Transporting the water from the source to the targeted pasture is the only challenge, and usually the decision is to use gravity-fed water. Only one rancher with a spring was also using a gasoline engine to pump water to a higher and frequently dry pasture on his ranch. In this latter case, the owner allocated an explicit sum of money every month to the gas fund for his water pump. His rationale was that given the natural flows of runoff he had observed during light rains, if he brought a low-flow amount of water to this high pasture, it would naturally drain to some of his lower pastures over time, improving the entire range of grasses covering the slope. The added expense of a gas pump, then, was justified in his mind because he used it only sporadically with a set budget for the added inputs of fuel and labor. One unanticipated expense of this plan, however, was that the hose type chosen to run from spring to upper pasture became brittle every two to three years given the remarkable heat in this part of central Sonora. But in fact this plan had its intended effect: the lower pastures were lusher in a single season than he'd seen in his lifetime. "My father would shit his pants if he were alive, this pasture was never this green when he worked this land," he remarked.

Stock Ponds and Retention Features. Of all the strategies used by ranchers, stock ponds and retention features are by far the most common. Any site located near an ephemeral wash or stream (arroyo) typically has one or more of these features as a way to interrupt flash-flood waters. In the rainy season, local precipitation events produce muddy torrents of water that can be diverted and stored for the subsequent weeks, even if much is lost to evaporation over time. Very few remain as permanent features, although longer-lived examples, properly located and occasionally fed by a raised water table or a perched aquifer near the surface, tend to be used as the central herding facility during times of drought. These are, not accidentally, also close to the central ranch housing structure, allowing for closer care and supervision by the vaqueros or the rancher. Three forms of these retention features are common in this region: On the upper slopes of drainages, ranchers will cross-bed the drainage with what look to be check-dam features to spread water onto surrounding local depressions or swales. These are short-lived water features that may last a few days or up to several weeks. Also common are upland ponds, where several dry washes converge on a plateau or mesa that may then be dug out to create an upland stock pond as a local feature. These tend to be close to the ranch facility or the small house and are longer lived as water features. Finally, in the lower-slope ranches approaching the river valley, ranchers frequently grade the floodplain with several depressions in the dry wash bed or to the side of the central wash to capture flood runoff during the rain season. Although also ephemeral, these features tend to last longer than the high-slope diversion swales and are crucial for livestock at lower elevations, herds moving through the small tributary valleys on their way to towns for sale, or seasonal grazing on the floodplain.

Natural Runoff. On the majority of ranches in Mexico, using precipitation and ground runoff to improve range conditions is unusual. Commonly known as *water harvesting* in the development literature, few ranchers practice this technique as it requires near-perfect timing and available labor and resources to guide runoff to an intended area of the ranch. Additionally, few ranches are so flat or even in terrain as to make this practice conceivable on a functional basis. It is far more prevalent in the arroyos at lower elevations, before these ephemeral streambeds join with the larger Río Sonora floodplain. Three ranchers in this study, however, practiced various forms or elements of water harvesting on their own properties. In one case, the owner had used tires on a gentle slope, arranged along the contour, to retard the rate of water runoff. He hoped this would allow more water to infiltrate into the upper soils and thus encourage some palatable grasses to return. The effort had limited success, in his view, but enough to justify continuing the experiment on some other slopes. He noted that although some grass cover returned in front of the tire line, grass flourished within the tire void and cattle could be seen grazing on this new source of palatable grasses. Appraising his row of tires, I remarked that he created a tire garden of *Bouteloua* grasses. His smirking response was, "well, I guess I'm a tire gardener, then."

Groundwater Resources. Apart from the springs, seeps, and surface water management techniques previously discussed, ranch owners and managers have also turned to the invisible water beneath their feet. Groundwater, in the last thirty years, has become a vital resource for maintaining herd size and animal health especially during the normally occurring drought cycles in Sonora. Without the new wells allowing access to groundwater, stock densities would be at least half of what they currently are on every ranch dependent on groundwater. This estimate was given to me by most ranchers, and there is no reason to doubt the figures. At first, few exploiters of this new source of water were conscious about the longevity or sustainability of withdrawal rates. They frequently extracted five times the quantity their ranches receive in precipitation, on average. Only in the late 1980s did the extraction rate begin to receive attention by both range extension workers and the ranchers themselves. Discussions with laborers, mayordomos, and vaqueros made it clear that they knew what was happening to their localized water table.

The arrival of new technologies, such as deep drills and hydrological monitoring equipment, has been greeted with optimistic caution; yet not all ranchers benefit from these expensive pieces of technology. In fact, out of the seventeen study ranches included in this study, only five boasted of their own deep-drill well, which depends on gasoline pumps for the extraction of precious groundwater. The consequences of these deep wells are felt regionally, affecting those who have drilled and their neighbors who have not. One of the most fundamental changes to the ranching industry and lifestyle in Sonora and northern Mexico, in general, has been the arrival of these deep-access rigs. Yet their very presence is an effect, not a cause, of changes within the larger industry dependent on the presence of so-called improved breeds. So while ejido members struggle to find and pay for groundwater in agriculture, ranchers face the same prospects; groundwater is a scarce and expensive resource (Wilder and Whiteford 2006). As an example, five ranches in this study had access to groundwater resources through a deep well, yet only three of those wells remained functional as of 2008.

Infrastructure and Access

For large ranches, no single cost is greater than the initial setup of road construction, fencing, and general ranch infrastructure. Annual maintenance costs also add up quickly. Given that many of these ranches are located up to forty kilometers (about twenty-five miles) away from the nearest formal town, the largest long-term cost is road maintenance. Ranchers will attempt to spread the cost and risk of road maintenance by cooperating among themselves, but also by influencing local, municipal, and state authorities to produce indirect aid through road maintenance or extension projects. Adding to the cost and challenge of these seemingly simple "ranch road" projects is the fact that many access routes follow natural dry wash channels, or arroyos, that are seasonally flooded during the late summer and occasionally in the winter. A single kilometer of road grading with heavy machinery can run into tens of thousands of pesos for new clearance and is still prohibitively costly for existing roadways.

Typically, road maintenance is the single largest, but occasional, cost ranchers face and also a source of friction between ranchers when cooperation is lacking.

Fencing is no longer the time-intensive project involved in building purely wooden fence barriers across semi-arid ranges. Since the advent of barbed wire in the late nineteenth century, and its arrival in Sonora during the twentieth century, the time-costs of fencing have plunged. As labor costs and needs declined, however, the capital input cost for purchasing fence materials skyrocketed. Even small ranches need kilometers of barbed wire to enclose their property lines; and kilometers more are needed to subdivide the land into pastures for rotational grazing, if practiced. The poorest of private ranchers simply cannot afford internal subdivision of their ranch and are reduced to manually herding their animals from area to area during the growing year. Fences, then, are one way to minimize high labor costs and inputs. One vaquero from a study ranch, Trini, illustrated the trade-offs and challenges of replacing human labor with fence infrastructure.

Trini and his son were leaving the ranch on a Sunday morning in November, heading to town to sell their homemade cheese at his boss's grocery store on the plaza and to catch the late church service.

"Stop by my house later, I should be done working by about ten o'clock tonight," Trini yelled to me as we crossed paths in our pickup trucks.

I asked when he planned on returning to the ranch. He looked blank.

"Well, tomorrow, of course." To take a day off, in his view, was unthinkable.

Trini is at ease with the cows in the corral. He knows their names. He knows which ones kick, and which ones simply refuse to have their back legs tied for a milking. He only gets the opportunity to make the cheeses in the late fall, once most of that year's clutch of feeder calves has been sold from the ranch. I met up with Trini at his house in town later that night.

"This ranch is too big for one man. I have to get my sons to help me sometimes, though Lobo doesn't know most of the time, but my son . . . especially my young one has to have a skill. If he doesn't do so well in school, he'll have something to fall back on. That's why I bring him out here. We go out to the high pastures and I quiz him on grasses, see if he can track mountain lions, though we haven't seen any this year thankfully. But every once in a while we got a few dead calves—it happens in threes as they say," he adds chuckling. He turns serious, however, when discussing the future of ranch hands, vaqueros, in the region. "I don't see a future in that," he quickly responded. The ranch owners, he argues, can no longer pay a living wage, and so there are far fewer ranch workers today than thirty or forty years ago. And these vaqueros, to be clear, hold local knowledge not commonly shared or comparable to the ranch owners. They work the area closely, know where ephemeral water seeps occur, how and where to herd the animals after a rain storm, when to move the animals down the arroyos to graze on the field crop stubble on the floodplain once the harvest is in. And few vaqueros transmit this knowledge to their sons (or daughters); Trini is one exception. But even he realizes the declining use for hands-on labor in the new Sonoran ranching industry; ranching as a domain of agrarian development projects has not been kind to labor.

Ranching as a Development Project

While the triumph of private cattle ranching in Mexico seems unquestioned, the role of the state has been vital to the survival, if not outright longevity and success, of the industry. Livestock projects as an important avenue for economic development were aggressively promoted during the latter half of the twentieth century. Parastatal government agencies in Mexico were created to extend credit, provide expertise, and promote the so-called improved breeds and pasture seed technologies bundled for creating a more productive livestock sector. International funding agencies were also intertwined with these activities and formulated much of the policy directives involved in these livestock developments. Just as Norman Borlaug, the father of the Green Revolution, promoted improved seeds for the agricultural crop sector in Mexico, the new agencies and bureaucracies of third world development groups promoted improved breeds to battle the seeming inefficiency and proto-historical nature of most cattle-ranching efforts throughout Mexico. These efforts were not restricted to a few states, but were widespread promotional actions, focused primarily on the country's herd structure and genetic makeup (Cotter 2003).

The famous criollo (or corriente) common breed slowly started losing ground as the dominant breed in most herds, first disappearing in the herds of large, wealthy private ranches, and then declining even in the humble communal herds of ejidos and comunidades. But the aggressive promotion, hybridization, and artificial fertilization of cattle was but one of the development "encounters" for improving ranching's efficiency and modernization in Mexico (Escobar 1995). These efforts were packaged as a total sum product for modernizing agriculture in Mexico. For livestock, the process was termed *ganaderizacion*, roughly translated as the "livestockization" of the country. In addition and intimately tied to the breeds came a raft of other pushed development "packages" that were to revolutionize cattle production. African grasses, improved feed crops for cattle, and livestock credits for ranchers were the complements to the improved cattle breeds. These were the conjoined development items to be incorporated in the "new" Mexican ranching economy (Chauvet 1999). Simply adopting the livestock, without new feed and water resources in place, was a poor decision for the vanguard of ranchers who attempted this move. As we will see in chapter 4, countless early "experimental" European herds met with a tragic end in Sonora; some were placed under metal roofs in the desert and died of heat exhaustion, while others were improperly inoculated against neo-tropical animal diseases.

Labor and Resources on Private Ranches

In addition to these qualitative portraits of the study ranches, the data gathered from questionnaires and interviews aided in understanding and explaining what informants qualitatively described. The following summarized estimates illustrate the important relationships between labor allocation, ranch management, and the important "sectors" so critical to managing a ranch.[2] While large ranches employ more people, the key difference is in the number of hectares per worker. On the small ranches in this study, the average was seven hundred hectares per person; for the medium ranches, this average increased to fifteen hundred hectares per person. On large ranches, fewer people are available on a per-hectare basis, and this difference is also reflected in the amount of time and type of activity in which they are engaged. So the large ranch average was just

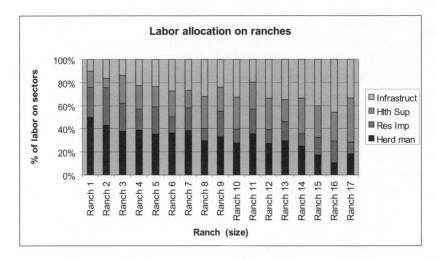

Figure 3.2 Labor allocation on ranches. The percentages are based on observations and tally sheets completed by cowboys and laborers working on the private ranches. (Adapted from Perramond 1999, 103)

under twenty-six hundred hectares per person, while the so-called mega-ranches averaged some four thousand hectares per person. These data illustrate the difficult choices owners must make in placing management decisions in priority.

When the data are broken into *factors* of land management, the information becomes more meaningful. Figure 3.2 displays data on labor inputs for all of the ranches in this study. The figures were in hours per week per worker in all cases and were then converted into a percentage for the figure. The total amount of labor expended, in other words, may be far greater on larger ranches. Normalizing the figures *per worker* provided a clearer picture of how management varies across the size continuum of private ranches.

These data were both observed and estimated. Direct observations and measurements were made by the author, complemented by both direct questioning and time-expenditure estimates tracked by cowboys and ranch laborers. Each cowboy (in charge) was provided with a simplified form to fill in the hours worked daily. These figures were checked weekly or bi-weekly. Despite some occasional gaps in record keeping, the memory of those involved ensured a good measure of success. A similar technique was used by Sheridan (1988) with smallholders and by Grossman (1984) in tabulating labor estimates for time allocation on specific tasks. Since these cowboys are the direct agents for land management on most of the ranches, they have a clear understanding of the time expenditures undertaken for each kind of activity described (Dary 1989).

Figure 3.2 illustrates several important trends in the data. First, note the steady decrease in direct labor invested in "herd management" as ranch size increases. Second, there is an observable increase in "health care and supervision" of animals on the larger ranches. An interesting and third revelation from these data is that "resource improvements" are given much more attention on smaller ranches, in terms of time expenditures, than they are on the larger ones. Finally and perhaps not surprisingly, large ranchers spend more time allocating labor to the maintenance of their ranch infrastructure (roads, fences, corrals) than do owners of smaller ranchers. Akin to the impact of scale in horticultural systems, the larger ranches display the trend of decreasing labor intensity, though with increased levels of capital inputs on these larger ranches. This observation parallels the arguments made by Netting (1993) for household versus industrial farms, in that actual measured efficiency by space and resource use is higher on the smaller properties than on the supposedly advantaged larger estates. This trend has been substantiated for the communal ejido sector as well (Kay 2002).

Resource Assets and Ranch Assets

Ownership of horticultural land, as explained, is a key to the success of these dryland ranchers. Canal irrigation systems feed most irrigated croplands in the alluvial soils of the Río Sonora Valley, and the maintenance involved is well worth the effort; ranchers depend on *la milpa* (irrigated fields) watered by the irrigation canal (*acequia*) systems of various towns. Without the milpa, they would no longer have the necessary, seasonal inputs from cattle feed crops or the access to field stubble after the summer and fall harvests. While large ranch owners generally have more irrigated pastures available to them, for food or feed, there is important variation. Some, such as ranch 3, owned by the Sarellas, have enough irrigated

Figure 3.3   Animals on *la milpa*. One of the linchpins of Mexican ranching is the agricultural floodplain support system, much of it now converted to cattle feed crops.

land to support large numbers of cattle. Their medium-sized grazing land resources are supplemented with over 36 hectares of irrigated cropland from the Banámichi district. This land is critical to the maintenance of the ranch and the survival of cattle, as these lands can support up to three animals per hectare when needed (fig. 3.3). In other words, over one hundred animals can be fattened when the timing is right. The overall resources of a ranch family are vital to the owner's decisions, and in overall strategy, for the particular ranch. They also play a strong role in determining the nature of the land market in the Río Sonora valley, as is common elsewhere in Mexico (Bresciani 2004, 213).

In addition to the grazing and horticultural assets of these households, other economic assets are, of course, vital. Put simply, the total assets available to ranchers increase with ranch size. The dramatic difference, however, is visible in the move from large to mega-ranches, especially when the total family assets are included. True to its past, Mexico still has a rich heritage of landed families, many of whom have successfully defended these private estates from communal takeover efforts. But "landed families" elides, as a category and descriptor, the wide range of resources available to them. Many of the truly wealthy have access to credit and revenue from a variety of sources: selling beer at a local *expendio* (liquor store), owning a small store or business, working as a middleman in the local wild chile market, or making some stiff *bacanora* (mescal) to sell during the holiday season.

Thus, ranchers hold more assets than the ranch resources and animals they own, and much of this is due to the accumulation of assets in the commercial sectors or because of the importance of family and inheritance as previously discussed. The difference between a one thousand–hectare rancher and a six thousand–hectare rancher, then, is not as great as the difference between a six thousand–hectare ranch owner and one of the true mega-ranchers. This difference was borne out by the data on animal numbers. Large ranchers have much more land per animal than do small ranchers. Those fortunate enough to maintain herd size through irrigated pasture "subsidies," like the Sarellas (ranch 3), can "cheat" the numbers of carrying capacity. Although frequently understood as a *fixed* number, carrying capacity changes on a weekly basis for most ranches, and so is sensitive to either natural inputs like precipitation or anthropogenic inputs (Sayre 2008). In this case, beating the fluctuating capacity involved feeding their cattle fodder crops from the rich irrigated lands of Banámichi. These additional resources, it should be noted, are never considered in official estimates for ranch or rangeland carrying capacity; of course, extension experts realize that ranchers move their animals back and forth between dry range and wet floodplain. But the normative picture of carrying-capacity estimates is a fixed estimate based on rangeland alone and does not include the feed subsidy that is now par for the Sonoran grazing course. The disparities in resources, however, were sharper when larger ranch properties were considered.

The mega-ranches examined in this work escaped the expropriation of rangelands during the late twentieth century, and if they have one advantage, it is that they are far removed from towns. Proximity to settled populations increases the chances of corporate versus private resource debates and battles. However, in labor control, owners of these ranches are faced with a double-edged sword. Ranch owners cannot oversee labor inputs from a distance, even though they are generally urban dwellers, impelling them to hire an additional overseer (again, mayordomo) for the vaqueros. That very same distance-decay effect, however, has been important to the long-term survival of these huge estates. They have faced little threat of expropriation because they are so distant from arable lands with access to irrigation. Most of these truly large estates were consolidated through family links, hiding ownership through kinship title arrangements, in order to proclaim them "small properties" under Mexican agrarian codes and laws. In other words, a ranch that covers tens of thousands of hectares may have twenty registered legal owners; agrarian reforms and redistribution were dodged tactically through a complex mosaic of land-tenure division. The vast majority of private properties, however, are more humble affairs. Many have been inherited or purchased by incoming migrants from other regions of Mexico in the twentieth century, while some have also been purchased more recently or divided amongst heirs. Countless others are creations of former ejido members who now own their own ranch outright. Yet the process of becoming a private rancher, or even qualitative profiles of these people, is rarely found in literature on ranching. Because the "process" of becoming private has remained elusive in the social science literature, it has reinforced the binary of "private" or "communal" in land-tenure discussions.

Becoming a Private Rancher

In the traditional order of dichotomous social science treatments, someone engaged in ranching is either a communal or a private rancher; the transition to private ownership, much less co-ownership, is ignored. In fact, the scholarship on land tenure has ignored land ownership as a flexible concept, a right or privilege in flux, where a range of options is possible. Property is not a simple object; it is subject to a process of negotiation over access, definition, and contention. Falling under a different arrangement of property law, a "new" private rancher can effectively change the governance structure of land and water resources, a point lost on most critics and analysts of cattle ranching (cf. Merrill 2002). For members of an ejido, land rights are usufruct, still federally owned in technical terms, and land users are still subject to the will and whim of the larger ejido organization and its ruling council at the local level. Ejido members must also negotiate with state-level officials and with the larger federal umbrella of the ejido as a federal commons still owned by the Mexican nation-state. With one foot in the ejido and another branching into private, simple title ownership, relationships become more complicated. The communal rancher can still run her cattle on the ejido, even as she is setting up her own private estate for the long term. This betweenness of land tenure is rarely accounted for in systematic studies and can muddle the clarity of the dichotomous property regimes, as communal versus public is no longer the only land-tenure contention.

One of the poorly understood facets about land ownership in Mexico is the decision and transition made by communal ranchers who become private owners of rangeland. Are they still communal, part of an ejido, or have they forsaken both the institution and the shared communal grazing lands? The answer to this often difficult question is generally both yes and no. Ranchers who own private land, yet remain part of the recorded householder list of ejidatarios, can still retain their role as a communal institution stakeholder. One of the wealthiest ranchers in Baviácora, for example, still runs cattle as a comunero in the small town of Mazocahui to the south. Because of kinship ties and the past registration of family members as comuneros, he has retained this right and membership even if locals in Mazocahui may grumble about his lack of presence in their town. Or, as one woman put it, "It's unfair that he still runs animals here—he has his own beautiful ranch near Sinoquipe!" Yet most comuneros admit this practice is the norm, that it is not unusual for private landowners to come from, and retain rights to, the commons in Mexico. When asked whether comuneros would prefer to see private landowners completely withdraw from their resource base, the responses are equally ambivalent. Some quipped immediately, "Yes, he should go," while others weighed the question carefully since they viewed his potential exclusion as problematic. As one of the comuneros put it, "Well, if he did leave Mazocahui with all his animals, it might be okay for other cattle owners but maybe not for everyone here, since he also maintains his ties here and will throw parties or be a godparent to some poor families. So it may not be good for us."

Typically, however, the transition from communal to private involves a gentle phasing out of communal role-playing into one in which private concerns are dominant. In doing so, they sever most of the rule-making institutional connections to the old commons, whether ejido or comunidad. And yet they may retain the social, kinship, and *compadrazgo* (godparenthood) ties that still link them personally to individuals within the commons. In becoming "private," communal ranchers hoping to make the leap to outright ownership face several challenges. First, capital is needed for the purchase of the property itself and any needed infrastructure such as a road or ranch house. Second, access rights must be at least tentatively negotiated with other private owners if a shared access road is in play. Finally, the person must be able to start producing some revenue in the second or third year after purchase to meet loan obligations and to start reinvesting in a larger herd. Because financial capital is in such limited supply, the examples I encountered of a transition from communal to private ownership were limited to a few scenarios. Some entered into co-ownership with an existing private ranch owner, unable to afford the entire cost of both property and a new herd of livestock. Others depended heavily on family loans and capital to purchase their first ranch and herd as they tried to avoid formal bank loans of any type. Finally, some returning migrant workers, having earned enough in the United States, were able to purchase ranches outright.

Migration from Mexico into the United States has been a constant thread of life, income, and seasonal practice in this part of Mexico since the 1940s Bracero program in the United States. Linked to the male labor shortage of World War II, the United States contracted Mexican labor for set periods. Many of these first Mexican workers created social migration and employment networks that their sons and daughters used in the 1950s and 1960s. This generational social chain has been maintained, and I met a family that linked back to the Bracero through three generations of their family: parts of their family now spent the entire year working in southern California in the San Bernardino area. The subsequent phenomenon of the *remittance effect* has had clear impacts in many parts of Mexico with a strong migrant tradition. The billions of dollars now flowing across international borders have led to rural construction booms, new housing complexes for extended families, and new capital availability for all manner of enterprises. The purchase of a ranch, especially for returning men, is usually one of the first return practices of this new migrant generation.

The livelihood is viewed as one of the few honorable income generators in an area with few other employment possibilities. Perhaps just as important is the lifestyle it allows, the mythology attached to ranching and rural life, for returning sons and daughters who grew up in a cattle culture replete with songs and a respect for the practice.

The Betweenness of Condueñazgo: Joint Ownership

One of the possible midway points for the transition between communal and private land ownership is the practice, still common, of condueñazgo. This form of joint ownership is common in Mexico, usually found in kinship arrangements to avoid partible inheritance, but little is known about the contemporary aspects of joint management, use, and ownership. Kouri's (2004) study of joint ownership as an important dimension in nineteenth-century Papantla, Mexico, is one of the few serious treatments on the subject. But his example is far removed, in time and space, from the current dimensions of this form of land-tenure holding. Two of the ranches in the Río Sonora Valley profiled in this book are under joint ownership. In the case of the Rábagos ranch, two brothers shared the small ranch property. In the other case, however, no kinship ties existed, a situation that has proven problematic for both owners of the property.

Jesús, one of the owners of ranch El Aguaje, bought into a partnered arrangement with an already existing private rancher, Nacho Morales, agreeing to carry three-fourths financial ownership in the enterprise. What followed, however, is less typical of condueñazgo as a theoretical land-tenure construct. In the fall of 1993, Jesús was falsely accused of "squatting" on the ranch without due title or co-ownership rights after money had been transferred. He was unceremoniously arrested once by the local judicial police and placed in prison for three nights. Although he was released after the long weekend stay, his co-owner continued to hound him using political and extralegal means. Jesús returned to a longer prison term of five months until a judge reviewed the arrest case and termed it illegal and unwarranted given their initial agreement and contract arrangements for co-ownership (see also chapter 6). These arrangements, then, carry special risk when little social or cultural capital exists between potential or real co-owners.

Figure 3.4 Jesús, back on the ranch again. After years of conflict, this *con-dueño* is back on his co-owned property. Co-ownership is a poorly under-stood dimension of the private/communal dichotomy in Mexico.

Even in daily affairs, Jesús was constrained in his abilities to manage the property and especially the infrastructure as a newly private land-owner in the valley. He complained only a little of his past legal prob-lems, but his attention was focused on maintaining the road that accessed his ranch fifteen kilometers east of Baviácora (fig. 3.4). "I wish El Lobo would help me pay to get this road fixed up, or at least the miners who cross this road on their way to Cumpas and Nacozari, but do they help? No, of course not, they never will . . . *conchudos.*"[3]

Maintaining this road was a serious problem for Jesús, with only him-self and occasionally his younger brother, José, doing most of the labor required on a weekly basis. He spent long hours on the ranch, frequently by himself, because he could not afford to pay any day laborers for extra work. Typically, extra help is enlisted from the towns to clear ranch roads after violent storms in the rainy season, which send heaping masses of colluvium, rubble, and boulders down onto the small dirt track. These become permanent roadblocks until cleared. Jesús, of course, could not rely on his co-owner, Nacho, for any help whatsoever. The latter had essentially pulled all cattle from the ranch, refused to sell the remaining quarter interest in the property, and rarely went to the ranch. Still, as a safeguard, Jesús kept a rifle at the ready in case he needed to flee the ranch again. Such is the life of this *condueño* (co-owner).

But the arrangement of co-ownership is still a common occurrence in Mexico, and has been one means to becoming a private owner, even if it is still commonly overlooked in discussions of land tenure. For many, it is the terminus; they will never wholly own a private property. For some, it is the intermediary point, a stopgap measure to build capital over time and eventually acquire title ownership. And for a tiny percentage, it is merely a grand experiment, as one former condueño explained to me. Outside the town of Alamos, in the south of Sonora, I met a man who had just sold his "share" of the ranch to two other people as he was never able to improve his financial circumstances being a co-owner. As he reflected, "I thought it would be a good way to make money, get land, raise cows; then the peso devaluation came and it was clear I didn't have enough land to make it. I lost money for three years, and then got out while I could. Maybe I was just unlucky." In many ways, it was a repeat, in the entire region, of the financial crisis following the crash of 1982 (Montaño Bermúdez 1991). Trial-and-error experiences have been common to ranching and to ranch owners; yet most land managers have held on successfully, able to sustain even small enterprises over the course of generations. Total failure is the exception rather than the norm in the ranching lifestyle.

Learning from—Not Preaching to—Traditional Ranching

I could not believe the size of the bird in front of me. The girl dangled the dead chicken in front of me, hoping that I would buy one, which I quickly did. I told her I had not seen chickens that large since Virginia. She tilted her head and asked me where in Virginia, in perfect English. I responded with my hometown, and she beamed at me, claiming that her brother Gerónimo had spent a year in the town just down Interstate 81 studying poultry science. Though I remained a little incredulous, I met

the boy not hours later in the main plaza, where El Güero was serving up
the best bacon-wrapped hot dogs in Baviácora. Gerónimo and I spoke for
a few hours, reminiscing over the Shenandoah Valley we both knew, and
the conversation turned to what I was doing.

"So you're here to see what we do, instead of telling us what to do or how
to do it?" He seemed flabbergasted. I explained again but he cut me off.

"No, I understand, it's just different." I asked him what he meant. His
face became serious.

"Everybody thinks we don't know what we're doing, like we're stupid,
and we're treated like idiots by the government and livestock inspectors
from Hermosillo. We know what we're doing and how to do it. It's just
that it's becoming harder to do."

A constant and bitter strain in rancher rhetoric is their opinion of the
so-called technical experts in range management. While the number of
visiting agronomists or range extension workers is still low in the state of
Sonora and throughout northern Mexico, their impact and the shadow
they cast is significant. Ranchers and cowboys alike constantly complain
that they are treated poorly, viewed as simple people, unable to express
their opinions and knowledge with the extension experts. There is great
ambivalence, to be sure, in these relations. After lambasting a recent visiting range scientist, one rancher quickly changed expressions and told me,
"but he gave me some new pellet poison that is supposed to kill *chiragui*
(*Acacia cymbispina*) in a month." These small technical packages and
samples are both appreciated by ranchers and a common currency for
range and agricultural experts. All of the ranchers featured in this book
clearly wanted to be thought of as "progressive" and informed about
their ranch: to try the latest products and to exchange information about
cattle breeds, water management, or the latest supplemental feeds. Yet
they are also highly conscious of the cost barriers to being a full and
first adopter of new technologies, a point now clearly problematic in the
development literature and a sore point from the so-called Green Revolution days (Cotter 2003). Simply put, few farmers and ranchers can afford
new and expensive technology. Fewer still have the income necessary to
be part of the local "vanguard" in adopting these right off the bat.

Much like Mexican smallholding farmers, Mexican ranchers have
adapted to this situation flexibly, according to income or opportunity,

yet still remain vexed by the lack of availability or poor information on new range products. They know their rangelands, know where water resources are located, and they have great knowledge as to the local flora and fauna nearby. Most private ranchers have a vision, an ecological-landscape ideal to which they aspire, yet they are limited frequently by the lack of resources, inputs, or simply raw capital. As this study suggests, range experts and extension workers should be working with and learning from, not always preaching to, these local ranchers.

There are, admittedly, ranchers less committed or interested in grassland conditions and cattle health. These types of ranchers are usually maligned, or at least constantly teased, for their lack of knowledge and for using the ranch as a hobby. They are not viewed as real *ganaderos* in local Sonoran society. So the prototypical stereotype of the "ignorant rancher" is both an early twentieth-century example, before Sonoran ranchers were aware of the multiple breeds or new technologies, and the latest emergent personality of a new "urban cowboy" complex unraveling in the country-side. The majority, however, are clearly interested in their ranches, ranch operations, and rangeland conditions. "It's still a business, you know," opined a rancher discussing the latest trends in ranching, "and we have to adapt economically to bigger markets and bigger players, just like a corporation or a company." And to do so, they have to negotiate success-fully the administrative and bureaucratic space that separates them from government officials and range experts in Sonora.

The negotiations between expert and "local" forms of knowledge and managers shape the social relations and dynamics of private ranch-ing, the ecology of ranchers, and the political norms and rules affecting physical environments through time. The state agencies exhibit a form of "environmentality," as Agrawal (2005) has defined it, that not only diagnoses and prescribes rancher behavior and actions, but also actively engages in physical reforms and proscriptions for future decision making in private ranching. To paraphrase Agrawal's concept: these agencies are interested in creating rangeland "subjects" that ascribe to certain norma-tive standards of behavior and landscape modification and understand-ing. For example, one of the ranchers in this study was visited by an extension agent from PATROCIPES, who kept referring to desertification of his pastures, which should worry the rancher. After about an hour of this deluge of information, the rancher simply responded, "How can you desertify something that is already a desert?" The extension worker shook his head with a smile and qualified his statement with "Okay, let us agree that it is now more of a desert in appearance than it used to be." The agent took the quiet glare of the rancher with a simple nod of acceptance that his point had been made, but privately the rancher was not satisfied. He later stated to me, "Of course, my father used to say that my ranch had more grasses, more oak on it, but I hate it when these *científicos* [scientists] come in and tell us a story of what has already happened. I want to know what to do now." Both parties in this case had a clear conception of environmental history or, better put, environmental memory, yet neither was willing to concede to the narrative of the other.

Admittedly, private ranchers are rarely held to the vast majority of recommendations or prescriptions and have found effective solutions or tactics to dealing with state "expert" knowledge purveyors. Just as they have developed ways of avoiding ecological damage to parts of their rangelands, they have avoided economic or policy recommendation damage by filtering out what is nonsensical to their circumstances or biophysical settings. This statement does not imply that everything "local" in ranching is superior or a better way of handling management. That viewpoint would be playing into what Purcell and Brown (2005) termed the "local trap" of development thinking. What ranchers do use, in effect, is a local filter. Ranchers sieve information, advice, and new technologies that are seemingly appropriate for them, ignoring what they find to be spurious, too expensive, or simply ridiculous. If they are cautious and skeptical now, it is only after a long and tired recent history of failed experiments, as many were naïve when first approached about improved rangeland technologies. And while ranchers have a clear understanding of the micro-scale changes in ecology and vegetation changes over the last forty to sixty years, they also note how important it is to be "careful about saying the wrong thing" when discussing these matters with state range management officials.

This chapter discussed the importance of ranch size in the decision-making processes of ranchers (owners) and those who work on the ranches. Clearly, ranches are not biophysically equal, rancher knowledge or ability is not equal, and the continuum of land-tenure variations is key to understanding both the physical spaces of ranches and the people who practice the livelihood. It is common for private ranchers to retain stake and voting rights in local communal institutions, be it ejido or comunidad. It is also common for private ranches to be split or shared, or even co-owned in the case of condueñazgo. Joint ownership is challenging within kin relationships and is especially tenuous when little social or kin capital exists between the joint owners, a clear reason why this kind of land-tenure holding is a minority in modern Mexico. Who makes the decisions, especially in joint ownership operations, quickly becomes a contentious issue on the range. These decisions, tactics, and strategies have an importance far greater than the mundane event of a decision.

The full impact of these decisions is visible in the ranching landscapes of Sonora. The next chapter addresses the biophysical impacts of management and, in many cases, mismanagement. The term *mismanagement* is not used for moral judgment, but rather to underline the strong role that political institutions play in the "authoring" of the environment (Robbins 1998). The label of mismanagement, used by so-called rangeland experts, strongly distorts and shapes how decisions are made on private ranches. It also provides a wedge, or entry point, for range experts to inject themselves into the complex mix of decision making. Few outsiders get access to actually shape eventual decisions. The bulk of daily, mundane choices and actions are executed by ranch laborers, vaqueros, and, in the case of small ranches, by the owners themselves.

4 Ranch Ecology, Landscape Change, and Power

The small, narrow canyon valley glowed with the orange-yellow hues of oaks and willow leaves turning, a few leaves brittle underfoot, as autumn arrived in the Río Sonora.

"I've got the most beautiful ranch in the Río Sonora Valley, eh?" said Señor Dariel as he elbowed me in the gut. I agreed, of course. No other ranch visited had its own reservoir complete with a canoe for boating. We passed by trilobite fossils in the canyon walls. The rise in elevation from the turn off the main highway to the ranch was noticeable as we left the shrubby thorn scrub of the Río Sonora Valley behind us and climbed into the grassy oak land once so expansive in Sonora. Adolfo's ranch was not the largest ranch I saw, but it was certainly occupying one of the most desirable locations in the Río Sonora cattle country. Precipitation was more reliable at this elevation, he claimed, and it was only in the past few years that he felt the drought economically.

"I normally get about 58 to 61 centimeters of rain every year, but not this year. This year [1997], it's been pretty dry, and the little rain we had was in the early spring. We haven't had enough during the summer. That's why the grass looks so brown right now. Normally, it's bright green at this time of year."

The ranch was acquired in the traditional way of patchwork purchasing, the original grant reaching back into the early national period of Mexico, 1836 to be precise, when the foundling nation-state was desperate for solid currency. Over a century-and-a-half of expansion, the size of the ranch nearly doubled, reaching its eventual 6408 hectares.

"The worst thing this year has definitely been the grasshopper plague. I haven't seen it this bad since 1983. Maybe it's because of all the winter rain . . . I don't know, but they absolutely devastated the *zacate salado* (*Leptochloa filiformis*) and left only the thorny bushes behind."

Adolfo was exaggerating, of course, because compared to neighboring ranches he was in good shape for the coming year. His ranch's pastures, especially those at higher altitudes, were underlain by rich brown topsoil rarely seen on the ranches in the Río Sonora Valley. Areas more level were filled with coarse sediments, and the hills were littered with rocks and pebbles. Again, the hills of this ranch provided a significant ecological subsidy to his enduring herd of cattle, topsoil that consistently produced high grass year after year. The biophysical diversity of this valley, the history of the region, and the management decisions taken by private landowners have all created a complex mosaic of favorable and less favorable ranching contexts. Adolfo is one of the lucky ones, if you can call it luck. He is a descendant of one of the more powerful ranch families in Arizpe, and his ranch is not some accident of good fortune. Son of an already wealthy merchant and rancher, he had little to do but inherit the ranch; Adolfo has nevertheless purchased a few small, additional range pastures during the last thirty years and has steadily made small landscape improvements to facilitate ranching.

The climate, ecology, and geographic setting of ranches does matter. But the geography of private, co-owned, and communal grazing lands is not accidental; it is not simple providence or fate that the best grasslands are in the hands of large ranchers. Ecology, power, and the uneven history and geography of access to resources feature prominently in this story. Part and parcel of the complex mosaic of land tenure in the Río Sonora is the role of the state in abetting the current situation. What once was a marginal, frontier-type activity, associated with mining during the colonial period, was reenvisioned and reinvented as a way for Mexico to become a livestock-exporting nation-state. The embedded nature of state politics in ranching was embodied as a "livestock-as-development" strategy pursued by several states in Mexico. Sonora featured prominently in this unrolling of development activities, abetted by international loan agencies and policies that encouraged the cattle export market in the late twentieth century. This process was less about *adaptation* than it was about *adoption* of technologies, development ideology, and new rancher strategies and tactics. It is why the landscape ecology, cattle and grass hybrids, and power are inseparable. They have been, intentionally, a conjoined project and process in the region. In this chapter, we focus on the interrelated nature of these factors and the profound ways in which they have shaped the Río Sonora.

As previously discussed, cattle ranchers and ranch laborers, as land managers, have transformed the biophysical landscape of the Río Sonora Valley. This truism belies the range or panoply of decision makers involved in the transformation of both landscape and society. These landscape changes reflect the shifts in political-economic, social, or governance forms. But landscapes and ecology also shape the contours of human decision making and governance policies. Accordingly, as landscapes themselves are constantly changing, they alter the range of choices and options available to ranchers, vaqueros, state agencies, and NGOs. These decisions made individually or in response to larger sets of sweeping policy recommendations and adoptions are directly or indirectly transferred to the landscape through a complex calculus of land manager decision making and bureaucratic interventions. Similar processes can be traced across the Borderlands. The power of these landscape changes and the difference between nomadic versus sedentary pastoral activities were all too vividly clear across the border during the large cattle boom in Arizona near the end of the nineteenth century. As external (largely British) capital subsidized a completely unsustainable boom industry, southern Arizona witnessed an open range grazing system that overtaxed local ecologies (Abruzzi 1995; Sayre 1999). A similar process, distinctive because of its unfolding in the late twentieth century, has occurred in Sonora.

The contemporary and recent decisions by ranchers have created altered and hybrid landscapes across the entire Borderlands. Two common trends in agriculture and ranching were visible in the latter half of the twentieth century. The first change, as mentioned previously, was a notable displacement of food crops for cattle feed in irrigated districts, essentially a decline in mixed agriculture that integrated livestock into crop horticulture. The second trend was the increased adoption of so-called improved breeds and grasses on arid rangelands, as both communal and private ranchers attempted simultaneously to add value to their enterprise by adopting breeds more in demand by the global market for meat and to stem the decline in carrying capacities due to localized overgrazing of native grasses.

Climate and Vegetation

The climate and vegetation of the Río Sonora are typically considered semi-arid. While the region receives more average rainfall than the hyper-arid Sonoran Desert to the west, much of the river valley now hosts species considered arid. Higher reaches of the foothills have milder, wetter regimes and vegetation that reflect the difference. Precipitation varies widely on annual and seasonal bases, averaging between four hundred and five hundred millimeters for the Río Sonora Valley (Dunbier 1968). Of this, more than 60 percent of annual precipitation occurs as violent thunderstorms during July and August, referred to locally as *las aguas*. Winter rains, or *equipatas*, consist of light showers, particularly between December and February. A marked dry period follows the equipatas, with the driest months extending from March through June. The traditional end of the dry season and the beginning of the rainy season falls on June 24, the feast day of St. John the Baptist.

Vegetation patterns in the Río Sonora watershed closely parallel precipitation and elevation gradients. In the valleys, between 400 and 750 meters in elevation, some stretches appear as true desert. Here the assemblages of cacti (*Opuntia* spp.), agaves (*Agave* spp.), desert shrubs (such as *Acacia* spp.), ocotillo (*Fouquieria splendens*), and trees such as mesquite (*Prosopis* spp.) and ironwood (*Olneya tesota*) dominate the flatter areas (Doolittle 1988, 7). Higher in elevation, leaving the valley east or west to 800–1800 meters, are found juniper (*Juniperus monosperma*), a variety of oaks (*Quercus* spp.), and native grasses such as black grama (*Bouteloua* spp.). These species are especially prominent in the northern areas of the study region, with greater amounts of *Opuntia* spp. and *Yucca* spp. in the rangelands of the southern municipios of Aconchi and Baviácora. A few subtropical species occur along the moister canyon bottoms and seasonally flooded arroyos of the watershed, including *torote* (*Bursera adorata*), brazil tree (*Haematoxylon brasiletto*), and kapok, locally named *pochote* (*Ceiba acuminata*), the latter clumping in larger stands around 800 meters in elevation on northern slopes (West 1993, 11–13; Field notes, Baviácora, MX, November 2–14, 1997). During the late summer rainy season, the native grasses can provide luxuriant grazing for cattle, if the rains are plentiful. In times of drought, annual or seasonal, animals will happily browse on mesquite pods, high in fats and proteins, and even venture into the thornier assemblies of acacia. Private ranches are found in a wide variety of vegetation and elevation regimes of the Río Sonora Valley, and depending on the combination of climate, grasses, slope, and topography, even gargantuan spreads can be marginal places for raising livestock. For example, ranches located on the western side of the Río Sonora Valley have less land cover and less precipitation on average. The more arid, degraded rangelands on the rain-shadowed western slopes of the valley lack the biophysical complexity of the other ranches.

Poncho is one of those unfortunate souls whose ranch is located on the west side of the Río Sonora, yet not far enough to be cooled by higher elevations.[1] His ranch averages 5 to 13 centimeters less precipitation than ranches located on the eastern side of the valley. The mountain ranges create the infamous rain-shadow effect in which the downwind side receives far less precipitation, the bulk of the moisture drops on the windward-facing slope, and the effect is certainly visible on his barren scrubland. He makes do with a herd of rangy, mixed cattle, content with his corrientes as they tend to be hardier under the Sonoran sun. The ranch is only a twenty-minute drive west of Baviácora and accessible by a decent graded road that goes to the old mines located south of the property. Poncho employs no ranch hands, doing most of the work himself or bringing a family member along at times. During roundup, branding, or other crucial times of the year, Poncho will bring in outside help. But those occasions are few and far between, and he makes the drive to and from the ranch on an almost daily basis. Poncho then faces two major dilemmas. First is the shortage of labor; doing almost all the work himself limits what he can accomplish in one day. Second, and by far the more important, is the location of his ranch on the rain-shadowed slopes west of Baviácora. In fact, his ranch adjoins several other rangelands that have only recently been put into use by communal ranchers, because these lands are notoriously bad grazing for cattle. The dense mats of nasty acacia rip at the animals and jeans alike.

"I don't want problems with the ejidatarios, but they want to take away what's mine, what's always been in the family, and that's why I have to go to court a lot," explains Poncho. More than most, he understands that not all ranches are equal, even if the animosity over land, even poor

quality land, can be just as heated. And the dimensions to these conflicts are complicated by the now necessary integration of floodplain feed
crops into the drylands ranch complex of the region.

The Wet and the Dry: Ecological Subsidies and Breeding Scarcity

Over the last fifty years, the integration of grazing livestock with field agriculture has declined in Sonora.[2] Rather than an example of mixed food
crop agriculture, the floodplains now produce feed for cattle and ranchers
increasingly dependent on an ecological subsidy from wet, irrigated fields.
The large, meat-bearing cattle species now common in the Borderlands
are a far cry from the rangy, tough criollo cattle that once roamed the des-
erts. Exotic, largely Euro-American crossbreeds, real hybrids, now lumber
across rangelands of northern Mexico. Forage scarcity on the ranges has
been "bred," created by the adoption of these resource-hungry breeds.
Ranchers were cautious about adopting European breeds too early, given
the failures in the history of livestock development initiatives. In the 1950s,
private and communal ranchers started to cross their animals with Zebu
cattle for better drought survivorship and retained value on the hoof.
Brahman breeds such as Zebu, modified from their South Asian ances-
tors in the United States, are quite popular for their heat tolerance and
are ubiquitous in the southeastern states of Mexico. They typically have
more sweat glands and can cool off more efficiently in high temperatures.
A touch of their skin quickly confirms how wet, even oily, their hide feels
when the temperatures reach triple digits. More recently, Angus, Brangus
(Brahman plus Angus), and Charolais have found favor on the private
spaces of ranching. These are hybrid animals, hybrid landscapes, and
hybrid livelihoods in the truest sense of the words. For a region already
well grazed and in localities overgrazed, the added burden of supporting improved breeds seems illogical. Economically, they have had a posi-
tive impact on the short-term livelihoods of both private and communal
ranchers, as the price per animal is higher for improved cattle breeds.

Ecologically, these temperate and new tropical breeds require greater
access to groundwater resources, and the water table consequences are felt
throughout northern Mexico. In other words, any scarcity experienced

by ranchers can be partly attributed to the adoption of the new cattle breeds. The irrigated floodplain of the Río Sonora, once planted in staple food crops and a diverse mix of vegetables and specialty plants, now grows almost entirely alfalfa in both planting seasons. The milpa has become the life support system of the dry rangeland, the wet subsidizing the dry portions of the Río Sonora, as crop horticulture encounters the wider market of imported grains and foods. The spatial fixity of true cattle ranching, with the decline of open range and transhumance, has created a permanently modified agro-ecosystem. With permanent boundaries for animals and an internal division of pastures, livestock must be consciously moved to mimic the natural herding impacts of native fauna. If domesticated livestock are spread across pastures or kept enclosed in any one pasture for too long, the condition of the grassland can change severely. This change in how animals are allowed or directed to graze across a pasture or the larger watershed has had profound changes on semi-arid rangelands (Sayre 2001, 24–25). The experience of Sonoran ranchers has paralleled those using transhumance elsewhere globally, and concordant increases in energy transfers have taken place (as noted by Gómez-Ibáñez 1977). Ranching has evolved in concert with the demands of local inhabitants and the historical consequences of their choices, as we shall see. These changes have also structured the agency of land managers in distinctive ways.

My argument is not based on a crude form of landscape determinism; nor am I arguing that environments in and of themselves drive landscape development or social processes. I view this approach as a more honest and explanatory way to describe the substantive nature and relationship between landscape and society rather than as a subterfuge for mild or biophysically disguised forms of determinism. This framework neatly encapsulates and recaptures the inherently political aspect of landscape, in that political actions or events influence land-use changes, and that landscape change can then be a mechanism for amplified or constrained cultural politics at the local level. Politics, after all, can begin when two or more people disagree and must find some form of culturally acceptable compromise or solution. Changing a field crop, converting a field from corn to alfalfa, or reinforcing a portion of barbed wire fencing—all these actions provoke a response or a change in tactical politics by neighbors.

The physical landscapes range from the floodplain of the Río Sonora with its assemblage of cottonwoods and mesquites, to the high-altitude oak stands on mountaintops, home to a wide variety of oaks and a few remnant pine stands. Ranging far and wide between the river and the mountaintop, cattle can be found on the flatter mesquite-dominated tracts in the southern portion of the study area and on the extensive ocotillo plains in the municipio of Arizpe, more typical of the northern sections of the study area. While these biogeographic generalizations hold true for the present state of grazed landscapes, much evidence suggests that these semi-arid plant mosaics are constantly changing. So while the Río Sonora landscapes are *sensitive* to climate, cattle, and floods, these same areas are also more *resilient* than conventional wisdom would have us believe. Compare any pasture in the wet and dry seasons in Sonora, and the visual difference is remarkable. But that resiliency, ecologically, is impinged by the decisions made on communal and private rangelands. In this way, the Río Sonora study region is typical of other arid regions, in that the nature of Clementsian ecological principles, so driven by the teleological idea of a final "climax community," may not ring true. In other words, ecological theories and frameworks derived from temperate lands may not be entirely applicable to more unstable (or more variable) semi-arid environments (Behnke, Scoones, and Kerven 1993; Bestelmeyer et al. 2004).

The central notions of ecological or ecosystem *stability* are then the genesis of cries of degradation, defined by traditional ecology as any process "thought to deflect the biotic system away from" stability (Sullivan 1996, 3). When one person's degradation is another person's accumulation, it is preferable to focus on a social definition of *environmental degradation*; the research presented in this study is based on this perspective, rather than on an ideal notion of what *should be* present (Blaikie and Brookfield 1987). For example, erosion from ranches upslope becomes the sedimentation and bounty of farms and ranches located lower downslope.

In semi-arid environments, nonequilibrium and stochastic processes may prevent any permanent or stable form of vegetation, a point that only emerged in range science in the 1980s (Westoby, Walker, and Noy-Meir 1989). This dynamic concept of biogeography allows for more openness, nonequilibrium explanation, multiple scales of analysis, and a focus on the internal factors or mechanisms producing the plant geography presently found in the Río Sonora study region. Because grazing is an interruptive disturbance process in almost any landscape, the plant communities are kept in a constant succession treadmill and are not headed in any particular *climax* direction—this is the fundamental importance, or bottom line, for the concept of multiple stable states (Westoby, Walker, and Noy-Meir 1989). These grazed surfaces may remain stable or unchanging for months or several years, but they are constantly in flux, as overviewed in the following section.

Vegetation Change in the Río Sonora

Historic vegetation change in semi-arid regions remains a popular and controversial academic research topic. Many have sought to comprehend, or at best document, "desertification" (Bahre 1991; Sullivan 1996). Contrary to the popular image of fast-moving sand dunes engulfing entire regions, this process of vegetation change is related to changes in species composition, density, and general biome types. For Sonora, this process of so-called desertification has meant the historic spread of thorny shrub species into areas formerly unaffected by such vegetation, usually grasslands, and in many areas a lowering of local water tables because of groundwater pumping (Brown 1982, 141). In this context, then, defining desertification by an increase in tree-form land cover is ironic. However, what is clear from analyses of the processes that can lead to more arid conditions is that the nature and definitions of desertification are relative. Shreve (1937) described this vegetation ecotype as "Sinaloan thorn scrub," and the locational adjective seems to be appropriate as many ranchers identify this new plant presence as coming from "the south" or "from Sinaloa" or even further, from "the coastal regions." Even Mexico's own national agency maps, produced by INEGI (Instituto Nacional de Estadística Geografía e Informática), have been modified to reflect this vegetation change over time. Parallel to this question of desertification are the twin processes of deforestation and climate change. Deforestation in the Río Sonora has been historically related to a few species, most of them oaks, though several accounts have suggested heavy pine deforestation of the Sierra Aconchi before the 1950s (E. Molina, S. L. Lopez, interviews by the author, October 15, 1997, Aconchi, MX).

Oral Narratives of Change

For some elder vaqueros and ranchers, such ecological changes remained fresh in their memory, and horseback rides with anyone over 70 years old could become a lesson in plant changes on specific mesas or arroyos. These elder land managers are an untapped source of information on ecological change. Pancho Gámez, 82 years old and from the town of Aconchi, provides an example of the sort of historical information available from oral interviews (Fogerty 2001): "Well, there used to be a lot of wood in the mountains, and good wood: pine, emory oak, oak. But now everything has changed because there isn't any more [wood]—and the carpentry business has gone away as well." [3]

According to old vaqueros, farther away from towns, but still within the communal lands, these tree species gave way to expanses of grassland dotted with oak and mesquite and the occasional cactus. Based on 79 interviews with older ranchers, vaqueros and "others" working on ranches, I tried to reconstruct patterns of vegetation. As the pattern of overall land-cover types changed substantially between 1940 and 1990 (see the following section, including note 4), these were approximate dates for the vegetation patterns reconstructed using participant cartography. The 1940 data, then, were from the interviews and collaborative cartographical input of older ranchers and vaqueros. The 1990 pattern was based on a land-use map by INEGI for the Río Sonora Valley. Informants described the initial conditions of specific gully washes, hilltops, and mesas circa 1940. The characterization of this vegetation was then matched to the 1990 INEGI map for vegetation cover, so that the categories of plant cover would be similar. The most dramatic shift in vegetation patterns is in the thorn scrub component, with informants collectively agreeing that scrub now covered some 60 percent more of the valley than as they remembered it from 1940 (fig. 4.1). Why has this general pattern of vegetation changed? When asked, most of the informants (65 percent) stated that people began cutting out the remaining oak species from these grassland areas, while others insisted that the climate has changed since the 1940s, contributing to a decline in oaks. A third and unmentioned possible reason was that low-income households along the Río Sonora had little access to

Figure 4.1 Sinaloan thorn scrub invading pastures. Vegetation maps have been modified in the last century because woody species (such as *Acacia*) have encroached into desert grassland areas. Here the low grasses have been increasingly crowded by the taller *Acacia* species in the background.

high-elevation forest areas and began cutting over riparian woody species in the floodplain.

Sinaloan thorn scrub has increased in coverage at the expense of oak grasslands. Private ranchers and vaqueros who worked on private ranches attribute this change to the founding of the ejidos and the subsequent overstocking that occurred. Fully 80 percent of those interviewed agreed with this interpretation of cause-and-effect. The few ejidatarios included in the interviews admitted that there were too many animals, but bemoaned the lack of greater resources to counter this change in vegetation. They rightly pointed out that few of them have the extent of irrigated milpas that private ranch owners have access to, and that mixture of irrigated cropland and dry grazing land has been critical for livestock in the Río Sonora because of seasonal drought and forage availability. Many of the old oak stands were cut over during the 1950s and 1960s.

Compared to other regions of Latin America, Sonora has very little forested area. The rate of deforestation as a percentage figure in Sonora, however, is very high considering what little is left (Vazquez-Leon and Liverman 2004). The areas left with substantial amounts of timber are the municipios of Cananea, Alamos, and the northeastern highland municipios bordering Chihuahua. Little of the pine-oak association remains today in the Río Sonora region, and what little pine remains is located in largely inaccessible pockets of the Sierra Aconchi, to the west of the town of Aconchi, and a few places to the east of town. There is a substantial amount of available fuel wood, but mostly in the form of mesquite, ironwood species, and other small trees. Within the communal ejido lands, the first few kilometers adjoining each town in the Río Sonora used to be covered with thick acacia and mesquite stands. The cultivation of sugar cane and the processing of cane using *trapiches* up until the 1960s were supported by these dense stands of scrubland: the trapiche process depended on large amounts of fuel wood. As in the tropics, forests fueled agrarian development, conjoined with the livestock industry (Hecht 1985). Unlike the tropics, however, these changes are long since past. Access to fuel wood more distant from villages has been cut off by the fencing of private ranches in the valley and the foothills, which has also created a spatial squeeze for the communal sector.

Tragedy of the Commons?

"How are we supposed to make a living with only two or three cows? We had to have more animals, and when the buyers [cattle buyers] started coming to us in the 1950s by truck, a lot of people began to keep more animals," explained one former communal rancher who was now retired. This highlights the multiple ways in which ejido members, in contrast to most private ranchers, are constrained. Ejido grazing lands surround the towns along the river, but are constrained spatially by the private ranches. Since so-called small producers are untouchable under past and current agrarian law in Mexico, there is little recourse for ejidos, as they cannot have small properties expropriated for communal use. Finally, the constraints of consumption levels are notable and well noted by most ejido members; few want to return to life as it was fifty or even thirty years ago. Thus they are unwilling to destock communal range-lands and lower their income, even if that means the range serves little purpose or that animals are undernourished on the shared range.

The overgrazing occurring locally on ejido rangelands, sometimes exceeding the recommended stocking rates sixfold, is reflected in plant composi-tions. While these rangelands, located along arroyo bottoms, can be resil-ient with rainfall and produce some grass cover, little is done to prevent animals from immediately plucking at the green peach-fuzz of early grass regeneration. Hence, the communal ranges are kept in a constant "early" stage of succession, and ejido members have unintentionally changed the balance of herbaceous and woody species on their rangelands. The communal rangeland exhibits a classic case of a multiple stable state, as the landscape has adjusted to current grazing densities, low annual grass resilience, and invasion of woody thorn scrub species. These alternative stable states then shape how sentient livestock adapt to a new landscape of scarcity: they have turned grazing livestock into browsing animals, as the mixed cattle breeds desperately seek out any source of nourishment such as mesquite seedpods.

Thus the plant geography of the Río Sonora Valley continues to be modified by private and communal rancher alike. But how does land cover vary on private ranches? And does the variable land cover reflect land-use decisions or, rather, management and decisions taken by those working on the ranch? Are private ranchers really more efficient than communal ones? Are there differences between private ranches? The next section addresses patterns of environmental variation on private ranches, in terms both of land-cover percentages and of the effects of animals on soils. One of the few ways to assess the impact of differential labor inputs on land cover is to actually measure land cover by percentage. I also wanted a clearer picture of the impact of grazing on soils in the region, because cattle are known to compact the ground and alter the vegetation density.

Ecological Contours of Ranching: Vegetation Cover and Soil Compaction

Chapter 3 demonstrates that labor inputs and ratios are far different on private ranches, depending on the size of the property. This section discusses the importance of property size in determining the land cover (as a percentage) on a ranch and the effects of cattle on soil compaction. To determine these qualities, I divided each ranch landscape into transect segments, consisting of differing terrain, to account for changes in topography, soil, and vegetation conditions. These segments consisted of flat areas (represented by F), mesas (M), and also hillslopes (H). These segments are defined by the slope angle, but also the aspect of the landscape segment. Flat areas and mesas shared low slope angles (0–10° slope), while the hillslopes were commonly steeper (15–45° slope). I lay down one hundred-meter transects on all study ranches, numbering between five transects on the small ranches to twenty on the mega-ranches. The results were not all that surprising. In essence, larger ranches had more land cover as a percentage of ranch surface and lower soil compaction rates.[4]

Smaller ranches, along with many of the medium-sized properties, have greater variation between landscape segments. Hillslopes on the small and medium ranches have lower densities of land cover, while the flats and mesas featured higher land-cover percentages. Three factors explain these trends. First, small- and medium-sized properties are generally located closer to river valleys and are more arid than larger ranches located at higher elevations. These conditions lead to less direct precipitation and less plant cover, as a result. Second, the stocking rates for small and medium ranches are slightly higher than those of their larger counterparts. Finally, small and medium ranches tend to have larger portions of broken terrain, with less flat-lying land (lower slope angles) than the larger ranches.

Variation in the quality of grazing lands is the norm. It is also dependent on the type of landscape unit involved. Land cover is higher in percentage on the mesa tops (M on the maps of transects), where organic matter may still be present in soils. Land cover is also typically higher on the flat washes (F) than on the hillslopes. The trends in land cover observed paralleled the data for soil compaction. Compaction was more prevalent on the smaller and medium ranches and especially severe on hillslope segments. The flatter areas along ephemeral watercourses (arroyos) tended to have slightly more compacted soils than the mesas. While soil moisture, putatively higher near these seasonal streams and washes, is critical to maintaining lower soil bulk densities, here too, cattle play a vital role.

The concentration and congregation of livestock around these flatter, arroyo portions, for at least seasonal access to water has eliminated the important undulations on the surface, or what soil scientists term *micro-topography*. This complexity in the surface height, variation, and terrain allows for greater soil moisture and a greater concentration of grass tussocks, the clumps of native forage so precious to ranchers. The frequency and density of grazing on these lower areas, close to water, begins to eliminate the landscape micro-complexity and topographical variation (Nash, Jackson, and Whitford 2003). This unintended consequence can easily accelerate not only soil erosion, but the slow, gradual elimination of these grass tussocks. Such ecological simplification literally "flattens the earth" in localized areas.

Lastly, the most compacted soils are those found on hillslopes. Cattle prefer grazing uphill, rather than downhill, and spend a disproportionate amount of their time on hillslopes. This tendency, plus the higher slope angles leading to increased soil erosion, helps explain both the low land-cover percentages and the high compaction measures for hillslopes. The standing weight of livestock further compacts soils on hillslopes, and any organic matter at the surface is broken by hooves and removed during strong precipitation events. In this context, the effects are recorded by landscapes, or as Phillips (1999, 121) has put it, there is indeed a "soil memory" operating within the complex interactions of animal-soil-vegetation.

Between ranches, then, and more notably between ranch sizes, there are also considerable differences. Simply put, the larger ranches have soils that are less compacted, in all terrain types (F, H, M). But many do not have any measurable topsoil, and the ground surface is littered with a substance that resembles coarse cat litter. Several ranches shared this predicament. For their respective ranch-size categories, land-cover percentages were less with these coarse soils, and their soil compaction rates greater than their similarly sized counterparts. In the case of ranch 3, owned by the Sarellas, 90 percent of the livestock were sold off in March 1997. In common with ranchers elsewhere in the Borderlands, debt and rainfall tend to be the primary motivations for changing stocking rates. With the peso devaluation in 1994, and a tough four-year drought, the Sarellas made the tough decision to destock their modest ranch until the range recovered. Others resort to perhaps less dramatic management decisions, such as planting exotic African grasses, in order to sustain their herds in the semi-arid thorn scrub. Selling animals before their time or owning an empty ranch is a decision few owners are willing to make.

One of the many recent trends in the Sonoran cattle industry has been the use of cultivated pastures to increase the carrying capacity of rangelands. Indirectly, this development was a reflection of the Brown Revolution coming at the expense of food crops in the floodplain (Sanderson 1986). Directly, exotic annual grasses were introduced into Sonora in an effort to stabilize soils and to increase the carrying capacity of ranches since native grasses struggled to produce enough forage. In areas where exotic grasses have been successful, the stocking rates have gone from 20 hectares per animal unit, to 4 to 5 hectares per animal unit, a four- to five-fold increase, although these were usually in the first two to four years after establishment. One of the common introduced grasses is buffelgrass, and the most common variety has been *Pennisetum ciliaris*. Buffelgrass has been a species of great concern in the biological and environmental sciences, and its arrival has been even more disconcerting to environmentalists (Yetman and Búrquez 1994).

The Miracle of Buffelgrass?

Cattle ranching in Sonora, Mexico, made use of seasonal pastures and open-range strategies until the twentieth century (Pérez Lopez 1993; Camou-Healy 1994). The introduction of barbed wire fencing in the twentieth century and the expansion of its use in the latter half of the modern era were only one of many new technological introductions made to promote a more commercially viable cattle export economy in Sonora. In addition, one of the most visible factors of landscape change in ranching regions is the replacement of native grasses and plants with exotic, cultivated grasses. This process has been common to most of Latin America (Parsons 1972), with the landscape changes even more apparent, more visible, in semi-arid regions. In Sonora, irrigated pasture grasses (such as alfalfa and ryegrass) and planted exotic grasses (such as buffelgrass) are increasing at the expense of staple food crops and native grass species, respectively. These changes are related to (1) the intensification of livestock production and feed grasses and (2) the economic decisions made by ranchers and government agencies. The twin processes of agricultural change and economic decisions have driven the dispersal and permanent use of improved and planted pastures.

Much of the controversy stems from the perceived threat that buffelgrass might have on biodiversity within the Sonoran Desert region. Given recent studies, the potential threat of buffelgrass on native grasses and shrubs will be all the more critical since about half of Sonora's land base is prime habitat for the invasive grass (Arriaga et al. 2004). Franklin and others (2006) demonstrated the effect of large buffelgrass pastures on the vegetation reflectance values of various ecosystems. Based on satellite imagery between 1970 and 2000, they found that reckless planting of buffelgrass resembled bare ground. In addition, Ibarra and others (1995a) noted that soil carbon and fertility decline after conversion to buffelgrass, although they argued that the spread of the exotic grass is not as rapid or as systematic as some early studies suggested.

A more clearly recognizable problem with buffelgrass is the potential for serious soil erosion because of the methods used in clearing and seeding fields for buffelgrass stands (Martín 1997). These assertions have yet to be tested in a regional-scale study but are dubious, based on the experimental data reported later in this section. The question of increased soil erosion is also dealt with in this section, but the impact of buffelgrass on biodiversity must be addressed by future research efforts and is not discussed in this study. The consequences of the land-cover changes associated with the seeded buffelgrass have been localized soil erosion and aggressive fire cycles beyond the bounds of a single field. Localized soil erosion occurs at the time of clearing the land for buffelgrass seeding and continues for ten to twenty-four months depending on the seeding success of the buffelgrass stand. Conflagrations are the result of dried buffelgrass, and because buffelgrass uses roads and paths to spread, the results are quite visible to human observers. The use of fire, in fact, is only now slowly returning to Sonoran pastures as a common practice for restoring grazing lands. The management of firing pastures, however, is tricky business in the broken terrain of these ranches. Most ranchers simply do not practice regular firing of their pastures (cf. Burwell 1995, 428). The practice is more common along the flat, coastal plain north of Hermosillo, where PATROCIPES is experimenting with new fire regime cycles. Factors that are not visible to the human eye are the state promotion of buffelgrass since the 1970s, the current rates of spread of buffelgrass, the effects of the exotic grass on regional biodiversity, and associated soil changes.

State Promotion of Buffelgrass

The Mexican federal government, the Sonoran state government, and international agencies have all speeded the process of ranch "modernization" in Sonora. As previously noted, importing the European "improved" breeds such as Hereford and Charolais, along with more tropical cattle lines such as Zebu, was accompanied by a parallel attempt to convert Mexican field agriculture into a feed agriculture. As late as 1985, a secretary of agrarian reform in Mexico claimed that Mexico "is not an agricultural country. We are a livestock-raising nation" (Sanderson 1986)—this coming from the official in charge of communal ejido affairs and agricultural land redistribution! The push toward irrigated feed crops in the Río Sonora was not long in coming. By 1970, the last traditional wheat mill in the Río Sonora Valley sold out to the La Fama wheat mill company of Hermosillo. The legacy of abandoned wheat mills from Baviácora to Arizpe is not forgotten by the older generation, who bitterly remember the beginning of wheat price fixing by the government, which dropped the price below the tolerable level of small production typical of the Río Sonora Valley.

Outside the narrow strips of irrigated land in the valley, an accompanying trend of land-cover change was also promoted by the "three states."[5] Buffelgrass was first introduced into the United States in the late 1890s, and the early seed test research took place between 1902 and 1940 at the Texas Agricultural Experiment Station. The most common variety in northern Mexico is from the Turkana Desert area of northern Kenya, but its origins lie in South Africa (Holt 1985). This grass was just one of the many tested by government range scientists and botanists after the Dust Bowl in a search for the "miracle grass" of the time (Cox et al. 1983). Most of northern Mexico was prime land for the ecological requirements of buffelgrass, and within its optimal range, it is able to actively colonize unseeded areas of soil as Ibarra and others (1995b) have demonstrated. Yet they also found that the rate of spread from initial establishment has been greatly exaggerated. The benefits of buffelgrass are that it grows during the dry season (when native grasses do not) and that it yields three to four times more biomass than native grasses. The Sonoran government began to push buffelgrass as the miracle grass for Sonora in the late 1960s, though it was not until the 1970s that financial backing caught up with rhetorical momentum. One of the first buffelgrass plots in Sonora was the one present in Las Delicias in the municipio of Banámichi.

Soil Erosion Rates under Buffelgrass

Although the controversy over buffelgrass is rooted in its supposed negative effects on Sonoran biodiversity, there are additional aspersions that buffelgrass may "increase soil erosion" or "destroy the soils" (McNamee 1996). Similar to many other assertions, conventional wisdom if you will, these statements are usually a matter of faith. In an attempt to provide quantitative data, I placed erosion pins in three different field locations during the summer rainy season of 1997 for experimental observations.

The three areas were set with pins at the same time, although a few precipitation events at the very beginning went unrecorded, for logistical reasons. These three areas included the private ranch of El Lobo (study ranch 11), located 12 miles northeast of the town of Baviácora; the ejido buffelgrass stands located before entering the ranch; and the newly deforested buffelgrass tract just north of San José de Baviácora. These data were the first available measuring the effects, or presumed effects, of buffelgrass pastures (Perramond 2000). The total measured precipitation for each site was 40.3 centimeters for the private ranch, 25.2 centimeters for the ejido, and 19.25 centimeters for the newly planted San José buffelgrass tract. These figures reflect a general decrease in elevation as well, moving from La Compuerta (680 meters) to the ejido (620 meters) to San José (450 meters). It should be noted, again, that precipitation figures are not reflective of the total rainfall received during the rainy season. Each site, however, was tracked through the included fourteen rainfall events of 1997. Slope measurements were determined through the use of a clinometer, and pin sites were kept uniform in distribution, relative to the slope position and degree of angle. The data produced, however, were not measures of absolute erosion—rather they were measurements of the *relative* degree of soil removal present at each site under different vegetation cover situations. To measure individual and collective erosion would have entailed a much more labor-intensive and difficult field run of experiments. Any statements made based on these results, then, should be taken as tentative hypotheses, not definitive summaries, of the effect of buffelgrass on erosion. Soil erosion was less, on average, in the buffelgrass plots than in the control sites (native vegetation). Only in San José, where newly planted buffelgrass was just beginning, did the exotic grass plots exceed the surrounding vegetation plots in soil erosion.

Buffelgrass and erosion do not necessarily go hand in hand, but soil erosion was problematic on the newly planted ejido site; however, this erosiveness was due to the relative youth of the stand, rather than any difference in seeding or planting technique used on the ejido. The most severe erosion occurring on the three sites was found on the new stands of San José. Some observers critiqued the shoddy seeding job performed by those on the work crew. Even the other ejidatarios from San José criticized the state of affairs on the mesa to the north of San José. This observation is not to dismiss the problem of *desmonte* (land clearance) involved with the initial establishment of buffelgrass, a real concern for rural cooperatives hoping to use the exotic grass and for those ecologists tracking the impact on native or endangered species (fig. 4.2).

Conservation rhetoric about the ecological consequences of buffelgrass introductions may be more complicated than previously thought. "Conservation conventional wisdom" certainly does hold up in relation to the devastating short-term soil erosion increase ascribed to the process of buffelgrass planting following the *desmonte* process (Franklin et al. 2006). Although limited in scope and scale, the data did suggest that after only two years of establishment, buffelgrass is an effective form of land cover preventing soil erosion—perhaps aiding sedimentation in most areas with less than a 15 percent slope (Perramond 2000). To be sure, the initial stages can result in significant soil loss due to the total lack of soil cover between seeding and the start of the summer rainy season. An additional factor in buffelgrass establishment success has been suggested, in the recent work by Brenner (2009), that excluding cattle

Figure 4.2   Bulldozer ecology and buffelgrass are an obvious ecological concern. One can even discern the darker soil layer over subsoil in this photo. The method removes all native vegetation, with devastating results.

from cultivated pastures for the first two years of growth is vital to the success of any pasture with buffelgrass. This outcome was the case in the San José fields. The key, then, is to avoid steep slopes (greater than twenty degrees) when planting buffelgrass. Why did these ranchers plant their rather steep slopes with buffelgrass? Many pointed to the relative lack of land cover (plant cover) and the nonexistent topsoil, and hoped that buffelgrass would help stabilize these erosion surfaces. As discussed earlier, hillslopes certainly lack good plant cover, and the soils, or what is left of them, are exceedingly compacted.

Ranchers attempted to improve the condition of their hillslope pastures by planting buffelgrass. In so doing, private ranchers have actually unintentionally started to reverse changes in plant geography on their properties, by using the exotic plant. The increasing prevalence of thorn scrub species during the twentieth century, such as acacias and mesquites, is being countered with buffelgrass and creating a landscape more akin to what may have been present earlier this century, albeit with an exotic species (Stoleson et al. 2005). Species composition, however, and the percentage or mere presence of native grasses is less of a concern for most ranchers. They want the original "look" of grassland, with better yield and higher pasture availability for their animals, even if this attempt at winding back the ecological clock may create disruptive new forms of ecological processes. Important tree species such as the original oaks and endangered cacti are left behind, but all vegetation is otherwise cleared from the eventual buffelgrass "fields" before the grass is seeded. This process involves a form of *bulldozer ecology* that has unintended consequences: it has opened up a thorny landscape and created new stands of oak grassland, albeit nonnative grasslands. The unintended consequences of the desmonte process are lower land-cover values and diversity measures in Sonoran Desert ecosystems, although little data exist on carbon impacts when native vegetation is cleared and then planted with the exotic grass (Franklin et al. 2006).

Areas that were steeply sloped and did not have good plant cover to begin with were further eroded after native thorn scrub was removed to plant the exotic grass. On slopes where "strips" of vegetation were left after the removal of thorn scrub, buffelgrass fared better and was able to provide a luxuriant mat of grass—as was the case on ranch 11. Species are not inherently evil, they are perceived as such, and buffelgrass seems to suffer an image problem, in ecological and environmental circles, because of its generalist tendency: it tolerates a wide variety of conditions. Like many African grasses, it has succeeded in areas long ago depleted of native grasslands, serving as a new and welcome complement to rangeland decisions (Vásquez-León and Liverman 2004). For most, if not all, Sonoran ranchers, buffelgrass is not a wholesale replacement species for mono-cropping; rather, it will serve as merely a tiny percentage of their overall properties, helping in times of drought.

Ranching has severely altered Sonora's diverse biophysical settings, and continues to do so. Smaller ranchers herd greater numbers, for the size of their properties, than do medium, large, or mega-ranchers. Accordingly, these smaller ranches also have lower land-cover percentages and higher soil compaction rates than larger ranches. Medium and larger ranchers are frequently able to plant buffelgrass as an aid to their ranch's carrying capacity, a practice uncommon for small ranchers who cannot afford the substantial costs involved with buffelgrass plantations (Vásquez-León,

West, and Finan 2003). The state of Sonora does provide indirect incentives to planting exotic grasses, but not all ranchers can take advantage of the credit system, either for economic or ecological reasons. The economic pinch is the initial investment many ranchers are unable or unwilling to make. The ecological limitation is the range for buffelgrass cultivation. Rarely does *Pennisetum* sprout successfully on ranches located at 900 meters or greater in elevation, largely because of killing frosts (Arriaga et al. 2004), though some researchers now caution that the grass may spread up to 1350 meters in elevation (Franklin et al. 2006). The species is also susceptible to various kinds of spittlebugs, such as the *mosca pinta* (*Aeneolamia albofaciata*), that first reduce the yield and then attack the root systems (Vásquez-León, West, and Finan 2003, 166).

Diverse Ranching Landscapes

The combinations of labor demands, unequal biophysical resources, and limited access to credit created a diversity of ranching landscapes in Sonora, just as the changing environmental geographies of individual ranches and the interaction between animals and rangelands created a complex theater for decision making. Political decisions did have an impact and continue to do so, affecting the ecology that ultimately sustains or threatens the viability of any given ranch (Walker 2007). The outcomes or ecological processes have been highly influenced by the changing political-economic strictures of government institutions and policies, to the point where ecological conditions are debated or used as an institutional fulcrum to effect further changes. This argument is not based on simple a priori reasoning as Vayda and Walters (1999) have warned against in their critique of anything explained as "only politics"; rather, it was an embedded process derived from state and financial influences that sold the species to ranchers. The bulldozer ecology of buffelgrass (the process of clearing mechanically and then planting) was *subsidized* by state policies and *abetted* by regional lenders in order to provide more grassland forage for cattle ranches.

Ranchers were also given loans or subsidies to establish the buffelgrass itself, usually drilled directly into the ground mechanically. It was a desired landscape, one actively sought by private owners, to match the

Figure 4.3   A lush green pasture is a landscape of desire for ranchers. A buffelgrass pasture such as this one was a dream under the "livestock-as-development" model for extension agents, and the full extent of using buffelgrass has yet to be realized. *Pennisetum ciliaris* has resisted most planting efforts above one thousand meters in elevation yet can easily spread beyond this elevation through fire and wind transport.

visions of restored grasslands of any kind (see fig. 4.3). After three to four good years of grazing, in which carrying capacity may have increased three- to ten-fold, buffelgrass tends to recede as *Acacia* and other woody vegetation, such as mesquite, begin to encroach in the bulldozed fields, a trend observed elsewhere in Mexico (Burgos and Maass 2004, 479–80). For regional foresters, the increase in mesquite among range grasses is a desirable outcome, one gleefully reported in state reports. For ranch managers and range extension agents, these are problematic tree species that can reduce some aspects of carrying capacity and invade pastures of buffelgrass. But the very fact that the process itself began with the desmonte process is almost never mentioned, and if questioned, the response is the all-too-common Sonoran expression "¿Quien sabe?" (Who knows?) or simply "Sabe." State extension range experts, refreshingly, now view buffelgrass as simply a minor component to a successful coping strategy for ranchers. They now recommend that less than 20 percent of a ranch be planted in buffelgrass, realizing that any mono-crop may carry more risk than benefit in Sonora (Vásquez-León, West, and Finan 2003, 16).

As an exemplar of an exotic economics rationale, buffelgrass was part of the ranching-as-development suite imported from the United States, and ranchers bought into the logic of what might be termed a *neo-classical species* of rangeland development economics. For a micro-economist, adopting the grass makes perfect sense if the conundrum is about pasture yields. For a Sonoran rancher, more interested in the longevity of a livelihood, the choice to adopt is more complicated, and the economic rationale has little to do with the long-term ecological consequences, intended or not, of using the grass (see Tellman 2002). Ranchers in this study realized that buffelgrass is useful for between ten to fifteen years, after which productivity plummets and soils are left depleted of micro-nutrients.

The use of buffelgrass, then, is simplifying the landscape ecologically to one of an exotic, flammable grass filled with invasive, native shrubs of the *Acacia* species such as *vinorama* or *chirahui* (*Acacia cymbispina*). If ranchers can allow and retain larger leguminous trees, such as mesquite (*Prosopis*), and fell younger individuals, the larger specimens will continue to produce valuable seedpods for the next generation of mesquite trees. Since buffelgrass in Sonora, like Lehmann lovegrass in southern Arizona, is grazed early and late by cattle during the growing season, it plays a vital role in maintaining livestock in a dry climate (Anable, McClaran, and Ruyle 1992). But since the exotic is largely ignored or disfavored by cattle when native grasses and richer forage are available after the rainy season, buffelgrass has the opportunity to produce seed and spread further beyond bounded pastures. Its spread can hurt any intended or unintended efforts to mix valuable browse trees within the grazing pasture. While grazing pressure in Sonora is generally high enough to prevent high rates of spread on ranches, the species is less held in check along transportation corridors, especially in areas with lower grazing densities. Buffelgrass has become an ecological fugitive and an aggressive transborder migrant.

This second type of spread is clearly visible along roadsides of Sonora, stretching into Arizona to the north and Sinaloa to the south, where the absence of grazing control has led to a visually linear mono-crop of the

Figure 4.4   Buffelgrass along a Sonoran roadside. In spite of many ranchers' dreams, not all buffelgrass produces the lushness desired. Located just south of Arizpe, this desiccated pasture filled with brittle, undesirable buffelgrass expanded by roughly 40 percent between 1997 and 2003. Compare with Figure 4.3.

grass (fig. 4.4). Only the intermittent and spatially sporadic harvesting of buffelgrass seeds by human collectors may keep the grass in check, because mowing may simply spray seeds larger distances from the roadside. Any traveler in Sonora will notice this humble effort after the rainy season, as seed collectors wade through waist-high buffelgrass along the road, hoping to sell the seeds to nearby ranchers for about 20 to 25 pesos (US$2–2.50) in large cloth bags. Easily spread by fire, disturbance, mowing, and flooding, buffelgrass can leap across the roadside corridor, creating more difficult fire-management conditions in the peak of drought months in Sonora. If the grass dominates and fires easily, it can also affect the vitality and numbers of important tree species that are used by cattle and wildlife for browsing during the difficult dry spells. Indeed, it is the demographic stand diversity of some trees that is so valuable, as they may complement the seasonal shortages of native or introduced grassland patches during drought periods. The creation of pastures also pressures small populations of rare species that depend on fixed spatial habitat, such as pygmy owls (Flesch and Steidl 2006). Thus this exotic, while having served some of the concerns of ranchers for greater pasture, is now less promoted than it once was.

Ecology, Politics, and Power: Natural Resource Struggles

The embedded nature of state-sponsored rangeland and agricultural experts adds complexity and a point of negotiation for local ranchers, depending on their long-term ecological and economic goals for the ranch. For many, the shift from productive cattle ranch to wildlife ranch for hunting is a logical choice, and they may benefit from incorporating increased densities of mesquite trees that deer will browse. These shifts in rancher decision making or goals create a ripple effect, politically, in small towns as neighbors learn of their decisions. The shifts in ecological-economic goals, political friction, and relations of power between ranchers are uneven in their effects. How does power reveal itself on a landscape? Does power have its own ecology, its own set of relationships that tie people, place, and economies together? Is it putatively the equivalent of the notion of *culture* in the landscape, serving the function of *justifying* difficult or constrained relationships, rather than explaining them?

Many of the early works that used terms such as "power" or "power relationships" did so without a detailed notion of how power might operate. Typical definitions for power have ranged from the ability to achieve certain goals, to using power as a synonym for influence. Eric Wolf (1999) has analyzed how power has been shaped, used, and manipulated by elites in society, but did not provide a framework for analyzing the visual-material embodiment of power in the landscape. Wolf's concerns were clearly centered on the structural nature of power, even as individual and wildly different cultures translated symbolic ideology into tangible and raw forms of state or ethnic power. Both Haenn (2005) and Nuijten (2005) have used novel approaches of dealing with power dynamics in their respective field sites, but I feel uncomfortable with the intangible aspects of their treatment. Power is not like the force in the movie *Star*

Wars, it is not floating around waiting to be used, and it is most certainly not a force field that people bounce off when suddenly faced with obstacles. The challenge is to reconstruct, elaborate, and detail the microphysics of power at the level in which most locals find themselves. In this case, the articulations between politics and ecologies are crucial, and ranchers refract and reflect on many economic and ecological decisions by neighbors to decide on their reactions. Such a situation accords well with a tiered understanding of power: as a capacity, as a resource, and as combined sets of tactics and strategies. Power can simply be acquiesced to, used as a flex-point or fulcrum in particular situations where obligations are either clear or understood between parties, but it can also be embedded spatially within the mundane actions of individuals. Linking power to ecological or landscape changes is, however, trickier.

A wildlife "rancher," for example, may tolerate or welcome woody species intrusion as an accommodation to browsing species that can bring a direct profit, even if the long-term outcome is a decrease in grass forage for domesticated cattle on the same ranch. For the die-hard cattle rancher, perhaps more traditional and occasionally disdainful of this "wildlife" focus, these *Prosopis* species continue to plague what he or she may see as an otherwise desirable ranch landscape, and many private ranchers are wont to use the term *war* when invoking the mesquite. If their neighbor chooses to allow or even encourage mesquite expansion, this change in landscape ecology can become a contentious political act. The choices in economic goals and ranch trajectory are mutually constitutive with the products in ecological landscapes. Thus the distributive networks and influences of capital and political economy also shape these ecologies in unintended and occasionally nefarious ways. Ranchers flex individual decision-making power, neighbors may acquiesce to these in seemingly harmless ways, and yet these sets of mundane decisions can scale up into larger issues that neighbors will eventually notice and frequently contest. These varied scalar effects of decisions, power, and ecological consequences are not isolated to just the social relationships between neighbors, ranchers, and farmers. State governance and intervention schemes also play their hand in these complex landscapes.

For example, range scientists working for the state's cattle-friendly organization PATROCIPES are constantly working on experimental

plots to find new ways to increase grass cover and minimize woody species invasions. Much of this research involves quick rotational grazing
strategies and the wise use of small batches of liquid or pellet chemicals.
But as Russell (1993, 10) has astutely observed, the "science is subjective.
The research on range management is not a chorus of agreement." This
honest assessment holds true in northern Mexico among private ranchers, as it does for range science and expertise in the Borderlands.

The political ecology of individual ranches and the relationships between
these political ecologies drive much of the complex calculus of power relations at the local level. It is certainly problematic to argue that behaviors or
actions are *adaptive* or *maladaptive* in a biological sense. *Adaptation* does
not fairly capture the decisions and options ranchers face, and it became
apparent during my field study that much of their true management, at the
micro- and macro-scale, reflected shorter-term choices that are clearly tactical and strategic in nature. For some, decision making should be viewed
as a "coping" mechanism, or a type of "buffering" against the risk of
recurring drought. Put simply, ranchers will make decisions that seemingly make sense to them in the short-term but may stave off long-term
concerns, even if this might eventually weaken their buffering ability to
deal with drought (Davies 1996). But ranchers are not interested in their
own biological adaptiveness; to put it bluntly, they are more interested in
staving off or managing the political, economic, and highly cultural risks
of maintaining their lifestyle. For example, the state of Sonora has consistently provided direct aid payment to local cattlemen's associations in
Sonora during years of drought. In the last twenty years, all of the ranchers in this study had received some aid every year. This situation illustrates
not only the struggles of an agro-ecosystem unable to sustain current cattle
numbers, it also demonstrates the relative influence of ranchers in political
circles (see also Yetman and Búrquez 1998, 93).

In the context of rancher and nonrancher social relations, then, local
cultural "power" is either relinquished or assumed, depending on the individual dynamics of the situation. A vaquero asking the ranch owner for
his monthly pay, in front of other ranch owners, is an entirely different
dynamic than when the owner goes into the cantina and is suddenly surrounded by vaqueros. Power is flexed, suggested, or acquiesced to in a
variety of ways and on a variety of levels. Certainly aspects of Foucauldian

power are visible in the lines, and between the lines, of this work. One example is the way that government agencies create their own subjects of study from among the ranchers, asserting agency influence on grass selection or advising on breeds, the rawest combination of Foucault's concepts of bio-power and governmentality—or "environmentality," as others have expressed this notion (Agrawal 2005).

Local hegemonic agents, in this case wealthy ranchers and local politicians, drive the local negotiations of power in the form of favoritism, political patronage, or debt-driven relationships. In this scenario, however, the hegemony of a landowner is never complete, not even with his or her direct employees. Rather, tactical negotiations and public assertions of influence depend on context, and the range of power depends on setting, be it on the ranch or in town. Of course, on a daily basis, James Scott's (1985) "weapons of the weak" components are more common, such as using snide remarks in a cantina against the mayordomo or ranch owners. In other words, power cannot be understood in a single way, as a one-way street, or framed in a context that is universal. Each type of asserted or documented power relationship has its own dynamics, its own time-space cultural envelope in which these actions take place. No single framework or theoretical toolkit can encompass the variety of differential power relationships in this region, whether based on class, ethnicity, or gender dimensions.

So let us label this agricultural hegemony, the sense shared by both private and communal landholders, that the private sector is more efficient and somehow superior. This shared assumption, referred to by both private owners and communal farmers and ranchers, may be, but is not necessarily, tied to neoclassical economic theory or the assumptions behind development theory. Local arguments about the superiority of private holdings have more to do about the sense of security with a private title. Ranchers, both private and communal, nevertheless extended this logic into the sphere of productivity, efficiency, and certain "scales of economy" arguments familiar to ranchers elsewhere. It is also this conventional wisdom, translated as "common sense," that is placed on prominent display when private landowners must face off or deal with nonprivate owners or the state in any form, whether municipal, state, or federal entities. If locals view private ranch superiority as a static assumption, it is nevertheless constantly reinforced through rhetorical acts and cultural practices. It is in this context that the concept of *adaptation* makes little sense to explain the behaviors of land managers. Instead, it is the range of daily tactics that is observable, sometimes reflected in a set of longer-term strategies vis-à-vis other stakeholders such as ejidatarios or agency experts. These actions go beyond the binary of acquiescence/force in thinking about power to a more spatially complex and diffuse sense of the concept. These immediate tactics, in the micro-scale of space and time, may not be readily apparent to the eye. But they are yet another form of cultural practice, one that embraces the political needs and immediacy of making decisions quickly, and one that fully links the local understanding of how ecology, culture, and politics tie in together.

Tactics and Strategies: The Political Ecologies of Ranching

We can relate these cases to ranching as an industry through understanding *local culture* as a kind of political practice. For example, ranchers are just as concerned with risk minimization as are horticulturalists. Blaikie and Brookfeld (1987, 8) suggested, however, that rotational grazing is based on "avoidance rather than control strategies." In other words, rotation and herding are necessary, in order to avoid pasture degradation rather than trying to control the actual biological production of that particular pasture. Buffelgrass and the overall bulldozer ecology process in Sonora posit an active counterpoint to this assumption of *passive land manager* (see Brenner 2009). The use of fences, salts, tethers, licks, and water impoundments indicates a great deal of control and management over the grazing and herding of animals, which is certainly the case for private cattle ranches. But the contrast remains, as cattle ranching in ecological terms attempts largely to avoid damage, or at least to avoid lower carrying capacity, more precisely, rather than to manage it, as in subsistence agriculture. In economic terms, however, the strategy is much more focused in ranching. Management on these ranches then is all about economics, not ecology. The importation and use of buffelgrass, after all, was a range improvement effort to restore carrying capacity. It was never a tool for "restoration ecology" or to preserve "habitat for native species." While Sonoran ranchers have had to take some precautions, de jure, when clearing new pastures in Sonoran desert ecosystems, they are much less constrained than their North American counterparts in terms of ecological considerations. Cattle remain, in Sayre's (2002) words, the "species of capital" for our concerns. There is not yet a tidal surge of ecological concern for endangered species in the region, despite the efforts of some NGOs based in Hermosillo or even Mexico City.

Ranch Time, Ranch Space

The time-space dimensions of ranch management are more sporadic, involving small pulses of coordinated physical activities during the year, rather than the daily inputs and toil of labor involved with field agriculture. The political ecology of cattle ranching is driven more by tactics and strategies of production, rather than by land management, much less by adaptation, per se. This suite of rancher decisions is especially true in northern Mexico, where local ranchers have viewed range management scientists and techniques skeptically. Regional adoption has been piecemeal and ephemeral for reasons that are clear. Ranchers rarely see extension workers. When extension workers do arrive, they often push improved seeds or technologies that few can actually afford to purchase. The recent memory of development-incurred debt from the 1980s is also still fresh on the minds of most ranchers. So the reluctance for further debt is understandable, as are the reactions of ranchers, and they deal with extension workers with caution. They do so by attempting to control the place of interactions, hosting experts on familiar ground like their ranch or the local cattlemen's meeting hall, or by dealing with them in more strategic terms. Finally, they employ rhetorical means to curry favor or ward off many of the measures that state or agency experts offer. Ranchers tactically and strategically negotiate these encounters, temporally and spatially, and rhetorically construct stories and justifications that may serve them well in the short term. These negotiations and rhetorical constructs are very much part of their culture as a subgroup that self-identifies, and perfectly in compass with their larger cultural strategies for survival and perpetuating their very presence in the region.

These two terms, *tactics* and *strategies,* also imply a difference in scale in both time and space. Tactics are immediate, momentary, or event-based practices that may (or may not) reflect a longer-term strategy, involving immediate or intermediate actions and decisions to gain some advantage or maintain position in the community (Perramond 2001, 2007). In addition to the physical, pragmatic reflections of these terms, tactics and strategies are also a theoretical toolkit. Ranching and ranchers have their own peculiar rhetorical discourse within Sonoran society. By *discourse*, I mean the mundane context of language and relations and also the more theoretical terrain this word implies. The tactics and strategies used by Sonoran ranchers are reflected in the discourse used to describe particular rangelands or ranch landscapes. My usage of the term *discourse* is similar to that presented by Schein (1997, 663–64), yet I refer more directly to the tangible and material aspects of the insights rather than to the more theoretical aspects of deploying discourse analysis.

An example of rancher discourse is larger ranch owners' insistence that they are better managers than small ranchers. A logical extension to this rhetoric is small ranch owners' insistence that they are better suited for ranching than their communal counterparts, who are forced to maintain high numbers of animals on smaller areas of land. This neat encapsulated rhetoric of managerial superiority, however, misses the geography underlying the logic. Communal spaces are simply squeezed in between private ranches, limiting certain options (fig. 4.5). Ejidatarios thus complain they have such poor pastures because they need a certain amount of animals to break even financially, and there simply is not enough communal land to support current stocking rates, a point supported by grazing density figures.

Grazing densities on private ranches in this study ranged between 5.0 to 25 hectares per animal unit. The federal agency responsible for setting desired grazing ratios, COTECOCA (Comisión Téchnico Consultiva de Coeficientes de Agostadero), usually recommends upwards of 30 hectares per animal. On the ejidos of the Río Sonora, the densities ranged between 2.3 and 3.5 hectares per animal unit. In other words, private ranchers have between two to seven times as much grazing land to support their herds, yet this reality is not part of their discourse. Rather they stress their supposed rotational grazing, a practice (they say) not commonly executed on the smaller ranches and certainly not by communal ranchers (see also Desmond et al. 2005). Small ranchers will, in fact, rotate herds among their pastures contrary to this rhetoric. In a set of four to five pastures, the norm

Figure 4.5 A fence does matter. This photo shows ejido lands on the right and private pasture on the left, separated by the fence line running down the middle. This area was under dispute during the 1970s, until the private owner fenced off much of the best grazing land. The result is an example of a socially generated "tragedy of the commons," not one created by the supposed ignorance of communal ranchers.

for most of the study ranches, the owners follow a straight 1-2-3-4(-5) rotation during the course of a normal year. Cattle may spend as little as two weeks or as much as three months in any given pasture, depending on rainfall and forage conditions. Animals are also frequently moved into town, to graze on stubble after the crop harvest in midsummer, and then moved back to higher pastures during and after the rainy season. If the summer rains are poor, they are moved back down to the floodplain and will graze (on a paid basis per head) on alfalfa and ryegrass hay for weeks; calves in a difficult year will be sold in November or December, and in a good year held until February and March. Those months are when local cattle sales spike and when greater movement occurs in the larger industry, as Mexican calves are shipped northwards across the border. Most animals in the Río Sonora exit through Nogales, Sonora, or through Santa Teresa, in Chihuahua, near the feedlots close to El Paso, Texas.

Communal farmers face a tougher challenge because much of the common land is unfenced internally. The rancher's perspective is well illustrated by comments made to me by large ranch owners in reference to ejido lands. Most of the private owners spoke of a landscape that thirty years ago supported luxuriant oak grassland, but that was now devastated thorn scrub because of land redistribution to communal owners desiring some rangeland for their livestock. The private ranchers blamed these environmental changes on the smallholders of the ejido and used landscapes as their proof, a point not lost on the ejido members. "Of course they manage better," quipped an ejidatario, "because they have more to manage!" He continued: "When these [expropriated] private or abandoned lands were given to us by the government, the bureaucrats never worried about the number of people and animals; they wanted to look good politically." The policies surrounding the dispensation of so-called *terrenos baldíos* (abandoned or unoccupied lands) have long been controversial in Mexico (Orozco 1895/1974). But one of the findings of my work runs opposite this conventional wisdom of the private ranchers: small private ranch owners actually spend more time on management than do the large ranch owners.

These material tactics and overall strategies employed by ranchers have everything to do with what has been called the "strategically relevant environment" by cultural ecologists (Knapp 1991). Private ranch owners use a variety of daily and longer-term tactics to succeed in the long run as part of their overall strategy. Their logic has so much purpose that some small- and medium-sized ranch owners buy into this ideology, this form of agricultural hegemony that dictates that "bigger is better." And for the last seventy years, private ranches that are sized to support 500 animal units have been protected from further expropriation (Bobrow-Strain 2007). But manipulating the recommended stocking rates of ranches is famously easy. Because the numbers vary seasonally, they can be easily elided if rural tax assessments merely analyze them by a single, annual average (Sayre 2004). Risk avoidance by ranchers is not just biophysical, it is also policy oriented and tax sensitive: ranchers worry about bureaucrats as they do about climate. The actions of ranchers, then, make a mockery of any concept of range carrying capacity. At a larger aggregate spatial scale, the supposed superiority of private management is questionable, as

Coronado-Quintana and McClaran (2001) have pointed out: little significant difference has been found between communal and private ranches
over large areas of Sonora.

The tactical choices made daily by ranchers and land managers may
reflect a larger overall strategy or may simply be one-off events without
any further reflection or motive (Perramond 2007). Certainly the approach
of ranchers in their interactions with communal landowners and with state
agencies is more reflective of their long-term goals. In dealing with nonprivate entities, their strategies become visible and clearly communicated,
orally, symbolically, and occasionally in textual forms. This conceptual
framework also embraces the variety of explanations and contexts for both
empirical and post-structural theoretical veins of research on ranching. It
also more satisfactorily addresses the real desires expressed in private and
public settings. In sum, it may help to clarify the geographies of intent, the
changes, and the goals actively pursued by these Mexican ranchers.

The French theorist Michel de Certeau (1984) expressed this thought
in similar terms, with the added dimension of scalar intent, although
not originally phrased in the spatial sense. Tactics are reflective of single
events, in time, without a larger context or spatial setting. A strategy is a
string or series of tactics set in motion over a specific spatial context with
a larger goal. The social relations that structure the interactions between
ranchers and local community members are driven not only by the clash
over and about natural resources, but also over notions of tenure territoriality and the implicit notions of property superiority. If private ownership is both coveted and zealously defended, it is not surprising that the
social and spatial behaviors of ranchers mimic the value placed in land
ownership. Private landowners may "adapt," but do so in a behavioral,
calculating way, to any attempts that may usurp either resources or tenure security. Changes in Mexican agrarian laws since 1992 have some-
what lessened the tension between communal and private interests, as
the understanding of communal has undergone dramatic changes. Once
a solid part of the political geographical ideology of the dominant political party in Mexico, the PRI, rural communities are now spun off into
a more supposedly decentralized role. And yet, as Karl Polanyi (1957)
made so clear, the embedded nation-state in local relations rarely disap-
pears even during decentralization efforts. Even if, as the saying goes,

"all politics are local," the fulcrum points are also intimately linked to the national debates discussed elsewhere in Mexico: land, corruption, bureaucracies, to name but a few.

To this day, the intertwined nature of national politics and local life remains intact; only the idea behind communal ownership has changed (see chapter 6). Little of the revolutionary fervor for land reform exists today in this part of Sonora, although notions of equity and justice are tossed around, and certainly the ideals of Zapata are less influential here than in parts of central and southern Mexico. Ejido land can now be treated as individually owned, if title has been acquired. These lands, although theoretically communal or usufruct in the past, have always been thought of as belonging to a particular ejidatario. Only when ejido members left or no clear heir remained did the ejido reassign plot ownership or access rights. Even then, some parcels remained vacant and fallow for decades. To decentralize its past duties as the national communal lands manager, the Mexican federal government had to re-embed itself in local communities and resurvey and remap the same places that were created as communal resources seventy years ago. The same process used to create the ejido after the Mexican Revolution is uncannily similar to the one now being followed to "liberalize" the ejido sector and its ownership (Craib 2004).

Ranchers in this part of Mexico have not, to this point, directly poached on these new policies of privatization in the twenty-first century. The "new ejido" is, in effect, a reflection of what is, rather than what should have been: the small land parcels have always been managed by individuals and households and rarely, if ever, managed communally. The new flexible rules, all the way to outright title ownership, recognize this fact in local rules. It does, however, create new rules for acquiring property that may serve, over time, the local agricultural hegemonic elite in Sonora (as suggested by Vásquez-León, West, and Finan 2003, 167). The economics and ecologies of ranching also create a unique geography of daily life for ranchers, their families, and those who work the property on a daily basis. To grasp the complex social geography, the roles of gendered place, space, and political roles are vital to explaining the current and future geographies of ranching in Mexico. They also go a long way toward explaining the spatial dynamics of these communities.

5 Gender, Community, and the Spatial Dynamics of Ranching

¡Por supuesto soy ganadera! / Of course I'm a rancher!
—Amalia Ruiz

Women, children, and the elderly are key characters in the dynamics of ranching as a livelihood, even as the importance of extended families has declined in maintaining ranch traditions. The gender and community aspects in forming the identities of ranchers are formidable, and social scientists frequently use the euphemism *social reproduction* to explain how societies create and re-create the confines and contours of daily lived experience. The daily geographies of ranching, ranchers, and ranch families are shaped by many mundane factors. The time-space routes and movements of ranchers and vaqueros, the role of plazas and social interactions, and the gendered dimensions of life on a local scale all serve to drive the social relations of production in the towns strung along the Río Sonora.[1]

Less visible to the eye is the importance of gendered local knowledge, and how the unevenness of that knowledge contributes to the success, stability, or failures of ranching livelihoods in the Río Sonora Valley. Steve Stern (1995) has referred to this ignorance of past gender dimensions in discussing the "secret history" of Mexico, one that has been lacking in broader works from geography (Massey 1994). There is, on a parallel scheme, a "secret geography" to gender in all societies, only complicated in Mexico by social conventions such as *machismo* and *vergüenza*. *Machismo* is a complicated concept, wrought with ideas about manhood, and can be used either pejoratively, usually by women, or proudly as a badge of honor, usually by men (Guttman 1996). The ambivalent concept and multifaceted understanding of the word *vergüenza*, including the notions of simultaneous honor and shame, enables some understanding of the way gendered codes and the social control of women and sexuality prove fundamental to the construction and legitimation of the cultural-political order in this ranching society. Even for the influential female ranchers in this study this concept matters greatly, as they have been largely removed from the political sphere at the local level because of the gendered understandings of political and apolitical culture. Not to mince words, ranching has always been about the ideology and geography of masculinity as well as the construction of gendered identity roles. And this firmament has shaped and enforced particular kinds of social relations as much as, if not more than, class and ethnicity have, long since the colonial period in Mexico (Alonso 1995, 230).

The Geography of Ranching Families

We have already seen, in previous chapters, how ranchers and ranch laborers spend their time on and off the ranches. Some, such as the absentee owners, rarely set foot on their ranches, save for key moments of sales and transactions. Direct land managers, whether owner or vaquero, spend much of their week or even month on the ranch itself. But other factors contribute to the spatial arrangement and dynamics of ranch life, and these are usually based around the pivot point of the small towns they typically occupy, the plaza (Low 2000). The spatial configuration of ranch family homes within the towns of the Río Sonora has several peculiar and important qualities. Most notable is the town layout-level distribution of ranching families; the houses of private ranchers are usually located as a second tier around the main town square (plaza), that is, one or two blocks away from the plaza. The houses of politicians and some local merchants usually face the plaza and occupy the first block behind it.

The concept and feature of *la plaza* play an important cultural geographic role in forming place throughout Latin America and provide one of the central points of contact for understanding the spatial quality of ranchers' role in the community. Unlike many of their New World counterparts, Mexican ranchers have long been urban dwellers, or at least town inhabitants. Since the partition of large estates during and after the Mexican Revolution, the trend has been toward increased settlement and concentration of ranchers within town cores. Plazas serve, then, as central nodes of interaction for ranchers, farmers, politicians, and merchants, be they male or female. My usage of the term is not a simple reference to plazas as a form of architecture or urban morphology. The plaza is a social phenomenon of singular importance for religious, political, and economic reasons. In spiritual terms, it is the focal point of the community, as the plaza faces the main church. There are exceptions to this, such as in the town of Arizpe, where the plaza is removed from the main church. Even in Arizpe, however, when church lets out people quickly migrate to the plaza to sit and chat. It is a way of accounting for those who attend regularly, typically women, children, and the elderly, and a way for information to flow within the town and region's social fabric.

The political and economic purposes of plazas are numerous. Candidates for municipal, regional, and state elections give their speeches on the main plaza. Cattlemen come together to discuss important events, rodeos, or auctions on the plaza. The annual fiestas held in each town plaza along the Río Sonora serve to reunite transnational migrants with their remaining local kin. One rancher joked that he had no need for a computer because he used the plaza, an easier medium, to acquire the information or news he needs on a daily basis. Economic functions of the plaza include most of the town merchants, the local bank or rural credit office, and the ongoing and informal economy of personal loans between kin and friends. The plaza is a way station for ranchers coming from and going to their ranches, as they will stop and get the latest news from those milling about the benches or those waiting at the Tecate expendio for a few cold ones. Every single time a visit was made to a rancher's property, during or after the provisions had been bought for the week's stay, a stopover at the plaza was nearly guaranteed. This pattern is due, in part, to the nature of ranching in Mexico—at least in northern Mexico. Ranchers live a double life: half their time is spent on the ranch, the other half at home in town on the weekends if they can manage it. Those who can afford to stay in town longer generally do. For the vast majority of these small town ranchers, however, their existence is dictated by running a "satellite" ranch household operation. And the gender dynamics of this practice are long-standing, consequential, and frequently complicated by the peripheral nature of some ranch household arrangements.

Satellite Ranchers and Masculinity

Rancho El Morro is one of two in the municipio of Moctezuma owned by the Soldano family, whose origins lie in the study region. At the time of fieldwork, the ranch was undergoing division and fencing, as the original property was subdivided into five different ranches—one for each heir of Carlos Soldano. The ranch is located in the mountainous ranges that parallel the Río Sonora northward, separating the municipios of Baviácora and Moctezuma. This region is also one of the longest-occupied regions in terms of cattle ranching. Many of the ranches in the Moctezuma area date back to the colonial and the early national periods. Yet this ranch and its neighbor, La Pamplona, are high enough to avoid any rain shadow from the mountain range separating the Río Sonora drainage from the Río Moctezuma Valley. None of the heirs of this Soldano property stayed on the ranch; that task was left to the vaqueros who complete the daily tasks, all seven of them. Because of the division in the ranch, two were to be released, and the vaqueros were nervous about who would be let go. Among the *mautos* (*Lysiloma divaricata*) and *pochotes* (*Ceiba acuminata*), the vaqueros exchanged stories about mountain lions and even jaguars they had seen recently, to change the subject of their imminent "restructuring" by the new owners. All of the vaqueros lived in Moctezuma, 50 minutes to the east by pickup, and were disappointed with the decision to split the ranch five ways. They had grown accustomed to this form of satellite ranching, and Miguel even joked that he was a "long-distance cowboy" and wanted to remain so.

"It would be better to keep the number of pastures they have now," said Miguel. He continued: "They could increase the number of animals, and we could rotate them more often. They would all get something more out of this ranch. By dividing it, they don't realize they are reducing their profits. But none of them know this anyway, and none of them will listen to us. They want to carve it up, maybe sell it, and live in Hermosillo and drive fancy cars."

This statement by Miguel, the oldest ranch hand, stopped the tall tales of mountain lions. They all stared at him momentarily and quietly nodded. Miguel continued, encouraged that no one disagreed.

"Now Don Carlos, he knew this ranch, and he knew animals. He could ride a horse like you and me. Well, he used to be able to ride a horse.

Anyway, he loved this ranch, and would never divide it like these kids are doing. Boys want to leave the country and girls want to study at the university in Hermosillo."

Miguel emphasized his distaste by spitting out instant coffee that became cold during his diatribe.

"Shut up you old fool, you talk too much to be able to drink coffee!" teased his old friend Vargas.

The point, however, was not lost on the other vaqueros that night. They knew full well that grazing the cattle in more intensive fashion, with greater rotation, would probably maintain if not increase the income of the ranch. The challenge of partible inheritance is that the law of diminishing returns begins to operate sooner at smaller sizes. In other words, a big ranch is much more profitable than two medium ranches, because of the necessary inputs to maintain any ranch. The economy of scale achieved by Don Carlos in building El Morro and La Pamplona was now slowly being picked apart. To maintain this lifestyle was difficult, they admitted, but it was preferable to unemployment.

Private ranchers in the Sonora Valley, as is common elsewhere in northern Mexico, are satellite ranchers. The spatial aspect of this livelihood is, in some ways, not dissimilar from the so-called Kansas "suitcase farmers" who hold one main residence in a nearby town while owning land and some form of housing on the farm itself (Hewes 1973). It is also a practice that dates back to the Roman period of absentee landownership and a leftover of the Spanish colonial period (Trens 1992; González-Montagut 1999). The daily spatial paths of a rancher depend on his or her economic standing as a rancher. Ranchers with small- to medium-sized holdings typically provide the bulk of the ranch labor, spending several days to the entire week on the ranch, returning to the main town of the municipio at week's end. Many will stay longer, spending several weeks, during critical times for livestock raising. The calving season, roundups, and hygienic-medical problems can take weeks at a time to address.

Large ranch owners can afford the luxury of relying on their vaqueros and hired laborers to handle most affairs, and most commonly avoid going to the ranch, except during annual roundups or particularly important seasonal events. Those involved with daily or weekly jaunts to the ranches stress the importance of companionship: they never go alone.

Although loneliness was a frequently stated reason for companionship, the issue of safety, should an accident occur on the ranch or on horseback, was also important. Others involved in ranching operations, the vaqueros or day laborers, express this sentiment even more strongly. The practice of temporary isolation has a strong gendered character to it, as well: cowboys are almost invariably male. And while suffering from the stereotype of being hyper-masculine loners with poor manners, they are meticulously tidy and obsessive about ranch details. Only one female vaquera was ever encountered in Sonora, and she was the daughter of the ranch manager (mayordomo) of a large estate in eastern Sonora. She was also a temporary hand, on call during roundups, branding, and the late autumn herding to winter pastures. She also cited isolation and social separation as aspects that did not appeal to her, that she would never be a full-time vaquera, even working for her father. So while many ranchers are female, there are few true female vaqueras: a gendered and socially produced construction of what the appropriate roles are for men and women in Sonora. Or as Moore (2005, 98) has put it, these are "highly gendered performative practice." Yet few studies even broach the topic of how these social formations are created, much less how gender is constructed or pitched to a certain livelihood in ranch communities.

These images and symbols for appropriate gender roles are engrained at an early age, witnessed in numerous festivals and street parades that include children, on the streets of rural Sonora (fig. 5.1). As the little boys are decked out in hard denim, miniature cowboy boots, some with pasted-on mustaches, the girls are put onto rolling carts or floats in their finest Sunday dresses (fig. 5.2). Occasionally, a girl or two are given a metal pail and some rubber gloves, to stand next to a faux cow as if she had been milking. It is truly one of the most vivid memories I have, and one that drove home the sometimes overly academic concept of "social reproduction." Their gendered roles are displayed, enforced, and modeled quite early, and this shaping of rural society has molded Sonoran ranching towns into bastions of social, gendered inequality based on these acceptable roles. Those who are uncomfortable in the small towns have flocked, en masse, to the larger cities of Sonora. For local women, higher education is viewed as one of the few ways "out" of the predictably gendered roles and towns of the valley. As one university student

Figure 5.1   Gender on parade and in the making: Boys sport guns, knives, toy horses, and ropes. Masculinity and ranching seemingly go hand in hand.

in Hermosillo put it, having left her native Arizpe, "El pueblo me gusta llegar, pero no para vivir, [porque] es muy sexista." To wit, although she enjoyed visiting, she could not imagine living in the sexist confines of her childhood ever again.

But the overwhelming majority of ranch labor is male, working the satellite ranches located kilometers from their permanent home, and in the rural cast of characters, cowboys are expected to have several qualities. Many vaqueros never go to town more than once a month, and the local expression directed to these individuals, "el es muy ranchero," underlines the possibility that the person is lacking in social skills or graces due to the long-term isolation of this livelihood. To be "real cowboy" is not necessarily a bad thing from the point of view of ranchers who value their expertise, but it is the kiss of death for any cowboy hoping to find some kind of relationship in town. Few women aspire to be the satellite spouse, at home with children, while the husband is gone for weeks or months at a time. In fact, on the larger ranches, and especially on the so-called

Figure 5.2 The construction of rural femininity: Decked out in old-fashioned Sunday dress, the girls are perhaps not quite as ready to assume the role being presumed for them.

mega-ranches, cowboys are kept on the ranch for long periods of time. Smaller- and medium-sized ranch owners, in other words, make more frequent visits to the ranch and also allow their vaqueros more return trips to town. This was a strange finding from the interviews conducted with study ranch vaqueros. To verify this finding, outside interviews were conducted with vaqueros working on other nearby ranches in the study region. Of the forty-two "reference" vaqueros interviewed, thirty-three were employed on small to medium ranches, and every single one of the informants visited their home town or house at least once a week. On the other hand, those nine that worked on large or mega-ranches reported a trip to town every two weeks (five out of the nine) or once a month (four of the nine). Vaqueros attributed this difference in frequency of visits to a better salary for the large ranch laborers and also to the greater distance the ranch owner had to travel from his main residence to the ranch.

Absentee landlords travel the greatest distance to visit their ranches, and among the study ranches considered here (n = 17), this fact was borne out by the travel distances. Small ranch owners are, on average, about 10 kilometers away from their property. Those owning medium-sized ranches are, on average, about 14 kilometers away from their properties. Finally, large ranch owners (17 kilometers) and those owning mega-ranches (60 kilometers), travel the longest distances. Large rancher owners, in other words, want their cowboys on the ranch—and are stricter about visits on weekends for their laborers. Small- and medium-sized ranch owners were also a bit jealous of this fact, indicating their preference for vaqueros who stay for longer periods of time, admiring the quality of being "muy ranchero." In addition, one of the ranchers commented that herding is "not a part-time job, and the animals always need protection from mountain lions." While the "muy ranchero" appellation has great respect among men, it is not a social trait sought after by local women apparently, and for these ranchers in Sonora, women are key to running this dual household economy and pivotal in the local community.

Gender and the Household Anchor: Interviews

"Ranching is definitely not men's work!"
—Ana Dellot, Arizpe rancher

One of the neglected aspects of cattle ranching, and livestock herding in general, is the lack of information and appreciation for the role of gender in managing daily operations. It may be that the rancher is a woman, to be sure, but it is still a highly gendered occupation, and more common to find women married to male ranchers and vaqueros. The contribution women make, whether as direct owner and manager or in assisting with household management, cannot be underestimated. Daily activities of the women again correspond largely to the general economics of the rancher's household and assets. Interviews were conducted with thirty women, who were either directly involved in running ranch operations or were married to ranchers.

Women's relative labor contribution toward ranch activities is based on the size of operations. The data collected clearly reflect the importance of ranch size as related to their daily activities and the importance of women in managing these households. A basic analysis of these data show that, in percentage terms, wives on small (60 percent) and medium (30 percent) ranches contribute more to ranch or ranching activities than do those spouses married to large ranch owners. Those women that contribute to large ranches are the owners themselves, while most (80 percent) of them are not directly participating in daily activities. Small and medium ranches depend on women heavily in the integration of ranch and household tasks. Larger ranches, and certainly the absentee-owner versions, can allow for a more discrete separation based on gender: the men handle the ranch; the women manage the household. Proxy labor on the large ranches is handled, nearly universally, by men employed for such purposes, not by the female spouse. The exceptions to this rule are few, but notable, and again illustrate the variety and complexity of ranching's social organizing. The difference is largely marked by income or asset levels: the larger the ranch assets, the fewer duties taken on by the spouse. Indeed, this trend is clear from the empirical information gathered from interviews with ranchers' wives (and the female ranchers), as well as from qualitative judgments and opinions offered by other female relatives involved in discussions.

This basic and frequently binary relationship extends also into the realm of local knowledge about ranching and the specific ranch environments. Among the 30 interviews conducted with women, 11 had knowledge of the local plants, such as their names and potential medicinal uses. These were all women from the small- to medium-sized ranches, with one exception (Ana Dellot; see the following section for more). Another important factor in the knowledge of plant names and uses was age. The average age of those who knew the uses of plants was 52, while the average for those who did not possess such knowledge was 34. Women were also talented at diagnosing illnesses in animals, especially if visible in cow's milk. Of all the owners of case study ranches, 12 out of the 14 in the Río Sonora Valley deferred cow illness diagnoses to their wives before going to seek the help and opinion of a veterinarian. While these brief, statistical perspectives provide a context for understanding the importance of women in ranching households, I have included three qualitative portraits in the following section to underline the multifaceted roles that women play.

Daily Geographies of Ranchers and Ranchers' Wives

Ana Dellot

In contrast to some female ranch-owning peers, Ms. Dellot is one of the most intense cattle ranchers I met in Sonora, a woman knowledgeable about every aspect of ranch management. She can discuss local plants on both of her ranches, knows the terrain, and is a widely acknowledged expert on Arizpe's history (both viceroyal and contemporary).

"Why do you think I haven't gotten married?" Ms. Dellot asked me point-blank. I wasn't quite sure how to respond to this one.

"No one around who interested you?" I shot back.

"No, it's because a man would marry me for my ranch and my store, and my house. Then later he could divorce me and try to take those things from me." Ms. Dellot is keenly aware of her place in the community; as the self-appointed historical matriarch of Arizpe, she guards both her possessions and her knowledge carefully.

"You see, my main problem with the ranches in Arizpe is that they are run by people who don't care. They come and go as they please from Hermosillo, and when they come to Arizpe, it's usually to have a party of some sort on the ranch. They know nothing anymore of breeds, of grasses," she finished disdainfully.

Ms. Dellot owns two ranches, one on the east side of the Río Sonora Valley, the other on the drier west side of the valley. She may sell the one on the dry side of the Valley, she said, as she is getting a bit older and may want to retire into town for good and leave the ranch work to her ranch hands.

"Someday I'll leave this all behind and my dear niece can start worrying about these things," she cackled joyfully.

Her grandfather Jean-Claude Dellot arrived in the town of Arizpe in 1889, indirectly from France, through Mexico City. Like many of the French expatriates who settled on the northern fringes of Mexico, Señor Dellot established himself as part of the merchant class, only investing in ranching incrementally. By 1910, however, he was one of the most important ranchers in the Arizpe region. His son, Manuel, expanded the ranch between 1930 and 1955 and purchased another ranch. Today, these two ranches are run by Ana Dellot, daughter of Manuel. She not only maintains the ranching traditions of her family, but also keeps mercantile interests in the town of Arizpe, where she runs a general goods store close to the main church. She also is the main repository of historical knowledge, lore, and cultural histories about Arizpe, and runs the small historical museum with archival documents, photographs, and material culture on display. She is one of the few female ranchers in the Río Sonora Valley—and is fiercely proud of the fact.

"Many of the men in this community do not respect what I do as a rancher because I am a woman. They don't like it that I've never been married—they think I'm cheap and that I don't want to share my ranches," Ms. Dellot quipped to me during our initial conversations about her ranch in the Arizpe municipio. We walked over to the store down the street from her main residence as she explained the problems of being a female rancher in a patriarchal industry and local culture.

"I remember when my father first passed away, and my sister and I inherited the ranches in the family. I attended the local meeting of the cattlemen and they completely ignored what we said about any issue—so for the next meeting I put on my denims and my hat—that got their attention!"

She did not understand, however, the reaction of most ranchers to her, as many simply expected her to get married and turn over the daily management of the rangelands to her would-be spouse.

"That never happened," she said with a sly grin, "and they still don't know how to deal with me sometimes."

She went on at some length about her true love for Arizpe, the former capital of Sonora, and the local history. In October 1997, Ms. Dellot was a key orchestrator for a conference on Juan Bautista de Anza, the Spanish explorer who founded San Francisco, California. While it is true that female-headed households in this region are rare, they are growing in number, and Ms. Dellot is conscious of the challenges faced by single people. She admired the few women she knew in Arizpe who were responsible for their entire families, including extended kin, and frankly discussed their futures or troubles. But this difficulty, noted by others, has been doubly so since the devaluation of the peso in the mid-1990s, even for middle-class households (Beneria 1992; Willis 2000).

Chevita Soldano

In the dainty reception area of her home in Hermosillo, Chevita showed me to a comfortable couch, as we settled in to discuss her ranch in the Arizpe region. She slowly plopped two cubes of sugar into her coffee, organic coffee from Chiapas she claimed, all the while sizing me up with one eye. Halfway through the long discussion, she stopped with the topic at hand and simply waved her hand:

"You know, I just don't know that much about my ranches, other than the number of animals, the size of it, and who works for me. I don't like dealing with details, and that's why Pancho serves as the mayordomo for my holdings."

She continued, with a pained look on her face.

"My sister and I inherited these ranches from our father, so we never had a very hard time of it. Of course we worked occasionally, but we never bothered to spend too much time on the ranch. We like our houses, I guess."

Chevita and her sister María each own three ranches, most in the three thousand–hectare category and all of them in the municipio of Arizpe. Her father is said to be a very distant cousin of the Soldanos who own two of the three mega-ranches in this study (El Morro and La Pamplona ranches). The original size of the father's holdings totaled over nineteen thousand hectares in the Arizpe region, in addition to several commercial enterprises and irrigated land in the valley.

"María is a bit more involved with her ranches, as she spends more time in Arizpe, but a lot of the time she spends worrying about the gas station and store she owns."

Chevita went on about her sister, suggesting that she never married because she works so much, and that there were no men who had as much as she did. The latter opinion is shared among the men of Arizpe as the reason for a woman to remain single.

"She doesn't want to share the wealth," claimed one old man in the plaza of Arizpe one night. The others in attendance on the park bench howled with laughter at this statement. Other women in the town of Arizpe also suffer the same fate of gossip, and Ana Dellot can attest to that.

Delicia Morales

"Ay Dios, por favor, cálmate Jesúsito," cried Delicia across the corral to her son, who was upsetting the milk cow, and making Mrs. Morales's job that much harder. Jesúsito, all of five years old, ran inside pouting to find his sister. Delicia shook her head with a smirk on her face, continued coaxing the tepid white milk from the udder, as the cow occasionally bellowed to her nearby calf. Soon it would be time to return the calf and cow to pasture, down the hill from the main house, and the children were ready and anxious to take charge in leading the animals. Cecilia and Jesúsito, sister and brother, stood waiting impatiently. Delicia untied the back legs of the cow after finishing her task, and the cow squirted free to join her calf, kicking her rear legs to stretch out. Jesúsito opened the back door of the house-lot's corral, a gangly but tough blend of mesquite branches and barbed wire, and Cecilia shrilled at the calf and cow, prompting their exit from the house-lot corral. Delicia went inside with the milk and put the fresh bucket in the refrigerator, began boiling water for some Nescafé, and washed her hands. She sat down with a cool, moist towel, and we discussed the last month's activities and what would soon follow. It was November already, and her husband, Jesús, had just sold ten animals to a neighbor to pay off bills and to have some spending money for the upcoming local fiestas in Baviácora.

Mrs. Morales grew up in Suaqui, a small hamlet to the south of Baviácora, and was not raised in a ranching household (fig. 5.3). Her family owned some irrigated land, about three hectares (7.5 acres), below the bluff of a Pleistocene terrace upon which the town is located. Most of her childhood memories revolved around life in the fields of wheat, beans, cotton, and peanuts the family cultivated. Wheat and beans were the family's staples, while cotton and peanuts were grown for cash, though cotton has long since disappeared from the fields in Suaqui. The man she was to marry, Jesús Morales, returned to Baviácora in 1984, after having been divorced in Los Angeles, California. He was flush with cash from running a tortilla business in downtown Los Angeles and eager to start his life over in more rural fashion in his hometown. They met, married, and settled in the town of Baviácora, and Jesús bought eleven hectares of prime, irrigated land below the new location, just downslope, and looked to purchase a ranch nearby.

Figure 5.3   Delicia, with her husband and son, in a discussion. Their recently irrigated field (*milpa*), key to ranch survival, is on the right.

As discussed in chapter 3, in the case of the co-owned Aguaje ranch, Jesús entered into a partnership with a local rancher, buying a three-fourths share. The quarter share was held by three sisters and a brother. The brother, in this case, refused to sell his fourth and would not recognize Jesús as owner of the other portions of the ranch, complaining that his sisters had sold him out. This disagreement led to a long legal and illegal battle between Jesús and the other rancher. In many ways, the case represents a persistent, misunderstood, and underestimated problem in Mexican land jurisprudence. The old owner used "inheritance law" arguments along with local bribes to defend his remaining portion of rangeland. The net result was that Jesús immediately spent some time in a regional jail, in Ures, downriver. They dispossessed his cattle and land on three separate occasions, driven by local police and *judiciales* (judicial police), and he was on the run for over a year from these same officials. All the while, Delicia kept quiet vigil over Jesús's location and kept the household running. "Those were hard times we went through, and I was scared Jesús was going to get shot by the judiciales, but his neighbors really helped him . . . helped him hide from them," Delicia explained. She described the experience further:

> I had to get my sister and brother to help out with the work in the milpa, since Jesús couldn't be in town during that time. That was very difficult, because they have their own families and things to take care of, you know? My brother-in-law also came by frequently to help, until that time when he was also wanted by the judiciales and had to hide on the ranches with Jesús. All the time I was alone, here with the children, but my mother-in-law helped a lot too so we got through it. Every time they forced Jesús and his animals off the ranch though, I'd have to pasture them on the milpa, and sacrificed the crops to take care of the few animals that we had at the time [around 40 at this time], and then of course I had to sell them for less than they were worth because we needed the money to survive and to pay the damn lawyers (*pinche licenciados*) who were trying to help Jesús. Thanks to God that's all over with. (D. Morales, interview by the author, Baviácora, September 4, 1997)

María Ruiz

The floor was freshly swept—the streak marks of the straw broom still visible on the earthen floor of the small ranch house María Ruiz maintains with her husband twenty kilometers southeast of Baviácora. They were in the process of selling their 550 hectares of dry rangeland, but had yet to find a buyer, and the droughts of 1996 and 1997 had made the prospect of finding a buyer slim. They still owned and ran about 30 head of cattle on the property, most of which were the mixed breed derived from crossing criollo and finer Charolais animals, and appeared happily plump after the August rains. The Ruiz family sold some 60 head of cattle in 1995, during the height of the drought, and the decrease in animals had led to a rebound in the grassy land cover of their ranch, but had also allowed for an unwelcome guest to sprout. The central challenge faced now by the family was the rebound of an invasive but native shrub, *Acacia cymbispina* (*chirahui*). This problem is common and increasingly prevalent in the Río Sonora Valley, when and where ranges are destocked significantly. The intensive grazing control of grasses and shrubs by cattle goes unchecked, and the more aggressive *Acacia* species are able to return quickly, decreasing the carrying capacity of ranges in the valley. Still, María and her husband Antonio make the weekly trek from the small hamlet of El Molinote, to maintain the small house and look after the cattle.

During the week, the Ruiz family operated a very modest general store, though this enterprise could shut down soon as well. They were considering a move to Hermosillo once the ranch was sold. "It's just not worth the trouble anymore," said María, "to keep the ranch is more expensive than what we can get out of it." In other words, the ranch was too small to keep enough animals to break even with the costs associated with maintaining the animals and the ranch infrastructure. "The ranch has to be kept clean, the fences repaired, the animals fed and watered. Then with the drought, we've spent a fortune on *pacas* (alfalfa hay bales) the last few years, and the price just keeps rising!" Maria also wanted to be closer to her two daughters living in Hermosillo, one a beautician, the other a law student at the Universidad de Sonora.

Roles of Las Mujeres de Corral: Politics, Religion, and Work

If local knowledge is the pivot point for cultures in relation to environments, then it can be safely stated that women and the household are the pivot point for ranching livelihoods in Sonora with few exceptions. Women, as ranchers and spouses, business owners, and householders shape the daily cultural geographies of life in the small towns of the Río Sonora Valley. What the feminist scholar Donna Haraway (1991) calls "situated knowledges" is what can be considered the form of gendered local knowledge so commonly expressed in the social sciences. Women have different knowledge realms of empirical and daily understanding, about ranching and in general. They are most commonly the ones who know about local, medicinal plants and their actual or theoretical uses. As previously explained, women are also more adept at diagnosing health problems in milk cows and calves they have daily contact with, and they are rarely wrong. Of the 48 health problems witnessed in cattle by the author, fully 35 of these were found and diagnosed by the female rancher or spouse, before being treated. Local veterinarians testify to this knowledge as well—their diagnoses are frequently questioned or disputed by women.

What do women mean to ranching? In the case of the Morales family, Delicia served as the stable household owner and manager, while her husband struggled through his peculiar dilemma. This ordeal, then, accentuated the pattern of life for Jesús and Delicia: that of spatial separation. Like most ranchers in the valley, Jesús spent most of his week out on the ranch, located some fourteen miles northeast of Baviácora. Despite the physical proximity, he was compelled to dedicate his time, because he was frequently the only person on the ranch at any given time. His brother would occasionally accompany him, especially for demanding tasks such as branding or clearing vegetation, but because of the modest size of the ranch he could not afford outside help or labor for these tasks. This practice is the case with most small and medium ranchers.

Linked in a way to the balance between gendered forms of labor, another distinction emerges between small, medium, and large ranch owners. Small ranch owners like María Ruiz and her husband spend less time, as a family, on the ranch as a rule, because of the size of the ranch and the necessity of engaging in other complementary activities. Typically unable to make ends meet with less than a thousand hectares of semi-arid rangeland, the small ranch owner invests in small businesses, directly as a merchant or indirectly as an investor in a larger pool of concerns. The geography of daily activities, therefore, is rather different for small ranchers and their families. Gender roles become segmented, with men spending inordinate amounts of time on the ranch, far away from their families. The future does indeed seem rather bleak for many of the smallest ranches that struggle with the so-called economies of scale, but frankly, most are no longer an important economic benefit to household incomes. Instead, they may remain as a form of family nostalgia, used for special occasions or celebrations, and minimally stocked with livestock.

Owners of medium-sized ranches tend to be the most active group as owners, performing much of the physical tasks by themselves or with family members, and spending the most time during the week (or month) on the ranch itself. The devaluation of the Mexican peso in 1994 combined with recurrent drought cycles typical of arid and semi-arid regions have hit these highly dependent ranches hard. Unlike the larger properties, this class of ranch outfit cannot afford to pay day laborers or to separate vaqueros for ranch maintenance and are thus highly dependent on family and extended family labor. Women retain the household management, as male owners have increased their labor allocations on ranch management. The large estates, especially those that adopted the finer breeds of cattle and linked with exporters in Hermosillo or Arizona, face brighter prospects interrupted by short-term difficulties such as water shortages. The size of herds, the range and diversity of their held assets, and their overall wealth serve to buffer them from the largest of market or climate shocks.

The Cultures of Gender: Inside/Outside Spaces

Concordant with what Stern (1995, 21) has written about colonial Mexico, there is a local understanding and implication of gender as being scaled, or, perhaps more properly understood, that there are differential levels of gender qualities. These levels are visible in the relationships between ranchers, between ranch spouses and other local women, and between family members. They also occur in quite different settings, geographically, separated by differing notions of where gender occurs, where it is appropriate, and how displays of gender operate in different ways. If women have operated independent ranches, they have done so with the understanding that certain parts of "male" livelihood social geographies will be closed to them. Few female ranchers engage in or view, much less bet on, local horse races, for example. This risky set of gender displays is culturally rooted in the prominent display of horsemanship as vaqueros and those who fancy themselves good riders compete not only for pride but for cash.

Anyone who spends time in the region can name at least a few songs about locally famous horses, though perhaps the tune most recognize is El Moro de Cumpas, a famous horse named after the town one river to the east in the Moctezuma Valley. The musical group Los Huracanes del Norte released (in 2004) an entire CD with nothing but *corridos* (ballads) of famous horses. "El Moro" is the lead track for the album. El Moro was owned by the descendant of an American settler in the region, Pedro Frisby, and the horse was finally immortalized on screen in a rather bad 1988 B movie; produced in Mexico, the film told the story of the race between El Moro and Relámpago, a competing horse from the border town of Agua Prieta. In the Río Sonora Valley, about a third of all the corridos typically played late at night are about horses; songs about hardship and the occasional narco-corrido are also typical grist, the latter more popular with younger listeners (Edberg 2004). The drug trafficker is now a stock-in-trade for most record companies, commoditized like the horses bought for racing and the cattle sold around them. And even if these ranchers and vaqueros are now usually more comfortable commuting to their ranch in a pickup truck, the lore and tales of fast, wild horses is still immutable and attractive. Corridos continue to be sung in cantinas, at the races themselves, and at local municipal festivals.

These horse races are always performed by male jockeys, largely wagered on by men, and while women are in attendance, there is an emphasis on heavy social drinking (fig. 5.4). Male-dominated horse culture in Sonora revolves around machismo and vergüenza, a display of horsemanship and riding prowess, and the general exclusive nature of the practice. Because of the occasionally high wagers placed on these races, upward of NP$10,000 (approximately US$1,000), patrons and participants are also engaged in a high-risk game. Fathers and sponsors will place their youngest, lightest sons on horseback, in the hopes that low weight may trump the experience of an older, larger rider. These races often end in tragedy. I still clearly remember the warm September afternoon in 1997 when a nine-year-old boy was placed on a horse, tethered in with thick rope, only to lose his mount and get trampled to death as the horse mindlessly sprinted down the dusty airstrip being used as a race track. Total chaos followed as everyone related to the boy tried to shoot the horse to halt its deadly run, and everyone else rushed for their trucks and cars to leave the scene before any judiciales arrived. The fear and grief at the end were as palpable as the machismo and greed at the beginning of the afternoon. While anecdotal, this event underscored many of the behaviors typical of the horse culture of the region.

In terms of power relationships, "higher masculinity" (or more) is attributed to prestige locals and elites, in relation to other men in community,

Figure 5.4   Male horse culture at a race: Betting, loose cash, and Tecate flow freely in between metal mug shots of *bacanora*. This leisure activity is typical of males in rural Sonora.

and a like "superior femininity" to local elite women much like their counterparts in late colonial Mexico. At the risk of heightening the myth of (colonial) societal continuity, the parallel runs to this day, as ranchers form the elite in both gendered categories. Thus, the local, elite ranchers are usually viewed as *muy macho,* and at the very least, they cultivate the image and reputation of being "more manly" than others in town. But in order to maintain the image, if not the geography, of masculinity, men must also engage in acts of "homosociality," as Irwin (2003) has put it: to avoid men in the street is to draw suspicion. To be out among men, herding or raising hell, is the expected norm.

Even a female rancher likened herself more to the male ranchers of her town by saying that many of her girlfriends viewed her as too masculine, too "country" to circulate in a large city. "Can a woman be macho," she seemed to ask rhetorically, "I'm not sure but sometimes I certainly feel it, and my friends do look at me differently when I have my chaps and riding gear on." Similarly, and to a person, all of the spouses of ranchers were

referred to by other community members as "muy buena gente" in a way
that was reserved for their social and gender status in the villages. And
spouses likewise cultivated the image of feminine honor, and the associated concepts that accompany it, notably that of shame (*vergüenza*).

Yet the distinction remains between the two types of cultural politics
at play here, in which one is viewed as ungendered (political culture), the
other as deeply gendered (gender culture). In the first context, village-
level ideas and commonsense notions of the concept of "political culture"
address the legitimate and less-legitimate local and regional authorities
created by the complex relations of publicly accepted and influential landowners and politicians (Stern 1995, 19). In the second setting, the local
assumptions of place-based and acceptable "gender culture" and gender
behavior include a wide variety of public understandings of manhood,
womanhood, and gender identities generated from household power
relations, between and within the sexes. These are viewed outside the
realm of local politics, as apolitical and separated from the identity roles
that people assume in their public capacities of "political culture." Yet the
conflation of authority and nonauthority, legitimate and illegitimate, is
too complex to dismiss with simple binaries. Or, in other words, as Stern
(1995, 302) put it: "Popular understandings of and arguments about
legitimate and illegitimate authority rested on profoundly gendered foundations. The deep interplays between the politics of gender and the gen-
dering of politics suffused popular culture." Disaggregating such notions
of gender roles within political and popular culture is important not only
for understanding ranching and ranch households, but also for a deeper
analysis of how rural Mexico changed in the twentieth century because
of these same gendered dimensions of struggle.

What Stern (1995, 337) described as a "decline of patrilocal custom
from hegemonic destiny into one among several trajectories of work, residence, and education" facilitated not only by the initiatives and agency of
women and youths, but also by a dramatically shifting terrain of technology, politics, and culture. One often-cited example was the importance of
the late nineteenth–early twentieth century arrival of the grain mills (*moli-
nos*) in small towns of the Río Sonora, which released women from the
grueling work of grinding grains with a *metate* (grindstone). The arrival
and popularity of this new form of grain processing was disdained by men

as providing too much "free time." In other words, men suspected that women would have this time for other kinds of gendered mischief, namely unfaithfulness. Quite apart from the commonly voiced aspect of sexual discipline, some also attributed a poorer taste to nonmetate-ground corn. Even if tooth enamel was prematurely worn because of grindstone traces in tortillas, men seemed to be more concerned about household control than dental health. Yet several important dimensions of this localized patriarchy fell apart, resoundingly so, during the late twentieth century. In the valley, it was also quite apparent that while men left for the summer labor markets, women were leaving permanently. Higher education has been an important outlet for younger women in the region, and any demographic profile of the towns in this area reflects this overall trend; young men are left behind in the villages, when they are not elsewhere in the summer. Migration has simply added to this more nuanced, gendered balance of social relations, as men have departed leaving seasonal affairs and much of local politics now more profoundly shaped by women along the Río Sonora.

After dozens of interviews with women ranchers, spouses, and extended household members, it became clear that certain aspects of gendered life and roles have changed over the last decades. One of the great paradoxes was that while there was general agreement that progress had led to greater ignorance of localized knowledge, the loss of agro-ecological skills and techniques, and the decline of local politics at the expense of greater regional and national awareness and interest, there was also strong consensus that gender equity had improved. Overly romantic notions about the prior "community-level" decision-making process, then, need to be tempered by these gendered testimonies. As Purcell and Brown (2005) have termed it, the "local trap" of knowledge and traditions is not necessarily progressive or even desirable, and in this case the overbearing sense of patriarchy has been lessened with the changes to the agro-industrial landscapes of the Río Sonora. While terms such as *conservative* and *progressive* must be used with caution, this dimension of livelihood transitions clearly deserves more attention, in light of the difficulties of capturing the scalar properties of economic changes.

As Mexico enters the final transition stages of adapting and adopting its own version of neo-liberal economic policies at the national level, local livelihoods are often at odds with the macro-political economies and policies in place. As the subsidies from PROCAMPO have slowly trickled out, as the price supports for corn and tortillas have disappeared, ranchers too face difficult questions and a disconcerting future. The impact of and on gender roles has been rather limited, at first glance, at least in ranching regions. Yet the seasonal out-migration of the local workforce along the Río Sonora is a relatively recent phenomenon, the implications of which are not yet fully understood. In the Mexico of free-market democratic initiatives, smallholder ranching will face new challenges in the economy, and old ones in the physical environment.

Women, children, and the elderly simultaneously face new geographies and economies of risk and opportunities if education and migration continue to be two of the few release valves for rural livelihood failures. The risk is in the form of gendered demographic imbalances, and yet these same forces create new places and spaces for opportunity, as women are filling in gendered niches that in the past were reserved or at least understood to be "masculine." Humble shops, *tiendas*, or small food stands newly owned by women are obvious signs in the Río Sonora Valley. Women with higher education from Hermosillo are returning as municipal civil servants and local teachers. Already, in the summers, the villages of the Río Sonora Valley become skewed demographically, as nearly 30–40 percent of the able-bodied male residents disappear for seasonal labor jobs in the cities of Hermosillo, or for longer contract periods in the United States.

The current impacts of transnational communities in both Mexico and the United States are difficult to assess even if they are common to the past (Truett 2006). What David Harvey (1989, 230–32) once called "time-space compression" is certainly at work in Mexico, as distances between places, national and international, are now easier to cross. If it is now a "smaller world," the inner irony in this change is the new time-space distance added because of migration opportunities, and Sonorans have certainly been quick to adopt longer seasonal migration as one other revenue source for their local household incomes. Migrants, in this new era of transnational communities, likewise typically maintain two homes. It is not uncommon for residents of the valley to retain a U.S. address, for seasonal use or for some social benefits. These transnational satellite communities, now common in the United States, have an impact on both their former village and their new residences. Ranchers still maintain satellite residences on, or near, their ranch apart from the central village home. In some cases, then, this means the maintenance of a ranch house, a village house, and a third international house for seasonal living.

The payments sent back to Mexico (termed *remittances*) have profoundly shaped some rural communities, evident in periods of booming housing cycles in the small towns of the Río Sonora Valley. In terms of daily lived experience, those without land and water resources in the region find themselves in a similar balance of gendered roles: men leave, and their spouses and children remain in the village, if the absence is seasonal. When asked about this seasonal and occasionally permanent migration stream, Sonorans usually identified the time period of the mid-1980s, the beginning of the economic restructuring period that has reshaped Mexico's economic geography. Hundreds of corridos now openly address this change; one currently popular, by a small group known as Los Tres de Sonora (the Sonoran Three) and entitled "Cien Cabezas de Ganado" (2005, Con Alma Sierrena), evokes a narrative typical of a successful migrant, who (logically) buys his "hundred head of cattle" as one of the first steps upon return. These are the audible, visible signs of profound changes under way in rural Mexico, as the country becomes increasingly steeped in the global economy. At the same time, the lure for returning migrants is the dream of ranching; ownership at the local level is a long-term desire.

Under the guise of new economic policies favoring decentralization, privatization, and new investment, Mexico seemingly embraced the so-called age of neo-liberal policies, or what some referred to as the "Washington Consensus," however confusing that misnomer may actually be. While these factors have certainly shaped rural and urban communities in Mexico, residents have creatively responded to these opportunities or simply not engaged with new federal priorities aimed at the communal, social sector. The ejidos were one prime target for government agrarian counter-reforms in the early 1990s, but change has been slow in this part of Sonora. It is to these latest changes and what they have done in the ranching communities that we now turn.

6 Private, Communal, and Privatizing Ranches in Neo-liberal Mexico

Despite Mexico's rhetoric of revolutionary land redistribution, the simple fact remains that the vast majority and the highest-quality grazing lands are in the hands of the wealthiest ranchers to this day. This resource imbalance, an unintended consequence of addressing large estate (*latifundio*) irrigated agriculture foremost among land resource types, translates almost directly into an uneven geography of political and personal power in the state of Sonora, and for northern Mexico in general. Even the largest irrigated estates in Sonora rarely qualified as a so-called effectible property, with few exceeding one hundred hectares in extent. But even in the current atmosphere that seemingly might favor private landowners and ranchers, the challenges to livestock owners are plentiful, and the so-called neo-liberal era has not been without difficulty even for the relatively fortunate private ranchers. Enduring legacies of land-tenure mosaics, debt, drought, even small pockets of narco-trafficking activity, have made the livelihood tenuous. Landscapes have memory, too, and they can be unforgiving.

The grandest agrarian reform clause in the Mexican Constitution, Article 27, was viewed too universally as a social cure; it was a political device for at least transient stability and patronage in the new nation-state, even if the article's geographic application could never span the range of conditions in Mexico (Morett Sánchez 2003). What is often overlooked is how conjoined the agrarian reforms were to the idea of private property ownership, as long as it remained "small." It is an illusion of poorly informed social scientists to think that Article 27 was only "about" the communal land reforms that followed its creation (Bantjes 1998; Robledo Rincón 2000). Yet the regulations, stipulations, and exceptions made for private ownership became far more complex over time. Rules that seemed logical to qualify private estates as too large along the Gulf of Mexico rarely applied as a solid land-tenure guideline for the arid stretches of northern Mexico. Even less attention, much less adaptive institution building, was given toward the differences inherent between coastal and inland areas of the country. This contrast is especially visible when driving east–west transects from the coast of Sonora to the inland, mountainous areas that border the state of Chihuahua. Once sprawling irrigation districts west of Hermosillo have notably contracted, withered, and turned to dust in the wake of groundwater depletion and soil salinization. The brief period of large, agricultural ejidos in these desert wastes reached its height during the 1960s and early 1970s, an aftereffect of Sonora's brief fling with desert frontier colonization schemes (Whiteford et al. 1998).

Coastal regions of Sonora dominate the international cattle trade, and the largest ranches along major transportation arteries and along the U.S.–Mexico border have fared the best in market accessibility, if not always in climate predictability. These coastal juggernauts of ranching have invested great sums of money into ranch infrastructure, through irrigation works, gasoline pumps, and buffelgrass pastures to increase their local carrying capacity. The interior regions, such as the Río Sonora Valley, generally find themselves already at a spatial disadvantage. They have neither the easy access to international crossings nor the means to acquire the big rigs needed to transport large numbers of animals to the border. Consequently, they sell to larger ranch owners, middlemen, and the occasional "coyote" at a lower price. Many of these are the larger, coastal ranch owners who must deal with increased drought variability, but have the economic means to purchase cattle elsewhere for sale on the border.

Ask any Sonoran rancher from the interior, in the foothills of the Sierra Madre, where all the political power and influence is, and the answer is invariably the same, "La Costa," "Hermosillo," and an occasional "Nogales" or "con los gringos," a sarcastic but, in their minds, realist perspective on their abilities to counter market difficulties. This imbalance deeply affected ranchers of the interior during the prolonged drought of the 1990s (Chavez 1999; Liverman 1999). Aid promised by state government, in response to recurring drought, first arrived in coastal regions—and primarily in municipios loyal to the PRI, Mexico's dominant yet slightly weakened political party of the twentieth century. Several fights erupted or were narrowly avoided during regional livestock meetings in the fall of 1997 because of the lack of government support during the drought. Members of livestock associations criticized their leadership for not instating quick disbursement or for not pressuring the regional offices in Hermosillo strongly enough, particularly in municipios dominated by the PAN, the right-of-center party in Mexico.

Micro-Geographies of Privatization and Agrarian Reforms

Léonard (1997, 2003) has provided some of the finest-detail data on how privatization practices have been embedded into the new agrarian reforms in Mexico and how these are disguised in various phases of rural development rhetoric. When the reforms to Article 27 of the Constitution were presented in 1992, there was little interest and great confusion as to what this set of policies would mean for both ejidatarios and for the ejido as an institution (Randall 1996; Cornelius and Myrhe 1998). The Mexican federal government arrayed new panoplies of institutions, a veritable acronym soup of new agencies, to speed the process of titling and certifying lands and resources owned and controlled by the ejidos. PROCEDE, as one new program, quickly became the focus of attention for both critics and proponents of this land counter-reform. This set of land-tenure reforms also entailed "selling the idea" of privatization under various guises or at least attempting to "construct consent" (Harvey 2005, 39). In some regions, simply calling the process the "privatization of title" was enough to attract interest from ejido members long frustrated with their community dynamic and the limits of the ejido bureaucracy (De Janvry, Gordillo, and Sadoulet 1997). In contrast, in states where participation lagged early (or continues to), such as Chiapas and Oaxaca, the government used the rhetoric of juridical security, stating that titling would keep holders safe from any legal contests or questions regarding their lands and resources.

Three aspects of the process within PROCEDE are notable: First was the similarity to past privatization efforts, such as during the Porfiriato and the liberal reforms following the Ley Lerdo of 1856 (Craib 2004). Consultation with state officials, measuring and mapping external boundaries, and agreement and consensus on internal boundaries for parcelization—all of

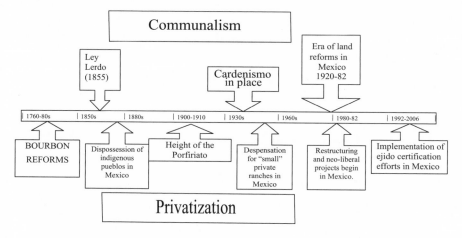

Figure 6.1 Long wave fluctuations between private and communal visions for Mexican land tenure.

these state-mandated steps and technologies were the same ones that the state used following the Mexican Revolution to distribute lands to the Mexican peasantry (fig. 6.1).

The second notable aspect was the speed of execution compared to the pace of agrarian reform in the mid-twentieth century (Escobar Ohmstede and Rojas Rabiela 2001). Following the revolution, ejido petitioners from Banámichi requested lands from the state, to be distributed among the new members of the agrarian nucleus (*núcleo agrario*). The process, because of measurement mistakes and bureaucracy, took sixteen years to approve (Sanderson 1981, 81–82). Now, the process of reversing control, devolving it back to the ejido for future decision making, can take as little as a year to finalize, although eighteen to twenty months has been the norm for ejidos along the Río Sonora.

The third aspect that has been elided or ignored in most of the literature is that few ejido lands are solid candidates for outright title ownership. Those areas given over to ejidos as rangelands are far from suitable areas for any kind of title acquisition efforts. It simply does not make economic or ecological sense to parcel three- or even ten-hectare plots of desiccated, frequently overused, rangeland. So while participation seems high, according to the national statistics disclosed at the end of the program in 2006, the "participation rate" did not mean that ejidos pursued full privatization. It only means they interacted with PROCEDE at some level, and in my case studies, only so far as certifying the outside bounds to the communal lands (Pérez Castañeda 2002; Perramond 2008).

Revolution, Counter-Revolution, or Counter-Reforms?

After the Mexican Revolution of 1910–17, irrigated arable lands were the primary goal and target for expropriation and redistribution to the landless or land-poor in Mexico. Similarly and perhaps not surprisingly, this valuable class of arable land (with irrigation) was the first identified for being parceled out by individuals, to secure individual property rights to the arable lands along the Río Sonora. As of December 1999, the municipios of Banámichi and Huépac had designated 107 hectares and 248 hectares of irrigated lands, respectively, as "parceled" and not for common use. While the eventual outcomes and results of privatization and neo-liberal land reforms in Mexico are perhaps nebulous and difficult to predict, the processes of decentralization and privatization are remarkably similar to those used in the land redistribution of the early twentieth-century revolution in Mexico.

Yet it is too early to call this new wave of privatization a counter-revolution; what is clear, however, is the intent at counter-reforming previous agrarian reform efforts (Yetman and Búrquez 1998; Kay 2002). In the Río Sonora Valley, there is little activity among private ranchers to simply buy out chunks of formerly communal land; indeed, in some cases, the defense of the ejido has been fierce, and members remain more than a little reluctant to engage in the privatization process now possible in Mexico. The new situation has encouraged an active rental market in most regions of Mexico, because the practice has now been legalized, but few people who are both ejido participants *and* private owners are involved in the rental market (Bresciani 2004). For ejidatarios pursuing privatization efforts, however, the expansion of pasture lands and the use of buffelgrass have proven to be alluring regardless of the prospects for long-term success (Yetman and Búrquez 1998).

In other municipios, the range of land classes now parceled is greater, as it is in Sahuaripa. In that municipio, the agrarian classes have more evenly claimed ownership to specific parcels with irrigation (16.2 percent), dryland or temporal (39.5 percent), good grazing land (21.9 percent), and dry/arid shrubland (22.1 percent). Some 27,638 people with parcels or rights to parcels were in Sonora by late 1999, and the gender balance strongly favored men, 71.1 percent for male ejidatarios and 22.9 percent for female ejidatarios, though these statistics do not speak with any definitiveness (INEGI 1999). They do suggest, however, that the land counter-reforms may be creating a new context for gender-based insecurity: at least one study has suggested that women may fare poorly in the new space of neo-liberal land tenure as they have in other parts of Latin America (Chase 2002). Yet empirical evidence, rather than assertions, has also been presented to the contrary: in spite of these reforms, women have gained increased claim and control over family lands (Hamilton 2002, 139). Mexico's last full agricultural census was in 1991, with the latest version from 2007 still being compiled, so any fuller assessment of the land-titling reforms in general will only be possible once the latest results are released.

While land-use and land-cover change in Mexico have been well documented for most of the country and remain dynamic, changes in Sonora have been small and incremental. Converted land use is now dedicated to the valley's livestock economy, at the expense of most staple, base food crops such as maize and wheat. Land cover, however, has not changed as significantly, with minor exceptions being small patches of buffelgrass pasture on private ranches and ejido plots. Unlike some of the dryer stretches of Sonoran Desert ecosystems, lying to the west of the Río Sonora Valley, the area has not witnessed a burgeoning wood fuel and charcoal industry (Taylor 2006). Forest clearance occurred in the 1930s and 1940s along the streambanks of the Río Sonora, as several informants discussed, and much of it was related to new field creation and a small woodcraft industry in the town of Aconchi, where close to twenty small furniture shops remain (as of 2009). Wholesale deforestation of primary cottonwood forests, much less the removal of secondary-growth mesquite, was simply not occurring in the Río Sonora Valley at the time of this writing.

At the municipio level, the preponderance and dominance of the live-stock industry remains unquestionable. As of 1999, in the last available data for reported "land use" by total land base, Banámichi, Baviácora, Huépac, and Sahuaripa (outside the valley) all reported 100 percent land use as livestock related (INEGI 1999, 27). The municipios of Aconchi, Cumpas, and Moctezuma were not far behind. Even including a generous margin of error for such statistics, which may conflate the percentage land use for a particular industry or activity, these numbers are remarkable. New forms of animal agriculture are making headways into the valley, such as aviculture and porciculture, yet these are not range-dependent activities. They are confined to the valley, close to the same feed crops that cattle depend on during the dry season, and thus use little geographic space. But in land-rent spatial efficiency, these recent animal industry efforts are far more profitable than cattle ranching even if they remain the butt of many local jokes. Only cattle command respect.

Changes in rural and urban land tenure, provoked and accelerated by the 1992 reforms to Article 27 of the Mexican Constitution, have been less dramatic or visible in the Río Sonora region. Unlike Vázquez Castil-lo's (2004) discussion of the case of San Luis Río Colorado and its rapid urban capitalization process, no such parallel is visible here, in the heart of rural Sonora. Indeed, West's (1993) idea of "new" and "old" Sonora, divided along an east–west transect separating urban, coastal Sonora with a more rural, foothill Sonora may have to be modified to incorporate the new proximity of capital in neo-liberalized Mexico. The border region, in other words, has become a new focal point for investment capital, and in this case, it is no longer isolated to the maquiladoras. In no small part, this increased access is due not only to the enduring difference between northern and southern Mexico, but also to the more egalitarian side of the valley.

The ejidos and comunidades along the Río Sonora have not aban-doned, wholesale, the principles of communal land ownership. They will variably benefit from the new titling process under way, as well. Ejido members in Huépac, for example, have been fortunate to have larger parcels of irrigated lands compared to their fellow ejidatarios in the other municipios of the valley. Already in the mid-1930s, this accidental con-juncture of land redistribution, a wide, fertile, and irrigated floodplain and generous reform benefited the landless or land-poor in Huépac. Still, the communal use areas are unlikely to be divided for risk-avoidance and logical reasons, mostly having to do with the mobile nature of livestock capital and the absurdity of a small, dry range that has limited capacity to support any herd. "You don't want title to five hectares of desert," was how one ejido member from Huépac so succinctly put it.

For some, this exceptionalism may seem too utopian or facile, yet the reasons for the endurance of common use areas are many. First, older ejidatarios rightly identify the commons as the basis for community organization and the original, political clout enjoyed by the ejido and its enrolled members. Second, younger ejido members recognize the importance of livestock, and how counterproductive it would be to parcel out small hectares of individual grazing plots in a region where precipitation is scarce and fickle in its distribution. Finally, if there is attention paid to the arguments for neo-liberal reforms, it is largely due to the historical and recognized value of irrigated lands along the Río Sonora. It is this last component where arguments for an outright title ring true and clear for both private landowners and ranchers, as well as the ejidatarios targeted with these reforms. And for those ejido members who have chosen parcelization, as in Banámichi and Huépac, the formalization of the land market is yet another addition to a diversified household economy. What is less clear, in those cases where parcel titles have been awarded, is what future the ejido will have as a local institution. Will it still serve a central, decision-making role? Is it likely to become nothing more than a social club, largely haunted by elders yearning for revolutionary memories of a former Mexico? As Simpson (1971) once observed, there are many Mexicos, and regional variation is still remarkable. So to paraphrase, there are also many *ejidos* and many *comunidades;* there is no single prototype for communal land and resource ownership rights.

Previously, the black market of ejido land rentals was the only route for adding some nonagrarian income in these latter villages. Yet in Aconchi and Baviácora, the difference is that the communal knot has not been loosened yet, and the ejido councils have proceeded far more cautiously into this terrain of private capital, private ownership, and neo-liberal logic. The vast majority of private ranch owners, however, are in no position to purchase titles or shares of communal lands. The very geography of ejido lands makes it unlikely that wholesale purchases will happen in the Río Sonora Valley. Ejidatarios no longer tied to, or practicing, field agriculture may first decide to rent irrigated lands to which they may now acquire title. They may eventually decide to sell that valuable, irrigated land to pursue other goals: education, migration, or urbanization (Durand 1983; Jones and Ward 1998). Most irrigated ejido plots, however, are surrounded by the arid rangelands of the ejido that will most likely remain as a communal resource, as the division of thorn scrub ranges makes little sense and is unattractive to even the most desperate of private ranch owners.

Certainly, Mexico's early twentieth-century agrarian reforms stand out when compared to other Latin American countries. In the span of seventy-five years, more than one hundred million hectares of national territory were returned or given to ejidos and comunidades. Some two million six hundred thousand ejido heads of household benefited. More than twenty-six thousand individual ejidos were created in the process, along with over two thousand comunidades. To be sure, there were exceptions for private landowners, as some million certificates of so-called inaffectability were doled out to protect small property owners (Manzanilla-Schaffer 2004, 844). Ranchers were among the most vociferous proponents to support amendments in 1947 to the Mexican Constitution, so that these small property owners could be protected from agrarian and land reform efforts. Their success has less to do with the principle of defending private property than it does with how this policy was successfully translated for ranchers. As previously discussed, a small property is one that can support five hundred animal units. And given the suggested stocking rates in Sonora, varying between twenty and thirty-five hectares per animal unit, this has given shelter to a wide variety of large estates in this semi-arid region.

Landowners use these tactics as part of their strategy to hold on to what they have inherited from parents and grandparents or what they have purchased outright. Many of the private ranchers in this study (nine out of the thirty-four surveyed) were once communal ranchers, belonging to either an ejido or a comunidad. To contrast private landownership with some vision of communal harmony within ejidos and comunidades does a disservice not only to the complexities of these institutions, but also to local realities. The sheer range of landownership and land-tenure arrangements, in the valleys of Sonora and in northern Mexico, are surely more complex than their caricatures in the social science literature. Freyfogle (2003) has noted that this dichotomous understanding of private versus public or communal, in the U.S. context, has been less than helpful in solving important conservation management problems. The implicit friction of using the either/or contrast between public lands and private lands creates a simplistic binary logic that helps no one. In fact, maquiladora-industrial and real estate ventures, like those found in San Luis Río Colorado (Sonora), the first community to use the reforms to Article 27 to privatize, may be a bigger threat than any agricultural landowners (Vázquez-Castillo 2004). Current development infrastructure popping up along the Sea of Cortez, presuming an explosion of condominium and resort-hotel development, is a clear indicator where private capital is moving.

While the study of private ranchers necessitates a more political appreciation of the cultural and political ecology of these places, the politics do not explain everything. This work makes clear the importance of understanding daily activities, labor management, and environmental quality and complexity on ranches. Certain aspects of private ranching remain, as of yet, unexplored. These include the steady decline of the smallholder ranching family, the increasing trend in absentee landownership, and the long-term effects of trade agreements and neo-liberal land reform policies currently in place.

Ranch Challenges and Opportunities

As Gabriel rode in, he kept his head down, until the last possible second. He presumed to know what I was about to ask.

"He's not here," he said, "and won't be until the weekend for one of his daughter's birthdays. They always have a little party here."

"That's all right," I responded, "since I wasn't looking for him."

He seemed puzzled, maybe a little bit bothered, and asked what I was doing. I asked if we could speak for a couple of hours that night, assured Gabriel that anything he told me would be in complete confidence, and gave him my word on the matter. He spit at his feet, squinted at me with one eye, and asked:

"What do you want to know about the son of a bitch?"

As the lone cowboy, Gabriel stayed busy on the 750-hectare ranch northeast of Baviácora, even when the number of cattle was down in a bad year because of drought. The current and next two years would be tougher for Gabriel because of an arrangement made by the ranch owner. He had rented out the ranch to another local, a mine owner for whom a drought was not particularly worrisome financially, and Gabriel found this arrangement aggravating.

"One tells me to feed the horses early in the dry season, and then the other one comes along and abuses me for not feeding the cattle instead!" While this rental arrangement was not common in the past, it is a growing trend in Sonora, as well as all of northern Mexico. Gabriel thought the owner gave the renter a raw deal: he was being charged NP$10,000 a year for three years, on a small ranch that could not support the number of animals that would make this economically feasible for the miner. Nevertheless, Gabriel spent his days watching and worrying about a herd of 129 cattle, of which 40 belonged to the rancher owner and the rest to the miner.

"These old goats are running over twice the number that should be on this ranch, and sometimes because of the terrain, well, I can't always find them. I've already had one calf killed by a lion!"

Gabriel went on about how 1996 was such a dry year, how they had lost five animals, but thought they would lose many more in 1997 because of the weak winter rains. The dual arrangement was a bad idea, he believed, because neither one cared what was happening on the ranch. The owner enjoyed the guaranteed rent, while the renter had no idea how to purchase animals to run on the range, much less what a good price to pay for a bale of alfalfa was.

"He [the miner] shows up here with a pickup full of alfalfa, then tells me to feed the horses first, then the bulls. Look at those goddamn horses—they're fatter than his mother! And the bulls do fine out there. It's the cows you have to look after, especially when they are nursing or pregnant. *Chingado.*"[1]

Gabriel faced two management dilemmas on a daily basis: the ranch's paltry water resources and the steep terrain, as the ranch is largely located on and around the flanks of the Cerro Gerónimo.[2] Two small wells provided plentiful water naturally for three to four months in a good year.

The one closest to the ranch even had a gasoline pump to extract and store the precious liquid in a small tank next to the horse corral. The one located on the northwest side of the Cerro Gerónimo was a mere trickle, except in the wet season, but did produce about two liters every minute.[3] The struggle for the cattle was to access this water; even when Gabriel tried to drive them to better pasture at higher elevations, most tended to wander back to the well sites. Consequently, these two areas were severely overgrazed, at least within a radius of about a half-kilometer. The landscape result was an opposite pattern from a center-pivot irrigation system, a nearly dry circle around the well, surrounded by a green, thorn forest.

A major change that has already occurred in the Río Sonora Valley is the near total absence of small ranches and ranch owners. Only seven small ranches were located within the study municipios, and many were simply held empty, rather than used for productive purposes. Five of the seven ranches were no longer in use. The remaining two were included in the case studies of this work. The other five were abandoned by the early 1980s, either because of the death of the principal owner or because animals were sold off in order to pay bank and commercial debts with the economic crisis of 1982.[4] Three of the these five abandoned terrains were in the process of being sold off to local ranchers, whose large ranches adjoin these small, arid rangelands. Importantly, these ranches were largely privatized from the so-called *baldíos* in the early years of the Porfiriato; these were the more arid stretches of rangelands that had been used for grazing, of course, but never claimed or titled in a formal sense.

These "abandoned lands" were the early and least controversial land reform targets under the Díaz regime, and their distribution did little to affect rural inequalities elsewhere in Mexico (Holden 1994). That they are difficult to manage, improve, or save as a ranch property was unsurprising to the private ranchers of the region. One noted derisively, "they [the federal government] should have converted those western [slope] ranches into ejido grazing areas, they're really dry and screwed up." This rather flip comment does illustrate the difficulties for small ranch owners, who face many of the challenges of ejidatarios in trying to eke out a living on arid rangeland, a problem noted by Camou-Healy (1998) in his study of the *poquiteros* of the Río Sonora.[5]

Absentee Landowners

By far the most powerful and complicated rancher icon is the absentee landowner. But the internal diversity of these ranchers ranges from isolated, elderly men who rarely leave the comfort of central air-conditioning in Hermosillo to young women keenly interested in applying new techniques to their ranches. While all private ranchers hold basic, common interests of private property ownership and defense, some ranchers are more bound to the private sector than others. Many ranchers not only own their own private ranch, but also continue to run animals on communal lands—whether they are in comunidades such as Mazocahui or on the ejido lands that adjoin Banámichi. Private ranchers, then, can also be ejido ranchers with access and full rights to the ejido membership and its resources. So while this group of landowners usually has much in common with the local private ranchers of their home or adopted hometowns, the internal divisions are highly prominent, and these fault lines of cooperation or conflict reflect complicated, localized social interactions. When there is a clear threat to any form of private land ownership in the towns, the absentee class can usually be counted upon to side with private interests (rather than the ejido or communal response). In contrast, when there are conflicts between private ranchers—for personal, political, or economic reasons—then the cleavages between and among the absentee landowner class are highly visible. Only a few remain sympathetic to the "small ranch" owners in and around the Río Sonora.

Camou-Healy (1998) has written persuasively of the difficulties that ejido ranchers and so-called poquiteros face with this growing inequity in both resource and herd numbers. Table 6.1 breaks down livestock ownership from the last full census in 1991. Animal units, usually defined as a cow and its calf, are a typical calculation for range capacity estimates on both sides of the international border. Clearly, the majority of livestock is owned by private ranchers, with a huge differential between those owning up to five, between five and twenty, and more than twenty animal units in the state (INEGI 1994a). While the aggregate data for Sonora mask the inequalities between the admittedly small animal unit producers (less than twenty) versus the largest producers, some notable differences emerge as much within the tenure groups as they do in between. Indeed,

Table 6.1. Livestock and ownership patterns of private and ejido ranchers

Producer type	Animal units	Household units	Mean*
Private			
≥5 a.u. owned	1,830	570	3.2
5–20 a.u.	18,646	1,489	12.5
20+ a.u.	1,110,108	6,182	180
Ejido			
≥5 a.u. owned	5,563	1,757	3.2
5–20 a.u.	49,610	4,112	12
20+ a.u.	312,514	5,033	62

*Average number of animal units (a.u.) per householder in Sonora.
Source: INEGI 1994a.

for producers with one to twenty animal units, the differences between private and ejido producers are negligible. It is only for the largest class of livestock owners, in both the private and ejido categories, that real and important differences become apparent.

NAFTA, Neo-liberalism and Economic Adjustments

Much ado has been made of the contemporary economic changes occurring in modernized, neo-liberalized Mexico (Harvey 2005). As part of the lingo of NAFTA, the discourse of neo-liberalism, terms like "economic adjustment" and "restructuring," tossed around the social science and public policy literatures have become the neutral-sounding euphemisms for real difficulty and livelihood loss in Mexico and elsewhere in the developing world. The terms and concepts, however, are rarely defined or specified in regard to the actual costs to the inhabitants being restructured economically. And they do nothing to account for culture change or for the range of possible local responses to seemingly crushing outside forces, as pointed out by Gudeman and Rivera-Gutiérrez (2002). For Mexico, Otero (1999, 46) has argued (following others) that these were sets of policies embracing both the retrenchment of state involvement as well as more aggressive pursuit of multinational dollars. Even if it was, as many critics claim, imposed from outside Mexico, private companies and neo-liberal reform promoters within Mexico embraced the proposed changes (MacLeod 2004). Yet the total retreat of the state has not occurred on the lines suggested by the promoters of neo-liberalism; nor has economic progress occurred evenly in Mexico (Cohen and Centeno 2006).

Rarely are these changes ever brought down to the level of communities—the actual impact of these economic changes in places remote from urban areas. Therefore, they can serve to dilute or hide the real power of these economic changes. I kept a log of price changes during fieldwork to document one example of devaluation and inflation costs to rural inhabitants. These prices are in Mexican new pesos (NP$), as revalued in 1992 from the "old" Mexican peso (P$). Between the beginning and end of the long-term fieldwork, September 1996 to November 1997, the value of the dollar to the peso increased from 6.7 to 8.5. This change in currency valuation, along with the inflation of real prices in Mexico, led to some dramatic price increases in local goods. The log includes both important food staples, as well as items necessary to local ranchers, as examples of these changes. The bottom line was chilling, as prices for these daily goods went up 32 percent in the course of one year.

The figures betray the effects of the peso's devaluation in 1995 against the dollar and the impact of inflation on local purchasing power, paralleling the shock that Mexican consumers everywhere felt after that event. For the decade following the crisis of 1982, most middle-class families recovered income and assets successfully, until the 1994–1996 period, when their purchasing power fell by some 40 percent (Gilbert 2005, 127). And as NAFTA has taken effect, rural communities from Canada to Mexico have struggled with falling prices for their commodities, even if general price levels for consumer goods have stabilized (Cohen and Centeno 2006). For Sonorans, this percentage increase was profound. Although not as devastated as Argentine households when that country's economy collapsed at the turn of the new millennium, households in Sonora struggled with the new prices for food staples. The Mexican federal government was also pulling the rug out from under price supports for major crops, which did nothing to alleviate stress in the rural countryside. These short-term economic blips can accentuate and aggravate the severity of short- and long-term debts, as interest rates rise, as indebtedness increases. For private ranches, the effects of currency devaluation and inflation can be severe. Indeed, when twinned with the Scylla of drought and the Charybdis of debt, it could be doubly difficult for any rancher, private or communal.

Ranches for Sale

With most scholarly attention focused on the privatization of communal resources in Mexico, little has been given to the failure of private properties, even during the crisis of 1982, the devaluation of the peso in 1995, and the economic recession of 2008–2009. Yet private ranches are actively being sold. To assess the magnitude, regional impact, and unevenness of sales, I conducted a telephone survey between 1996 and 1997, and then again in 2005, to track ranch ownership and sales patterns. Cattle ranches are sold for a variety of reasons, and the wholesale exit from private ownership is an intriguing but unaddressed aspect of these economic problems. To assess the short-term futures of ranches in the state of Sonora and the long-term intentions or plans of ranch owners, I first consulted the classified section of the daily periodical *El Imparcial,* based in Hermosillo, tabulating the "ranches for sale" section every week for a year's worth of sales (advertisements) within the state. I then contacted the phone numbers provided in the ads for further information.

In most cases, these ranches were sold indirectly through real estate companies and brokers within Hermosillo. In about 20 percent of the cases, though, the number was that of a private ranch owner within a specific town or city. A brief description of my interest was extended, after informal introductions, to either the agent or the rancher. The interest in eliciting their long-term desires and short-term trends was explained, and the rancher or agent was almost always willing to discuss some of the finer details of why the property was listed. Only five respondents declined to talk to me, usually for personal reasons, occasionally for legal ones. Those informants who agreed to discuss the sale of their ranch provided the location of the ranch by municipio (at least), the size of their ranch, whether they had buffelgrass on their ranch, and whether any livestock would transfer with the sale. The principal reason for selling was given, and usually fit into several generic categories: debt (35), drought (29), death of the former owner (21), and the occasional ranch facing problems with drug trafficking (3). Rancho Zetazora is an example of the latter challenge, a ranch that was fully immersed in what Astorga (2005) has called the "century of drugs."

Living with Risk: Narco-traficantes

Victor greeted me in his dentist's office, thinking I might be a potential patient, and the slight sorrow that I wasn't one was visible in his eyes for a moment. Señor Saguado is an example of the "back to the land" rancher, generally middle-class, who has their professional education and career on track. Many then return to their agrarian roots, as either landowners of irrigated agriculture or ranch operators. Victor is literally his "brothers' keeper," as he owns the ranch Zetazora along with his brothers, though he is the one who stays in Sahuaripa supervising the daily operations and needs of the property. Gargantuan in size, Zetazora is only one of many properties that Victor's father carved out of the state of Sonora, the balance located along the more arid coastal regions of Hermosillo and Caborca. Interestingly enough, Victor is also the only rancher in this study who demonstrated an appreciation for *conservation* in the globalized sense of the word. This observation does not imply that ranchers do not practice good management, only that certain ranchers are more sensitive to the still rather minor role that conservation and related organizations are having in Mexico; Victor was familiar with both the staff and missions of the environmental organizations already present in Hermosillo as of 2007. To be sure, Zetazora did not display any distinctive characteristics because of Victor's awareness, but his decisions to manage or not to manage certain areas of the ranch were influenced by his stated belief in conservation. A follow-up conversation in 2009 showed a subtle shift in Victor's atti- tudes—new protected areas that make use of private ranches are appearing in northern Sonora. And local ranchers are now paying closer attention to the work of NGOs as they acquire open spaces, reclaimed from former rangeland. Conservation is beginning to compete for space with the more illicit practices that were of greater concern just five years ago.

The thirteen thousand–hectare spread operated by Señor Saguado and his vaqueros is located north of the town of Sahuaripa, situated in east-central Sonora on the western flanks of the high Sierra Madre Occidental. Victor and his vaqueros are wary of the new presence of "certain ranchers" in his words. By this term, he was referring to the recent trade in "outsiders purchasing ranches for the shipment of certain goods." In 1997 alone, for example, his vaqueros had caught 15 people crossing his rangelands carrying plastic bags full of marijuana, either on the backs of burros or horses. A few of them were armed, and it's this aspect that spooked the vaqueros. Two ranches adjoining Señor Saguado's terrain were bought within a year of each other, by the same person, in cash. A phone call in 2007 confirmed Victor's initial suspicions of these transactions, and he added, "Three more places have also been sold to some dubious people, none of whom are local if you understand my meaning." These ranches were constantly buzzing with small aircraft on the landing strips. Federal troops mounted a raid on one of the ranches in 2003 but came back empty-handed. Victor understood the attractiveness of his ranch to the drug trade, with its location on the spine of the Sierra Madre Occidental and proximity to the state of Chihuahua. He just wished they would do it somewhere else. On top of the risky geographies of drought and debt, ranchers must now also deal with the dimensions of human smuggling and narco-trafficking in Mexico.

Long-Term Trends: Drought and Debt

From the data analyzed on ranch sales, the hypothesis that ranch sales were correlated with drought and debt depending on location within Sonora seemed to have merit. Of those ranches designated as "coastal" (C) and ascribing the sale to drought, 71.4 percent correlated with both location and drought as the main reason. The results for the interior ranches (i) ascribing the sale of their ranch to economic debt, was similarly convincing, at 59.6 percent. These data suggest that coastal ranches and ranch sales are more seriously affected by drought than are the interior ranches. Conversely, economic insolvency and long-term debt are the prime movers for ranch sales in the interior, where access to credit is notoriously difficult. It is rather interesting to note that this line is similar to West's (1993) division between "new" and "old" Sonora, largely a difference between the "older" interior and rural lifestyles and the "newer" urban and coastal regions of the state.

The future of ranching, private ranches, and the geography of land tenure in Mexico are not settled issues. The rural Mexican producers, farmer and rancher alike, have repeatedly been sold a bill of goods by government agencies and disembodied "market demands." They responded, and field agriculture has quickly turned over, crop to crop, to maximize profits, yield, and competitive advantage, much to the detriment of local and regional food security, to say nothing of local livelihoods and rural sustainability. For example, in the municipio of Alamos in southern Sonora, wild rumors circulated in the summer of 1996 that a nameless Japanese corporation was supposedly buying all the sesame it could get its hands on. Local farmers responded to this aggressively and overplanted sesame, only to find out that the original information was optimistic at best. No such company even existed. At least four farmers were ruined by this simple movement of erroneous information, broadcast through local speculation, and two of them completely removed their households from Alamos to Navajoa to take up wage labor industrial jobs in the nearby city. Ranchers have faced similar difficulties when rumors of special breed purchases, such as Black Angus, are said to be taking place with preferred prices for these prized animals. Two of the ranchers in this study had gambled on a meat-packing initiative in Hermosillo, said to be concentrating on well-marbled Black Angus, with catastrophic economic consequences in the early 1990s. The plant was never built, and the breed establishment was difficult along the Río Sonora with frequent health problems and vet visits, and the ranchers lost thousands of pesos in the process.

Private ranchers in Mexico, especially the larger, landed estates, did likewise when cattle finally acquired a commodity market price in the Borderlands. They have gradually diminished the number of tough, rangy, criollo cattle once rampant on the semi-arid rangelands of northern Mexico. In their vacuum, the improved breeds have profited with Angus, Brahman, Brangus, Charolais, Hereford, and Zebu strains now running through the bloodstream of range livestock. These landscape modifications and genetic improvements have a long-term cost. Larger animals, with more demanding diets and water needs, required supplemental feed in an arid landscape and the concurrent development of water resources. By development, I mean the depletion of groundwater supplies, which are now so taxed that local wells on ranches may drop six to fourteen centimeters a year during droughts. These are, despite their bucolic appearance, very much industrialized landscapes with meat machines walking on the surface, fed by pipes bored into the Earth to keep them alive for at least the near future. Some ranchers have this change pegged, and see the long-term prospects of productive agriculture as quite dim. They have already adapted their livelihoods to emphasize what they see as the future of Sonoran ranches in a changing neo-liberal regime: wildlife preserves for hunting and alternate forms of livestock.

Neo-liberal Natures of Ranching

As an alternative, those more interested in diversifying into other livestock have quickly entered the porciculture and aviculture markets in Mexico, and the number of pigs in Sonora has increased at a dramatic rate. Between 1970 and 1990, for example, the number of swine shot up from 117,944 units to 1,219,505, an increase of 934 percent. This occurred in the context of a slow growth rate for cattle numbers, only 13.9 percent larger in 1990 than in 1970 (INEGI 1994b). Industrial production and investment strategies found a new set of species for capital during the 1970s. More recent efforts by ranchers to supplement incomes highlight the difficulties of providing a livelihood through cattle alone.

Already in the Río Sonora Valley, two ranches commonly accept American hunter-tourists, who arrive to hunt and claim a trophy deer. The prices paid are exorbitant, relative to what most Sonorans can earn, and are thus complementing the current function of a cattle ranch with that of a game reserve. American hunters on vacation are paying upward of US$1,000 to hunt and kill a buck (white-tailed deer). While these are not the so-called canned hunts on ranches, typical in places such as Texas, ranch owners do facilitate access to wildlife and actively guide American hunters on their properties as part of their venture.

These game preserve ranches may be one short-term solution to the long-term problems that private ranches face in northern Mexico. It is likely that some modified eco-tourist ranches may also appear in the near future to accommodate the nonlethal counterpart to game preserves: the appreciation of wildlife. As various forms of capital spill over into

Sonora from the U.S. side of the border, an interest in seeing and appre-
ciating desert and endangered species will likely blossom, as has already
occurred north of the border (Sayre 2002). Yet very few federal areas
exist in northern Mexico for wildlife protection, and it may very well be
that conservation in this semi-arid region is beholden to private efforts
and private ranches to link wildlife, landscape, and a livelihood for some
form of future ranching. Certainly the introduction, experimentation,
and expansion of Savory's (1988) so-called holistic management techniques are largely taking place on private ranches, and many of these are
integrating natural landscapes and species along with their domesticated
livestock to continue practicing this livelihood, even if the management
strategy is controversial or the results variable (Cohn 2005). Groups
across the Borderlands are following multiple paths of experimentation,
including rancher-conservation collaborative efforts and public-private
partnerships, to find some sort of future path to ranching. In my last
visit in 2009, several ranchers from Cananea to Aconchi noted the recent
purchase of private lands in Mexico by the Nature Conservancy and the
Austin family, some of which lie directly on the U.S.–Mexico border.

By way of comparison, I witnessed a few parallels in a recent visit
to the Chico Basin Ranch, fifty minutes southeast of Colorado Springs,
Colorado. Here, in an arrangement between the Nature Conservancy, the
state of Colorado, and private ranchers, eighty-seven thousand acres are
being managed in a way largely foreign to past ranchers. Ecologically, the
current managers of the Chico ranch have adopted the so-called Savory
(1988) method of holistic resource management, using livestock to intensively graze small portions and pastures with quick rotation, using cattle
as a "disturbance event" to incorporate manure into soil and break soil
crusts, and then swiftly removing the cattle for an extended period of pasture rest. What makes this potentially attractive for the Mexican ranchers
studied in this work is that the Chico receives about the same amount and
distribution of rainfall as some of the Sonoran study ranches. The problem with this method is that it can attract a cult-like following, and much
of the language used to explain particular environments (e.g., *brittle*) does
little to explain why the techniques might result in improvements.

The ranch manager, Duke Phillips, who spent much of his childhood in
Coahuila, is a firm believer in the practice of holistic resource management,

mainly involving short-term use and rotation of animals for grazing. These are similar grasses, similar soils, and largely the same animals as the neighboring ranches. So the key, interestingly enough, is the management of space over time. The cattle are not left on a pasture or set of pastures for weeks at a time, but rather moved with mobile fences, every few hours to every few days. They are viewed as conservation tools. The animals are used as mimics of past buffalo behaviors, and the short-term results in most areas are promising. Even if the language or terminology of holistic resource management, in its original conception, is problematic it is at least forcing producers to pay closer attention to their goals at a landscape level. For example, when I asked one rancher in Carbó, Sonora, what he thought of the term *brittle* to describe soils as Savory does, he simply chortled. "It means nothing to me, but I like the way the plan makes me think. It makes me more alert to changes that may be occurring. But soil is soil, whatever you wish to call it." Traditionalists in the Río Sonora mock even this distinction, calling it just another breed with a different name. There is no wholesale adoption of this management style for clear reasons: it does not work well in all environments.

Even if Mexican ranchers have never faced the equivalent of a public lands grazing dilemma as their U.S. counterparts have, they remain intrigued at the kind of civil society networks getting established across the Borderlands. The Quivira Coalition, based in Santa Fe, New Mexico, is a loose-knit organization of private producers and public conservation, and is focused on finding new ways to create collaborative yet economically productive ranching efforts. The annual conference brings together an eclectic mix of people who, just twenty years ago, would have stood in clear opposition to one another's goals. Their unofficial motto of representing a new "radical center" for land-use compromise and conservation is at once refreshing and highly problematic for the stance the organization does or does not choose to take. The coalition is resolutely anti-lobbying in nature and strives to be apolitical in questions that are inherently political. It is an odd paradox for a set of land managers that have always engaged the ecology of rangelands as a political prospect (Merrill 2002). Yet the field activities, demonstrations, and instructional materials available through Quivira are well respected by both conservationists and ranchers in the region.

Finally, the Gray Ranch and the larger organization of the Malpai Group are well-known efforts intended both to preserve ranching as a way of life and to conserve open green space in parts of southern New Mexico and Arizona. Like Chico, the Malpai Group area is a patchwork of ownership, a mosaic of private, state, and federal lands covering large areas of the San Bernardino Valley in Arizona, across the Peloncillo Mountains, and into the Animas Valley of southwestern New Mexico. As detailed by Nathan Sayre (2005b), the group has focused much of its efforts on reestablishing natural fire cycles in the area with the hope of promoting natural grass-lands. In contrast to state and federally owned lands that still require or at least promote fire suppression, the Malpai Group has reached consensus in establishing protocols for the seasonal presence and removal of cattle in areas that are now fired as part of a larger management plan for the region. Its hope is to reverse the century-long trend of woody plant inva-sions across the desert grasslands of the Borderlands. It is too early to suggest outright success, as the work has only been in place for the past fifteen years, and it would be foolhardy to recommend the same plan for other areas because of the unique convergence of personalities, events, and conservation organizations in the Malpai case. These groups are attract-ing the attention of some progressive-minded Mexican ranchers from the Río Sonora Valley, even if, as of 2009, how to work these arrangements into a highly privatized landscape remains a challenge.

Apart from these novel ranching arrangements at the Chico, the Qui-vira Coalition, and the Malpai Group, the ecology and economics of a ranch offer a partial window into what the future holds for ranching in the drylands of North America. Economically, the Chico ranch managers view ranching as only one stream of income in a larger portfolio of assets that can be used to produce "new values" and a stronger connection between rural residents and urban consumers. Nearly as important is the success of the ranch's "working vacations," in which nonranching folk pay to stay at the ranch and work with the cowboys, whether branding or herding. Folklore and the romanticism of ranching, after all, are com-modities just like cattle. Shorter visits and educational talks, charged on a per person basis, also provide additional cash income.

Whether this form of agro-tourism will succeed or could be dupli-cated in Sonora is unknown. These alluring examples all face a common nemesis, the problem of land rents, or put more simply: suburbanization. Fortunately for these inland Sonoran ranchers, no such threat exists from any nearby city, even if a few privately grumble that Hermosillo has long dreamed of another dam on the river. But certainly there are other policy and practical measures that can lead to greater ecological and economic flexibility for ranch owners. These strategies and arrangements are rife with human agency and highly flexible. So land managers are not standing by, watching economic policies grow increasingly unfavorable; they are individually, and sometimes collectively, responding to the larger proddings of market, economic policy, and new trade arrangements. But they have always done so, regardless of how pundits have decided to label a set period of time: liberal, neo-liberal, or reformist. For ranchers, these terms mean little, as they are concerned about the mix of actual policy impacts rather than the *dominant economic paradigm* of any period.

During a visit to Sonora in January 2003, a gathering of eight ranch owners provided a sounding board for their concerns about the macroscale economic changes occurring in the industry. When I asked what changes were influential for their daily lives, the results were revealing even if limited as a representative measure of these perceptions. NAFTA, the Mexican federal government, PATROCIPES, the local municipal governance changes, and even one mention of neo-liberal policy changes were all discussed. While there was no clear consensus, the eight men singled out NAFTA and the removal of grain tariffs and crop subsidies as clearly important to the local economy, even if when pressed, they then specified the lack of support from the state of Sonora. They clearly understood the shifting scale of governance, rightly understanding the important macroeconomic policy changes such as neo-liberalism, but also more vitally linking this euphemistic and opaque concept to the administrative failures or weaknesses of regional and local response mechanisms by way of price supports or new policies. Less visible to them, but perfectly understandable to a critical political ecologist, was the long-term impact that improved breeds and exotic seeds have played as a corollary to the economic difficulties they mentioned. Yet these ranchers are also not stubborn, and a few have found yet another means to produce income in an era of increasing transborder mobility of goods.

During a visit with one of the case study ranchers, this new set of economic entrepreneurialism was front and center. Eduardo was yelling above the din of the swamp cooler in the small room, describing the work the women do in his small ceramics shop. He took me into the front display area, where two porters from Hermosillo were loading up boxes with the ornately painted load of the week.

"You see, we can't make it on the ranch alone, not these days. The last time we had a decent price for our animals was ten years ago. Now we have to diversify, have other businesses and interests, since we can't depend on our ranch anymore." Eduardo is now the de facto manager of both the ranch and this small ceramics business. While his father's father became wealthy off the hides of his animals fifty years ago, and his deceased father off the calf trade, the balance sheet for his ranch has changed over time, making it necessary to branch out into a merchant's world. Although the ranch is small, Eduardo and his father were able

Figure 6.2 The "fat ranch" of the Sarellas in Banámichi, Sonora. Cattle and calves fatten up either for reproduction or for the last feeding before sale and eventual slaughter.

to eke out an annual profit from the ranch, largely due to their substantial holdings of irrigated lands in the village. They owned 36 hectares of irrigated land, a generous amount for any family in the Río Sonora Valley, and an increasingly critical link between the ranch and the market. Eduardo calls it the "fat ranch," as they typically graze the animals on the luxurious irrigated pasture before selling off any of the herd (fig. 6.2). But Eduardo now estimates that some 60 percent of the extended family's income is due to this ceramics business.

It is unclear whether the new suite of ranching alternatives and economic adjustments is enough for ranching to survive as a primary form of livelihood. Some form of private ranch, a mix of livelihood, conservation and development activities combined, will surely survive well into the latter half of our century. Although a great deal of research is being done on "whether" ranching will survive in semi-arid North America, perhaps the questions should be refocused on "how" ranching will continue as an option for rural inhabitants caught between the squeeze of rural isolation and drought and the pressures of land speculation and suburbanization on the fringes of major urban zones in Sonora and elsewhere in the Borderlands.

7 Trail's End: Ranching a Continent

Ranching continues to survive, if not thrive, in most parts of the Americas. From the colonial-era Bourbon Reforms, through the so-called liberal reforms of the mid-1800s, large private estates were consolidated in Sonora. After the Mexican Revolution and its period of land distribution, private producers still remained; irrigated agricultural areas were the first targets for expropriation during agrarian reforms. From the Green Revolution and the arrival of its new hybrids, to the Brown Revolution and its emphasis on livestock-as-development project, and to the latest effects of globalization or neo-liberalization, private ranchers remain. For each wave of newfound interest in communal efforts or redistributive economic attempts in Mexico, private landowners have pushed back in multiple waves of private, reactionary revolutions. The earliest practices of territorial control in the colonial period have clearly waned, yet ranchers have continued with their spatial gains, while minimizing losses, even during periods of progressive land reforms or aggressive *agrarismo*.

Surviving on even the toughest of frontiers, the urban and suburban fringes of North America, "the ranch" as an entity has not remained immutable and unchanging (Sayre 2002). More scholarly attention is needed on how place or region-specific ranching cultures have changed, historically and more recently, to avoid the single-category generalizations so common in the social and natural science literature. The sizes of ranch outfits do matter, as do the variety of grasses available, as do the cattle breeds. These are obvious points of departure for any narrative; less obvious are the qualitative management decisions taken by landowners and herders. But these decisions have resulted in a cumulative set of landscape changes that is hard to ignore.

Living Landscapes: Economic and Ecological Exotics

As we have seen, the keys for private ranchers are managing for ecological complexity and economic diversity, if not adversity. In this context, *complexity* refers to the biophysical attributes of the ranches and the difficult tasks to maintain or limit the loss of carrying capacity, not to the more abstract realm of *complexity theory*. The decisions made by land managers are reflected in the landscape over time, as we have seen, and yet the consequences of intended landscapes are frequently unintended. Planting an exotic grass led to a set of consequences not anticipated by ranchers: they hoped for better pasture, not a more aggressive fire cycle, one of the results of using buffelgrass. These hybrid landscapes have bitten back, producing complications for future decision makers, local residents, and ecological policy wonks (Tellman 2002).

Buffelgrass pasture development in the Sonoran Desert region has run counter to a rather odd shift in land cover change occurring in Mexico and in parts of dry Central America, from tropical to semi-arid forests, a type of mid-grading of ecosystems (Bass 2004). Large tree stands, for example, give way to secondary forests in areas under frontier or population pressures. Alternatively, in areas with once-rich semi-arid grasslands like Sonora, the woody species are making their presence felt. What is being produced is a variety of Mexican landscapes held in a midpoint of successions: no longer primary forests, a richness of secondary growth and low-lying woody species, and a poverty of undisturbed grasslands. Yet these are landscapes of economic activity constantly held in a state of disequilibrium, and our understanding of them has been flawed by temperate climate ecology models. The transborder perceptions, while different on each side, produce particular kinds of rhetoric and ecological practices. The visual irony is striking: While poor Sonorans collect buffelgrass seeds to sell to ranchers nearby, locals in southern Arizona are aggressively uprooting the grass; paradoxically, the species is both an economic opportunity in Mexico and an ecological villain in Arizona (fig. 7.1). Local news stories report help is needed in the "war against buffelgrass" (Poole 2007). Citizen groups in southern Arizona are aggressively pushing for

Figure 7.1 Buffelgrass narratives: Wanted dead, not alive. This poster is one common representation of buffelgrass by a southern Arizona citizens group hoping to eradicate the species in the region. *Source:* Pima Association of Governments, 2007. Used by permission.

the elimination of buffelgrass in the region, due to increased fire risk and impacts on native species, while ranchers in Sonora still pine and hope for increased forage from "better versions" of buffelgrass hybrids.

Ecologically, ranchers have quite specific goals, and these vary from ranch to ranch. And while the desired or utopian ranch landscape, to the rancher at least, is usually apolitical in nature, the decisions made in management or relationships with their ranching neighbors remain highly influenced by these profoundly political dreams and acts. One rancher's desire for mesquite, for example, may be a nightmare for her neighbor if the ranch goals are disparate. Even imagined landscapes are political in this case, and the expressions of these goals ripple through the semi-arid rangelands and small towns of the Río Sonora Valley, even if the ecological outcomes of these choices are not always visible. But the overall impacts of ranching are difficult to assess empirically, given the extent of scientific protocols used in range science (Curtin, Sayre, and Lane 2002).

By diversifying economically, ranchers are able to participate and invest in various enterprises or business opportunities that are not related to ranching to maintain their economic base and to make them less vulnerable to the price shocks and droughts so typical of the region. Those unable to conduct a complex of economic activities, such as smallholder ranchers, frequently exit the ranching strategy to a small business and in many cases, retirement. Medium-sized ranch owners lacking environmental diversity on their ranches, or enough vegetation in the milpa for animal feed, are pushed to their economic limits. Many subsidize their dry rangelands with feed crops from their irrigated lands, even at occasional economic losses in the short term, hoping to maintain ranching as a livelihood or at least a lifestyle in the long term. The landscapes they work with and create are literally, not theoretically, "hybrid landscapes," profoundly shaped by cattle breeds that demanded higher feed and water inputs and profoundly reshaping the geographies of rural production in the dry valleys of Sonora by displacing human food crops. The new breeds with their higher daily water needs have also indirectly forced ranchers to drill and tap new groundwater resources. Ranchers have now responded by cross-breeding cattle in more creative ways, emphasizing where necessary and possible the semi-arid breeds that can succeed in

Sonora, even marketing such hybrids as Sonora 17 to accelerate adoption by other private owners. Their version of the so-called development encounter has led to some savvy branding of their own; one Sonora 17 cattle marketer was quick to emphasize his version is "a process," not an end point "like the government's version of livestock development."

By sheer numbers of hectares and animals, large cattle operations make out well in Sonora. Not even large ranches are created equal, however, and many are faced with reducing the number of cattle on their pastures, after decades of artificially high stocking rates. As a result, many are exploring other options that maintain the land base, but may complement their ranching activities, such as wildlife stocking. Built specifically as hunting preserves, particular pastures are stocked with wild game, for canned and highly lucrative hunts. Two of the study ranches had recently adopted such an approach for at least one of their major pastures by the late 1990s, and another two of the case study ranches had done so by 2003. More ranchers are likely to try this route, some out of desperation, and others out of simple curiosity.

The happenstance of ranch location, such as being in the rain shadow of a mountain range or the distance between ranches and buyer, can largely determine the success or failure of even large ranches. The cattle ranch is as much about culture and ideology in northern Mexico as it is about economics. In fact, culture trumps economics in ranching, until the breaking point. The day-to-day decisions by the owners are almost always centered on economics. However, when it comes to keeping the ranch at a loss or selling it for some amount of profit, many ranchers refuse to sell or simply never consider it. Ranchers view their private rangelands as covetously as Mexican farmers view irrigated farmland: to sell it would be like selling a relative. In this, Sonoran livestock ranchers are similar not only to their counterparts across the Borderlands, but also to herders across the Americas. They will, indeed, subsidize their ranch economically by balancing the ranch losses against another business making a profit elsewhere, or do so ecologically through hay bale purchases.

Every single rancher in this study practices this wet milpa subsidy for the dry ranch, providing extra feed for cattle during the early spring and summer, another factor in pushing human food crops off irrigated lands in the Río Sonora Valley. Every single rancher also claimed that they had only recently begun this practice and nearly all believed they would have to continue it because of ecological obstacles, such as drought, and market concerns for the weights of live calves at market. A few elderly ranchers bitterly complained they were sold a model of ranching that was clearly not meant for a desert, one dependent on year-round irrigated farming and constant animal supervision. As one disdainfully remarked about his prize Charolais bull, "Oh sure, he's big and beautiful, but he can't make it up most of the hills around here, so what's the use?" In this, he also noted that many of the new "better" breeds could only use small portions of the ranch, as their size and bulk affected their spatial mobility. His parting shot was "and of course they are more expensive to buy and maintain, which is why everyone here is poor."

Most of the ranchers I interviewed, around 60 percent, were plagued by long-term debt to formal state-subsidized institutions (such as the now-liquidated BANRURAL), commercial banks, or private individuals (especially other family members). Of the ranchers interviewed and surveyed, twenty out of the thirty-four claimed they were in "serious debt" (59 percent). All those who claimed indebtedness pointed to the national economic forces and policies, such as peso devaluation, as well as to the more general financial institutions involved in original loans and the recurrence of drought in the mid-1990s. A full 85 percent of the ranchers held *formal* debt from financial institutions, taken out in response to government initiatives such as improved farm equipment, improved European cattle breeds, and water resource development. This wave of state-sponsored development occurred in the latter half of the twentieth century in Sonora, as Sonora became tied not only to the U.S. regional economy, but also to the global economy of industrialized animals. Very little work exists on the consequences of re-regulating a reformed sector, such as agricultural commodities, and what may have been lost with the reforms both to crop subsidies and the ejido itself (Thiesenhusen 1995; Toledo 1995, 1996; Snyder 1999).

Just as significant to these ranchers is the amount of informal, sometimes familial, debt they have accrued. All of the ranchers had borrowed personally from family and friends, in amounts ranging from US$500 to nearly US$25,000. If the nature and timing of informal debt is certainly more flexible to manage, it is no less stressful for ranchers as they are bound to new relationships that make local logistics and daily life burden-some. As one rancher bluntly stated, "I'd rather screw a stranger, or be in debt to a bank, than be held hostage by my uncle who personally reminds me of my debt to him every day!" The story of Garucho, one of the ranch-ers in this study, is illustrative of this set of economic challenges.

It was early March 1997. Garucho was in town to meet Don Pesqueira, who, he hoped, would visit his ranch near Arizpe later that month to buy the animals he had in mind. At that moment, however, Garucho was biding his time and being patient, as he visited his cousins in Banámichi. Then he heard of the sale of animals on the outskirts of town. Although 1997 was turning out to be a decent year for cattle ranchers in the Arizpe region, many were still struggling with the aftereffects of 1994, such as new debt burdens from the peso devaluation and a plague of grasshop-pers common every six or seven years. Garucho was one of those strug-gling ranchers. He overextended himself on a bank loan that he might not be able to pay back for another 20 years, because even in a good year, cattle ranching no longer turned over the amount of profit it once did.

Last year I only made NP$29,000 (about US$2,900), which isn't much but it got me through the year. I don't have a family, so I can make it on that, you know? But I wasn't able to save anything for this year, and my first payments are due on the loan, so I'll have to sell more animals. Why am I in such debt? This guy in Hermosillo promised me that the new strain of buffelgrass could grow in elevated regions, like where my ranch is located east of Arizpe, and I believed him. I should have known better—the seed never took, and now I owe NP$58,000 (US$5,800) for the work on 300 hectares of completely razed land where nothing is growing except for weeds.

Garucho told me that a lot of ranchers in town had made fun of him because he had been taken by the salesman in Hermosillo. Garucho was a younger generation of rancher, who was quickly learning the ins and outs of making a living in ranching, and he admitted that he had much to learn. His ranch may also be up for sale soon, Garucho readily admitted, frustrated with the costs of maintaining the herds and the infrastructure of the ranch. His uncle left him the ranch back in 1993, and he has since decreased the number of cattle on the ranch, although not always by choice. While his uncle used to run nearly 350 head on the ranch, Garucho sold over 80 in 1996 to begin paying for the buffelgrass fiasco that landed him in enormous debt.

"I would have gone back to reclaim the money from the man [in Hermosillo], but I was so ashamed, and there really was no guarantee. It was only his word and I was stupid."

"I'm getting tired of worrying about this ranch all the time. The trouble is that I don't really know what to do with it. I didn't grow up on a ranch—I don't like to spend much time on the ranch—so I'm not really sure how to manage it or what kinds of animals to buy or who to sell to," added Garucho. So quite apart from the frustrations and challenges of almost every rancher in the region, his challenge was not only material but intellectual: running this kind of operation is "not for dummies," as another rancher put it. Even for those savvy to past changes and current opportunities, this is a difficult way to make a living in a frequently unforgiving environment (Food and Agriculture Organization [FAO] 1993).

Farewell to the Poquiteros?

As the title suggests,[1] this section discusses the precarious existence of small ranchers in Sonora. The three key changes to cattle ranching in Sonora—technological innovations and diffusion barriers, government policies, and market demand for feeder calves in the United States—have all led to greater levels of indebtedness for different reasons. Small ranchers, known as *poquiteros* in Sonora, could not afford most of these, and certainly the communal ranchers were largely unable to adopt these quickly and did so only by going into debt. By *technological innovation,* I mean simply the range of introduced and bundled technologies geared to increase animal and pasture yield. A few of these innovations, namely the so-called improved Euro-American cattle breeds that guaranteed more meat per animal carcass and the improved grasses such as buffelgrass meant to subsidize this increase in animal mass, resulted in dramatic changes in northern Mexico. The product was a whole suite of landscape and land-use changes necessary to support this new complex of industrial landscapes. As the geographer Lakshman Yapa (1996, 263) noted, innovations as objects are not the only items that move across boundaries, but also "the nexus of production relations and associated innovation bias" inherent in such neutrally termed "transfers of technology." These challenges are not completely dissimilar to what U.S. ranchers struggled with on the other side of the international border. A borderland ranching lifestyle still faces many potential nemeses, from suburbanization, to restrictive policies based on endangered species acts, to an increasingly militarized border (Adamson 2002; Sheridan 2007).

The shift from food crops to animal feed crops, for one, is a notable change in the land-use portfolio of the valley that does not escape notice. Some 80 percent of the valley is now dedicated to supporting livestock feed, not human food. Government policies, both federal and Sonoran, ensured a steady supply of loans to subsidize the introduction and permanence of these new forms of innovations in cattle ranching. Lastly, market demand in the American Southwest pulled feeder calves out of Sonora, and it was this change in the 1960s, when cattle began to acquire a real commodity price amongst local cattle ranchers in Sonora, that reshaped the physical and cultural landscapes of ranching. This increased demand was a boon to all of the ranchers, but consistently benefited large ranches first, because of their available capital to meet increasing demands such as that in the retail market for meat from improved cattle breeds. The smaller ranches struggled in the wake of these changes and took on larger debt burdens to increase the size, quality, and infrastructure of their operations. Even if the changes were incremental, small ranch owners could easily spend 20 percent of their income in a year on barbed wire, posts, and gate materials for the ranch.

But even in northern Mexico, where eking out a living has never been easy, "hobby" ranching has taken hold and seems to be replacing rural-industrial ranching as the dominant form. Like ranching elsewhere, livelihood and hobby ranching are taking complementary turns at the table and are not mutually exclusive (Starrs 1998; Sayre 2004). One of the ranches not included in the case studies is owned by a local pharmacist, who spends well over 80 percent of his time in town, away from the ranch. He leases out the ranch house, and its relatively spacious and luxurious accommodations, for parties, weddings, and other celebrations. The income received from this activity is about double the revenue derived from pure cattle sales revenue. He jokingly calls this his "beer subsidy for ranching," as the hosted celebrations underwrite some of his larger cattle-ranching expenses during the course of a year.

Future Trails: Policy and Recommendations

Walker (2006) has recently reminded geographers and political ecologists that few of our findings and fewer still of our recommendations are taken seriously in environment and development circles. The writers, creators, and practitioners of policy need some learned feedback, not endless and sycophantic sarcasm about the process of development work. To that end, there are policy decisions that would help both communal and private ranchers in the Río Sonora Valley and in Mexico in general. Academic geographers, like most social scientists save perhaps the economists, have been shy about handing out advice, either because they are unabashedly recalcitrant to participate in policy measures or, more commonly, because they view policy and prescriptive work as "not their job." That reluctance is, of course, forgivable, given the track record that development advice has left in its wake. For the aggregate success of higher yields and better breeds at a national level, the agricultural revolutions for both crops and animals have a very mixed local record.

Indeed, after comparing and contrasting the context of ranching in Mexico and in the U.S. West, geographers must view and treat these findings with logical caution. Instead of viewing Mexico and other developing states as a sink for advice, expertise, and recommendations, we should flip the coin and think of these places as additional sources of information, if not inspiration. If landscapes, species, and livelihoods are similar enough, why not take the time to monitor and understand what others have done in likewise difficult environments? Let us reverse the presumed or real direction of information migration; we should consider the calm and reasoned expertise of others who have a long record of experience in a semi-arid place (e.g., Reed 2004). Even those systematically promoting a "kind" of resource management know that these efforts can fail miserably when applied in highly unpredictable environments (Savory 2002). While any prescription for development is problematic because of the financial, juridical, and ethical burdens involved, I have summarized eight prescriptive changes for development practices as points for consideration. Many of these changes were also suggested by the informants and participants of this study and thus are part of the ongoing dialogue of what could be done in the Río Sonora Valley.

1. Reintroduce some form of agricultural and development credit for local, rural communities in Mexico, preferably credits that are not necessarily bundled to specific technologies.
2. Allow agricultural and range experts to serve as consultants to the goals of rural producers, rather than as extension agents for the state who are only responsible for the implementation or introduction of chosen technologies.
3. Assess the desmonte process of buffelgrass expansion in Sonora with an eye toward slope and soil stability in local context, rather than promote a generic "bulldozer ecology" that ignores the importance of ecological place (Franklin et al. 2006).
4. Promote agricultural and technical vocations in rural areas that are losing population to encourage local children interested in rural livelihoods and to stem the loss and migration of younger generations to urban areas.
5. As another way to stem the flow of migration and the resulting depopulation of small villages, reintegrate and revalue the importance of the extended family in rural Mexico and provide tax incentives for family members working in rural households.
6. Understand that international migration, from Mexico to the United States (and Canada), is only one mechanism for local households to stay local—that rural Mexicans view migration as one possible route to land investment back in their home community (VanWey 2005).
7. Conduct a regional assessment on local food supplies connected to ranches and how ranches may cooperatively buy and sell at least a portion of their product locally.
8. In connection with the last recommendation, emphasize the importance of local foods for local markets and a growing sensitivity to organically produced meats and foods. This local shift would involve the implementation of new regulations in the wake of food and crop subsidy withdrawals, especially for corn, begun in the 1980s and culminating in 2008.

Although the discussion of these findings, at least in rural Sonora, is difficult to frame around the concept of sustainability, it is this aspect that provides a foil for the changes wrought to the ranching industry during the last fifty years. As described throughout this book, rural producers are more concerned about sustaining their livelihood, and less about eco-logical sustainability writ large. But the fallout from disappearing trade tariffs, the crisis of the early 1980s, the withdrawal of food and crop subsidies, and the politics of NAFTA and economic liberalization have highlighted the need for certain aspects of re-regulation in the Mexican economy (Snyder 2001). That the suggestions for policy change were also participatory, in that ranchers, cowboys, and other stakeholders dis-cussed these openly with me at meetings, highlights the need for geogra-phers to pay attention to ethical practices in our work (Jarosz 2004).

Conclusions

The central challenge of this book was to explain the various political ecologies of ranching in northern Mexico, so actively shaped by indi-viduals, biophysical factors, and socio-economic externalities. These are not disconnected groups, processes, or economies. I hope the largest of my arguments are not lost. First, private ranchers should not be used or viewed as a binary opposite to communal farmers and ranchers or cast as simple villains. They are not some monolithic, oppressive class of rural Mexicans, hell-bent on the privatization or destruction of the ejidos. Many are still ejidatarios. Many are former ejidatarios and have only recently become landowners, either because of inheritance or a newfound source of funds that has allowed them some purchase in the valley. Most are what they are through circumstance, accident, or kinship ties.

The articulation of private, communal, and co-owned (condueño) properties in Mexico has always been complex, whether formal or infor-mal. And the contrast in ranch purpose, or goals of each rancher, is likely to stand out even further with the changes in tenure regimes in Mexico. This does not excuse, in any way, the landed elites' abuses of the agrarian code. Many of the gargantuan private ranch owners did engage in some form of chicanery, by understocking ranges, by hiding cattle, or by legally parceling out rangelands to relatives (*parientes*), even when no wholesale ownership change occurred. These tactics are well known in this part of Mexico and practiced elsewhere. But their apparent or seemingly unquestioned "hegemony" in rural Mexico has always been contested by neighbors, farmers, politicians, and even their fellow ranchers. Each ranch is intimately tied into the social fabric of local kinship, physical landscape, and local-to-global market relations.

Second, because ranchers are not a single hegemonic class of landowners, they perceive matters and make decisions in different ways. To reiterate, not all ranches are equal, nor are all ranchers (or cowboys, for that matter) equal. Their ranch locations matter, the ecology and setting of their ranches matter, in spite of rancher creativity, and they are as constrained by pasture quality and rainfall as by anything else. The biophysical properties of any given ranch are, of course, important to whether a rancher will succeed in the short or the long term. But this is not to argue for some simplistic determinism in relating "who wins and who loses" in this narrative. Ranchers with small, poor pastures simply have more work to do to compensate for the unevenness of ranch quality in the valley. Small and medium ranch owners spend more time managing their herds, while large ranch owners obsess about their infrastructure, market access, and relationships with middlemen. The latter are not perfectly rational economic thinkers existing in some theoretical isoplain of decision making: they are related, they are emotional, and they are human. Logically, the local conventional wisdom, ironically concordant with much neo-classical economic theory, of "bigger is better" in ranching does not translate to management or ranch quality conditions. Some small ranches, in other words, are in much better shape than many of the larger-sized neighboring properties. These landholders rarely collude as an entire group of stakeholders, except when faced with demands from the ejido or when faced with new agency rules by various bureaucratic functionaries.

Ranching households depend not only on local day labor, vaqueros, and connections to the market; they also must integrate family members in a logical way to support the livelihood. As we have seen, the gendered roles within ranch households become more complex. The industry continues to be dominated by men, predictably, but this apparent dominance is made possible only by the support of women, children, and the elderly in extended family support networks. Yet the variety of these extended networks is rarely drawn out in stories of and about ranching. This dimension is complicated in most writing about human-environment relationships. These are not simply stories or narratives of "struggle, resistance, and conflict" in a globalized world set in a locale far removed from the cosmopolitan. New social chains of migration in the Río Sonora Valley, linked to extended transborder families living in California, Arizona, and Texas, have provided a new source for livelihood resilience. And this ebb and flow across the border has produced a return wave of new ideas, conceptions about the area and its relationship to the outside world, and a new appreciation for the regional landscape. The cultural ties and roots of returning migrants are also shaping a new political landscape at the local level (fig. 7.2). Municipal elections are now closely scrutinized and followed by local representatives of the three major Mexican political parties, even if the PRI and PAN swap leadership roles regularly.

My third and final point has much to do about how we cast the set of relationships in the continuum of society and nature. There is no single

Figure 7.2 A political march under way. Many of the most active participants now in the political process are women.

"struggle with nature," even if ranchers decry on a daily basis the lack of rainfall. There is no single account of "struggle over resources" that can satisfactorily explain the private and public geographies of land use and water resources in this area. The false binary of "human/environment" also breaks down further when cattle are considered: while animals are sometimes viewed as passive recipients of human decision making, they have their own will and ideas about where to go for water and where to find the best pasture. All of ranching's practices are a complex assemblage, "linking human agency and nonhuman efficacy" (Moore 2005, 99). These nonhuman agents of change are rarely vilified, save by the most radical fringe of environmental organization, but are vitally important to understanding the full dimensions of livelihood changes in the Río Sonora Valley.

Class, ethnicity, family roots and relationships, extended kin disputes, and the localized negotiations of all levels of governmental power play a role in the cultural geography and political ecologies of natural resource use and abuse within the Río Sonora Valley of Mexico. Culture is omnipresent, not as some form of superorganism but as local politics, daily compromise, and the ritual of life in a highly religious set of communities. These social relations of production, as a political ecologist might put it, are as much cultural relations of production. Yet without paying close attention to cultural matters, or worse yet, cultural ethical practices in our work, we stand to lose traction or even face at the local level. I could not have addressed ranch hands and cowboys using the "division of labor" as my lexicon: doing so would have entailed, frequently, a discussion of "division of family labor" that such language only awkwardly captures. There is still a strong place and valid role for considering culture as a set of beliefs with its own landscape imprints, and not viewing culture just as a suspicious version of status quo folklore as some cultural critics would have it (cf. Crehan 2002, 106–9). Less than ideal practitioners and observers of even minor cultural mores simply make it more difficult for future scholars to participate meaningfully in the region (e.g., Burwell 1995). There is also the danger of simplistic treatments or advice that can affect the very people that were the "subjects" of study (Turner 2004).

My arguments should not be interpreted as geographic fatalism or as a presumptive carte blanche for the rural upper-class residents who have abused local politics to their advantage. Instead, this book has argued against simple caricatures of villainous ranchers, simplistic assumptions about private versus communal, and the notion that there could be such a thing as a singular "political ecology" of ranching. Assigning blame to any particular livelihood "sector" is more troubling than pointing out individual abusers of the system; nevertheless, I remain in full agreement with Taylor's (2005, 130) statement that "causality and agency are distributed, not localized" in the often chaotic complexity of cattle ranching. But what then is the future for ranching and ranching families in Mexico? How will private ownership evolve, develop, or accommodate the most recent changes in Mexican land-tenure reforms? Finally, what can scholars, ranchers, and policy makers learn from all this?

Postscript and Exodus

Landscape analysis is a common practice in fieldwork for cultural and environmental geographers. Like anthropologists, we tend to spend a great deal of time listening to, and trying to understand, the perspectives of local residents. Similar to historians, geographers are also sensitive to the importance of change over time, but often with a particular emphasis on how these changes occur over space (Williams 1994). Perhaps less common, yet no less important, is our attempt to understand how societies are, and have been, structured—a common goal for sociology. Unlike any of these fields, however, geographers love to "read" places and landscapes. There is *still* much to be gained from paying close attention to a particular place or region over a long period of time, especially with repeated visits (Parsons 1977, 3). One of our greatest challenges is how, when, why, and to what purpose we read landscapes. A cultural geographer may pay closer attention to material culture, housing types, or the contemporary ritual landscape of religion in a place. Almost every ranch has some form of Catholic shrine, either in the housing structure or embedded in some element of the physical landscape (fig. 7.3). In contrast, a critical geographer will be much more sensitive to issues (and appearances) of class, social injustice, and the visual footprint of capitalism. Even these small towns have had an industrial maquiladora present at one point in time, creating wage labor opportunities and conflicts

Figure 7.3 Religious iconography embedded in the landscape. Deeply held beliefs are carved out, literally, in the local geological formations leading to a ranch. La Virgen de Guadalupe is depicted in this photo, but dozens of saints in the shrines pepper ranch landscapes.

inherent in this form of industrialization. Is one any more correct than the other as a way to approach, explain, or understand a place? This is doubtful, yet many of us are reluctant to combine two or more viewpoints in our academic treatments of place, of region, or of livelihoods. This is wholly unfortunate. For too long, we have forgotten the conjoined and complex nature of our geographic vocabulary toolkit, mostly engaging one set of ideas while "tunneling" older ones thought to be unworthy or "dated" in some way (Turner 1997, 199). Many geographers view the term *landscape,* for example, as either cultural or political; this splitting of hairs has helped no one. Landscapes are both cultural and political, products of human customs and a belief in how local communities view their own polity (Olwig 2002). Sonora's cultural landscape is both producer and product of its own political geography, and ranchers understand this well.

Some years ago, Delal Baer (1997) wrote a small piece for the journal *Foreign Policy,* in which he analyzed and dismantled North American misreadings of Mexico. The article still resonates for me for three important reasons, in spite of its pro-globalization, pro-NAFTA, elite U.S. vision of a Mexican society (Aguayo Quezada 1998). First, academics and frequent visitors to Mexico cultivate a particular vision of the country, based either on images of a colonial past or on unfair comparisons of development indices such as education, income, or gender equality. As geographers, we can point people in the right direction by emphasizing the baggage we all carry: the colonialism, capitalism, and pop cultures that are the birthrights of most global citizens. Too few are explicitly self-aware of this permanent luggage. Fewer choose to write about it in books and articles. But elitism or landed elites are not a new phenomenon in this era. Hart (2002, 507) has noted how interconnected the elites in both Mexico and the United States have been and remain to this day. In other words, the past is not "gone," and neither is the landscape produced by geographic and historical processes.

Second, if the nation-state of Mexico has been and continues to be "misread," I would argue that so too have its landscapes and inhabitants. Because geographers are wont to promote the "reading of landscapes" in some tangible way, we need to be more attentive and participatory in the way we approach our tasks. It surely is just as easy to misread a landscape, of any kind, as it is to "read it" in any sense of the words. So too can people be completely misread or misunderstood. Mexicans continue to suffer a wide brunt of stereotypical caricatures: the immigrant, the drug trafficker, the day laborer. These are all comfortable roles that both media members and politicians love to reinforce. Indeed, this region of Sonora attracted such media attention most recently in May 2007, when dozens were killed in a series of strange actions triggered between warring factions of drug traffickers and regional and federal police. Cananea, home to one of the rural-industrial spurs of the original Mexican Revolution, was descended upon by drug gangs based in northeastern Mexico. Gun-toting enforcers took local police hostage after killing several in town and then dispersed into the surrounding ranches to seek cover from federal troops and helicopters.

I learned, after the fact, that two of the ranches included in this study were used as a temporary refuge. The same two ranch owners, however, admitted in phone calls shortly thereafter that they had helped round up the narcos hiding on their rangelands. The two general sets of opinion on these incidents, in the U.S. media outlets, were either (a) Mexican President Calderón could not control his own "drug war" in Mexico, or (b) Mexico is hostage to a new level of violence based on drug interdiction and aggressive tactics between regional drug cartels. The binary portrait was stunningly simple, simplistic, and comforting for most readers. And as McCarthy (2005, 954) has written, the maintenance of binary categories is "surely an ironic way to go about insisting on the importance of differences."

In this vein, ranchers and ranching households have also been misread in Mexico, internally by fellow Mexicans and externally by academics and long-time visitors. Visiting tourists to the Río Sonora Valley expected to see revolutionary *pistoleros* or at least men wearing large sombreros embroidered with signs of the Jalisco-based charro culture so familiar to moviegoers. I watched, with no small amount of amusement, the disappointed reactions of visiting urbanites from Guadalajara when they saw ten-gallon hats and ranchers talking about their particular brand of cell phone. Like American tourists in Tombstone, Arizona, for the first time, these visitors expected to see a bucolic, rustic, and proto-historical image of the cowboy, the rancher, the gunfighter, only to come away feeling disillusioned or cheated that these people seemingly live in the same century.

Academics, too, have left with their preconceptions shattered. I was no exception. I could not reduce local relationships to a simple case of wealthy ranchers versus poor farmers, in spite of our long tradition of framing rural Mexican contexts in this way. We need fundamental understanding of these people, an old goal for humanists, before we can even begin to form a cogent and valid critique of any practices they may have. It is then an even greater stretch to go from critique to forming any set of notions of policy recommendations that hope to predict or at least anticipate changes in a place. These ranchers remain astute, political, and highly connected to the information circuits they depend on for their livelihood. I found little romanticism, except from a few elderly ranch folks, for the past. And most rode horses because they had to, because their old pickups could not reach remote areas, not necessarily because they enjoyed it (fig. 7.4).

Third, the final misreading has been the mislabeling of certain outcomes in Mexico or at least too readily identifying the process *guilty* of changing rural and urban landscapes. For most scholars, the era of "neo-liberalism" has entailed using the concept as prefix, a preordained explanatory tool to explain or at least illustrate what has changed. Yet, as Castree (2006) has warned, what we term neo-liberalism is in fact a collection of processes, ideas, and philosophies that are rarely, if ever, coherent. So has Mexico changed because of neo-liberal policies? The easy answer is yes, but only in the sense that these are quite Mexican neo-liberal policies and practices. In theory, they may share similar goals with other "neo-liberal" Latin American projects or national trajectories, but in reality, they have created their own forms of landscapes, livelihoods, and outcomes that are dangerous simply to call neo-liberalized.

Is neo-liberalism a problem for Mexican farmers and ranchers? Again, the answer is absolutely yes, but only in certain sectors, such as whole grains and specialty crops and vegetables. But Mexico's neo-liberal agrarian experience is just that: its very own record of recent capitalism. It shares little in total sum characteristics with other forms of neo-liberalism, even if certain policies such as the decline of grain subsidies are commonly shared among many developing countries. Trying to compare records of

Figure 7.4 Ranching is still revered and is one of the most desired lifestyles in rural Sonora. Private ranches also remain dependent on multigenerational labor.

neo-liberal policies in Latin America, however, could be frustrating. There are notable differences, say, in how Mexico and Chile have pursued water rights "liberalism"—aggressively in the case of Chile, reluctantly and only on the urban fringes in the case of Mexico (Bauer 2004; Rap 2006; Wilder and Lankao 2006). Are ranchers actively being "neo-liberalized" by some weird process of which they are only partially aware? This possibility is unlikely, even if they are "coping" with changes in their industry by trying to find new ways to generate revenue. In between a weak peso, market price pressures to create well-marbled but cheap beef, and a frequently unsparing climate, what choice do they have? More important, when have ranchers not changed with economic or ecological pressures? Change is the constant, not the exception.

Mexican tourists and visitors of the Río Sonora Valley often remarked on how peaceful and rustic the landscape was, how undisturbed and friendly the locals were during their stay, as if rural Mexico were some form of theme park. They frequently remarked that cattle ranching must be remarkably profitable and voiced the desire to have a ranch themselves. North American (Canadian and U.S.) visitors were ambivalent about their readings of the local landscapes. Birders and some geologists remarked at how much "environmental degradation and soil erosion" was visible, as if rural Mexico was some kind of nature preserve, as if natural fluvial erosion and tectonic activity had not shaped this landscape prior to, and contiguous with, human presence. Tourists to this area thought the landscape was "beautiful to look at, but I wouldn't want to live like they [Sonorans] do." These readings, or misreadings, are shared and voiced openly. Environmental perception, then, is recursive in the sense of both being a process and a product of local insiders and outside observers (Walker and Fortmann 2003). To illustrate this, let us take the premise of "profitable ranching." While visitors from Hermosillo perceive local ranchers as being wealthy, for example, these same ranchers malign the lack of real income from their ranch. They incessantly supplement their ranches with subsidies from other sources, if available to them. In other words, many ranches are now income sinks, not income sources.

When the local ranchers' association in Baviácora threw a party for representatives and dignitaries from Hermosillo, one of the visitors opined that he would love to own a large ranch nearby some day. To which three ranchers, otherwise occupied with the grilling of carne asada, simultaneously faced him yelling "¡Te lo vendo!" ("I'll sell it to you!"). While expressed good-naturedly, all three ranchers told me (after the event) they might sell their ranch immediately if they could. This anecdote simply underlines the empirical findings from chapter 6, and the increasingly difficult nature of ranching as a livelihood, squeezed between regional climate changes and increasing debts. As an old ranching expression puts it, "If you want to make a small fortune in ranching, start with a large one, and then buy a ranch." If ranchers are now forced sometimes to think like economists, for the balance sheet of their livelihood, it does not mean they are ruled by economics. For most, it involves the lifestyle. Listen to the latest corridos and I think you'll agree.

Ranching continues to be valued locally and jealously treasured as a livelihood in northern Mexico; it shows no signs of disappearing as a form of land use. The intentions of owners, however, are much less clear. Ranching will change, no doubt, and if the speculative frontier of private real estate development reaches the Río Sonora, the similarities with states across the international border will be even more remarkable. The new laissez-faire economic policies of Mexico certainly point to a continued presence for private ranches, even if these new policy directions are more uncertain for communal forms of land tenure and land use. Here, at the end of this particular narrative trail, my hope is that academic friends and faithful readers will read these landscapes and livelihoods differently, recognizing the hybrid, inherent complexity and tenure diversity these places have always shared, to recognize and explain simple truths where possible and the equally complex gray areas, without simplifying the people or places.

Appendix A
Ranching and Regional Literature

Although the origins and growth of cattle raising are not the principal focus of this book, it is useful to point out some important works on these related topics in the literature. In the preparation for this work, it became quickly apparent that someone needed to comment on the current research and merits of existing studies on ranching. At the fundamental level of pastoral systems, see the works by anthropologists Tim Ingold (1980), and Barfield (1993), who clearly and eloquently distinguish between types of pastoralism, from nomadic to permanently settled forms. For the British Isles, the studies by Carrier (1936) and the research of geographers E. Evans (1942, 1957, 1973) and P. S. Robinson (1984) reveal the complexity of traditional sheep pastoralism and the dearth of open-range cattle traditions in Ireland and Scotland. On the Iberian Peninsula, Butzer (1988) examines the pastoral precursors to eventual New World grazing complexes, and Jordan (1989) ties patterns from Spain to Latin America in general, suggesting a highland/lowland model for most regions of the Americas.

The advent of domesticated livestock in the Western Hemisphere began with the Caribbean, yet no single study has addressed ranching explicitly, so we must glean information from Sauer's (1966) study and the largely unheralded, but remarkably comprehensive, work of David Watts (1987). Some anecdotal information for the Caribbean can also be extracted from Crosby's (1972) work. The eventual dispersal from the main islands of Hispaniola and Cuba resulted in a network of coastal savanna grasslands (Olive 1952–1953; D. Harris 1980). Most research in the Caribbean comes from historians, and their contributions for this region are important for understanding the diffusion and adaptation of various livestock strategies in the southeastern United States and countries lying next to the Gulf of Mexico.

For the more relevant Mexican origins of the pastoral system in Sonora, there are several important regional studies in geography and history. For North America, in general, Donald Brand (1961) and Morrisey (1950, 1951) elaborate the northward spread of livestock raising out of the core of New Spain, and Gerhard's (1972, 1982) contributions serve as a template of sources and maps for future ranching studies at the regional or local level. Indeed, we already have fine analyses at the regional scale by Butzer and Butzer (1993, 1995, 1997) who make careful use of archival records while remaining aware of the field conditions in each region. Additional work by Bensin (1935) and Doolittle (1987) suggests an eastern lowland Gulf Coast component as a key source region for later pushes in the cattle frontier of Texas. West's (1949) examination of the Parral mining district in Chihuahua serves as a model for illustrating the close ties between extractive industries on the northern frontier of New Spain and Mexico, and also details relationships between land use and land tenure. Brading (1971) focuses on the mercantile-miner aspects that West does not treat with some discussion of livestock. Many of the earliest cattle ranches in Sonora and Chihuahua were established concomitantly with these early mines. For a more updated, modern interpretation of industrial cattle ranching in Chihuahua, I recommend Machado (1981), who does a commendable job for the bulk of the twentieth century until 1975. In Spanish, Ascencio Franco's (1992) work on the meat industry in Guadalajara is a great complement from an economic anthropologist's point of view.

The Pacific Coast roots of later Sonoran ranching initiatives are treated in detail by Jordan (1993). A more specific case study analysis is provided by Meigs's (1935) work on the Dominican missions in Baja California, but ranching is the central focus of his study and is complemented by Henderson's (1964) later dissertation on agriculture and ranching in Baja. A notable Mexican contribution to the Pacific literature is Serrera Contreras (1977), whose monograph on the Guadalajara region is an extended treatise on economic history, including some focus on livestock. The Serrera Contreras volume also demonstrates the possible source of current ranching patterns in Pacific Mexico, namely that cattle dominated the hot lowlands, while horses and mules were far more common in the *altos* of the state of Jalisco. This pattern does not hold for Sonora. The

Jaliscan altos are the highlands in the state of Jalisco, and the cultural phenomenon of *charrería,* cultural performances centered on equestrian skills, is thought to come from the Guadalajaran highlands. Two of the greatest Mexican singers, Pedro Infante and Jorge Negrete, brought the combination of mariachi and charrería to the popular culture and attention of Mexicans at the national level. Although mariachi is not present along the Río Sonora, the local version of charrería is termed *jaripeo,* and many of the contests involved are the same as those found in typical charrería performances. Notably, most of the ranches famous for producing fast horses are in the foothills of the Sierra Madre, not along the coast of Mexico. The transition into California and North American ranching frontiers has been treated by geographers, from California pastoralism to vegetation change (Burcham 1957, 1961; Nostrand 1966; Hornbeck 1978; Starrs 1989; Blumler 1995). Comparative regional analyses of livestock economies of the Americas are illustrated by Deffontaines (1964) work, even if Jordan's (1993) treatise remains the only definitive, comparable work for North American ranching frontiers.

A larger body of work on ranching is available in the field of history. Though research articles and monographs are available for all of the regions discussed, more attention in history has been paid to the role and functions of ranching and land institutions. These emphases are partly due to the influence of select historians, and also to the fact that documentation of the mechanics of ranching is notoriously lacking for the scale of analysis desired.

Bishko (1952, 1978) is to thank for his research on the peninsular nature of livestock and the early institutions, such as the mesta, that regulated sheep activities in Spain, although Klein (1920) was the first to treat the institution to historical analysis in English. Its later implantation into Mexico is handled by Dusenberry (1963). A much broader and more important work is Vassberg's seminal book on land institutions of Castile during the sixteenth century, still a key reference and a magisterial work. More localized studies for Spanish ranching communities are Cortés y Vásquez (1952) and Camacho Rueda (1984). There are few syntheses, however, on the evolution of Spanish pastoral activities. Broader works are certainly forthcoming from the British Isles. Celtic contributions to the New World are explored by McWhitney and McDonald (1985) and Berthoff (1986). For England in general, Trow-Smith (1959) is a good beginning, as are the works of Parry and Slater (1980) and Haldane (1952) for Scotland. A similar study to Haldane's exists for Wales, Colyer's (1976) book on cattle trading markets.

Africanist historians have been remiss in leaving the work on ranching to anthropologists, whose main focus has traditionally rested with the pastoral nomads of North Africa and the cattle complex cultures of East Africa. Group and tribal histories are common in the French literature of North and West Africa (Marty 1921; Borricand 1948; Bernus 1974). Possible connections between African pastoral societies and New World ranching practices are sorely lacking, but possible Jamaican influence in the southeastern United States is elaborated by Otto and Anderson (1988). Boyd-Bowman (1964, 1968) has provided the best reference works to track individual Iberian migrants to the New World, and by extension, the possible influence of different regional variants of cattle or sheep ranching practices are now easier to trace. Rouse's (1977) popularized history of cattle in the New World should also be kept close at hand, to aid in reconstructing the variety of criollo (the animal, not the New World elite!) dispersals and changes once on the mainland of the Americas. A variety of work on comparative ranching experiences in the Western Hemisphere abounds in history (Jessen 1952; Sharp 1955; Gongora 1966; Baretta and Markoff 1978; Steffen 1980). For the early Caribbean land grants and the evolution of institutions (encomienda, hacienda, etc.), the studies by Corbitt (1939) on Cuba and by Lockhart (1969) are essential reading. The definitive work for Cuban land-use histories remains the fourteen-volume set by Marrero (1972–1988). A smaller study also exists for land use in Puerto Rico (Nadal and Alberts 1947).

For New Spain, historical works are bountiful, though specific land-use analyses of ranching have been slighted—the emphasis again returns to institutions related to livestock activities. To understand the early spread and implantation of ranching, see Morrisey (1950, 1951) and Matesanz (1964), both of which provide good beginning points. The two more comprehensive works (often cited, often criticized) are those by Chevalier (1952) and Simpson (1952). The work by Dusenberry (1963) on the Mexican mesta is helpful and discusses the transformations that the institution needed given its original Iberian context. The clutch of articles by

Sluyter (1996, 1997, 1998) is also worth consulting for its use of spatial-archival materials and consideration of ecological consequences.

For the northern expanse of New Spain, a dated regional overview of daily life is provided by Jones (1979); it once boasted the best genre de vie and ethnic descriptions of the inhabitants of the frontier, now displaced by Radding's (1995, 1997, 2005) monumental works on aboriginals of Sonora in the mission economies. Ranching trails splinter moving north-ward out of Mexico. See Baxter (1987) for some work on the arrival and evolution of sheep ranching in New Mexico, and the work of Lehmann (1969) that addresses the same animal in the context of south Texas. For Arizona, first consult the work of Wagoner (1952), Morrisey (1950), and especially the article by Mattison (1946) that has useful, detailed infor-mation on the private land grants during the late Spanish colonial period (1780–1821). A similar work on land grants is also available for Alta California (Cowan 1956). More informal works on the herders (vaque-ros) of California can be found in Mora (1949) and Rojas (1964). A large pool of ranching-related topics is now available for Texas—start with Jackson (1986) and Myres (1969), although more specifics can be found in the excellent work by de la Teja (1995), in which he details the strug-gles of a frontier livestock community in south Texas (San Antonio).

Historical work on the more eastern shores has been lacking until recently. South Carolina, Georgia, and Florida have the largest available corpus of works. An overview of ranching in South Carolina is in Otto (1986, 1987), while for Georgia the best work to date is Stewart's (1991) article on the early environmental history of cattle in the state. For Flori-da's ranching past, I recommend consulting Arnade (1961) and the more contemporary insights of Dacy (1940) for historical perspective. Slatta's (1990) comprehensive volume rolls in the abundant folklore and imagery of the cowboy with all of its cultural contradictions and complexities.

A problematic point for some works in history is the tendency always to compare historical events in the New World to some Old World model, something that geographers have also been occasionally prone to do. The belief that upon settlement most of the Americas became "feudal" in nature, as Morner's (1973) work posits ("economically capitalist, but socially feudal"), is difficult to support much less understand. The large landed estates did employ a system of debt peonage for cheap rural labor, although this practice was no longer common in northern Mexico by the early nineteenth century. Yet the peones were not "tied" to the land as they had once been in Europe. The tie came in the form of debt, not the outright ownership of land with labor already provided; only the *repartimiento*, the institution and practice of granting local native labor with land, was modeled on this particular understanding, and this particular institution was outlawed in the sixteenth century due to the abuse already visible in the indigenous communities tied to such land grants. Certainly some estates in the more isolated parts of New Spain were more feudal with respect to the ones closer to the core of population (C. Harris 1975). The gross characterization, however, that all of colonial society was "feudal" or even neo-feudal, is clearly untenable considering the evidence of regional and local contrasts (Van Young 1981, 1983). And the variety of single-estate histories, such as Konrad's (1980) or Harris's (1975), give lie to the generalizations found in earlier work.

Geographers have long been interested in material culture, and early contributions to the ranching literature underscore those interests, as seen in Dunbar's (1961) work on South Carolina's cow pens or Jordan's (1981) work on the roots of ranching in the American West. These contributions are invaluable because they focus on the tangible landscape aspects of visible material culture, and agricultural technology. While the work of historians is less focused on these aspects, the estate studies, private or mission based, also echo this interest. Only the unique aspects of single-estate histories are problematic, as they require some additional regional comparison, or context, to understand their importance or representative nature. One exception is the fine-grained and deeply sensitive analysis by Aguilar-Robledo (2003) in the Huasteca Potosina of San Luis Potosi, Mexico.

The environmental relationships between ranching and ecosystems, as a process, are still not fully understood or appreciated. Thus historical work is lacking on such topics and, when available, is only applicable to a specific situation or historical setting. More relevant ecological literature on the aspects of pastoral nomadism is available for Africa, though nomadism and ranching are clearly not the same topic (Barfield 1993). Using historical methods of reconstruction with archival documents for a region in Hidalgo, an anthropologist has suggested that widespread environmental degradation was the result of sheep ranching in that region (Melville 1990, 1994). The evidence used in the reconstruction is not in question, but rather her historical and theoretical interpretation as applied to that particular area and based on an Australian sheep live-stock model. Continuing research by geographers is clearly needed on the environmental consequences of livestock raising (Butzer and Butzer 1993, 1997; Sluyter 2002).

Recently, scholars interested in North American cattle-ranching issues and questions are tackling the political options; geographers are promi-nent in leading this charge and call to action and understanding. Still, these works highlight the current difficulties that ranchers face as a consequence of frequently stringent federal U.S. policies regarding grazing permits and lease access (Starrs 1998) as well as the role of the Endangered Species Act of 1973 in reshaping ranch-agency-species relations in parts of the United States (Sayre 2002, 2005b). For a larger picture on policy options and policy history, see especially Charles Wilkinson's (1992, 75–113) treatise on ranching's place in the American West and the more recent and highly sensitive treatment of the relationship between ranchers, the federal agen-cies, and public lands by Karen Merrill (2002).

Previous Scholarship on the Region

The burgeoning mass of books and articles on ranching is centered upon the historical events of its origins, evolution, and adaptation in New World environments. Ranching today, it should be stressed, is far different from its historical antecedents. The current environmental debates surround-ing cattle ranching in the American West have little counterpoint during earlier periods, when management strategies and institutions were a far cry from today's animal industries fully incorporated in global capital flows. Much of the existing research on cattle ranching with an alarm-ist bent emphasizes more tropical contexts, accentuating development problems related to recent commercial ranching, when the vast majority of this land use occurs largely in semi-arid and arid regions of the world. Finally, little of this more recent ecologically oriented research has been focused on areas with a long-standing ranching tradition. Despite signifi-cant landscape changes, ranching regions in the Americas have survived,

as have generations of private ranchers who handled the vagaries of ecological and economic boom-and-bust cycles (e.g., Sayre 1999). Sonoran
desert landscapes have been altered for centuries by the economics and
ecologies of cattle ranching, land speculation, and later suburbanization
(Sayre 2002; Sheridan 2007).

The truly authoritative works on Sonora capture both the long-lasting,
visible impressions of human-environment relationships, as well as the
ineffable quality of aridity that can render livelihoods in the region so
challenging. David Yetman's (1996) stirring short stories about life and
land in Sonora, vivid portraits of daily existence, are one avenue for
understanding the region in question. Much more impressive, frankly, is
his growing body of work with ecologists in the southern parts of Sonora
(e.g., Yetman and Van Devender 2002). The approach of this work is
also quite distinct from earlier research on the region and topic. Doolittle (1984, 1988, 2003) has examined the impacts and geography of
agricultural change, pre-Columbian settlement and agriculture, and more
recent fluvial modifications to the Río Sonora. Historian Cynthia Radding (1997, 2005) has produced two monumental works on the Spanish
colonial period that tackle how indigenous peoples in Sonora responded
to missionary activities, Spanish lay settlers, and varied colonial policies. Her work is so comprehensive that any work on the period before
the late nineteenth century in Sonora must use her sources and archival documentation. Two anthropologists, Ernesto Camou-Healy and
Thomas Sheridan, have also provided important structural and ethnographic approaches and findings to Sonoran livelihoods in the twentieth
century. Camou-Healy's (1994, 1998) study of livestock-raising centers
on the effects and actions of ejidatarios, small-scale, communal affairs
that largely center on the ejidos and comunidades of the Río Sonora, but
at the scale of the entire state. Camou-Healy's structural analysis of cattle
ranching and the persistent inequalities within the industry nearly made
my work obsolete but for the fact that he did not focus on the actual
management of ranches and how private owners have adapted and created political and ecological shortcuts in this area. His work is, by far, the
best available in the Spanish language.

Sheridan (1988), working one valley west of the Río Sonora, was also
focused on the trials and difficulties that ejidatarios and comuneros faced

in the small community of Cucurpe and how they managed to persist in spite of private ranches that surround the communal lands. But while Sheridan's portrayal of the corporate community, and political ecology, of Cucurpe shares many similarities with the communal counterparts on the Río Sonora, its main focus is not private ranch management or practices. The private ranches in Sheridan remain on the far side of a dark mirror, important because of their local and regional monopolies of land and water, and he nicely outlined their activities in the area. Ruiz (1988) gets my vote for best title about Sonora and how it has resisted and coped with its neighbor to the north.

These are all foundational works for the region, though they focus on thematic, structural aspects or a small percentage of the land and water resources. Yet private owners have retained, if not usurped at various moments, the bulk of the study area. Indeed, much of northern Mexico remains firmly in private hands, largely unaffected by Mexico's early twentieth-century land reform efforts. This retention of property has happened in spite of the fact that they are a small percentage of the regional and local population; ranchers in the Río Sonora Valley are among the elite, after all. And they are unabashed about this fact. But their stories, like those of private landowners elsewhere in Mexico, cannot be simply reduced to a story of resource control through thievery.

Appendix B
Research Methodology and Sources

In most scholarly works, the exact methods, sources, and techniques remain obscure to readers. This appendix, based on a small set of notes, describes how I conducted the work, performed interviews, and made notes on biophysical changes and the political-economic aspects of private ranches in Sonora. I hope that readers will find it useful in their critique and appraisal of this work. While I have consulted historical archives, such as the Archivo General de la Nación (Mexico City) in 1996, the lack of detailed documentation specific to ranching in Sonora was remarkable. My early impressions were confirmed while visiting the Documentary Relations of the Southwest Collection at the University of Arizona in 1995, 1996, and 2009, and my later archival check in the Nettie Lee Benson Collection at the University of Texas at Austin during the summer of 1998 and a return visit in 2006. This confirmed, officially, my envy of colleagues who work in central and southern Mexico and who have a far richer inventory of archival manuscripts to consult.

Calendar of Work

An early visit during the summer of 1995 consisted largely of reconnaissance fieldwork, getting up to speed on Sonoran Spanish, and making some basic observations on ranches that I happened to visit (two small, three medium, and two large ranches). I also spoke with a dozen experts and institutional representatives in Hermosillo, the state capital, during this first visit. Officials at SARH, SAGAR, PATROCIPES, and the Unión Ganadero were especially courteous and offered logistical help and numerous other contact names. During the long-term fieldwork, between September 1996 and November 1997, I returned not only to these ranches and the experts consulted on my first foray, but also began the process of visiting ranchers in the Río Sonora Valley, in Alamos and in Sahuaripa. A chance meeting with the owner of two large ranches in the municipio of Moctezuma was fortuitous and provided the first exposure to the differential economics and political power of the truly absentee landowner class in Sonora. For the sake of comparing apples with apples, however, I quickly threw out the decision of regional comparisons in Sonora and focused largely on the middle watershed of the Río Sonora for most of this period. I still maintained contact and returned to visit one large ranch (number 15) on the outskirts of Sahuaripa, but the differences in land tenure and ecosystem types made Alamos stand apart from the other two areas, and comparisons would have been more tenuous (Vásquez-León and Liverman 2004). Alamos was and remains a slightly dangerous place for people interested in land tenure or roaming far from the central town. The place taught me my first lesson in using a GPS unit in open fields, while running away from the sound of bullets ricocheting, presumably headed my way. For graduate and undergraduate students planning on any fieldwork, especially in a different country, the bottom line is this: No matter how well you plan ahead or create a master proposal for your work, it will change no matter what. Keep what you can or what is feasible, and chuck what may be dangerous or unrealistic, even if you know the place well.

Brief return visits to the Río Sonora area occurred in the summers of 2002 and 2009, with a winter visit in 2003 as part of a conference field excursion. I was able to see many of the ranchers again during these returns. Four owners had died between 1997 and 2009, and the ranches passed on to their heirs, but the other ranchers are still in operation to this day. Finally, the vast majority of what you have read was rewritten and updated with a visit to the Benson Collection (UT–Austin) in the summer of 2006.

Documenting Politics and Ecologies

Authorial power, gender relations and complications, and the increasingly personal nature of my relationships with people in the Río Sonora Valley explode the pretension of lab-coat objectivity. This aspect of long-term ethnography is, of course, well known to most anthropologists and geographers who work away from home. Natural scientists use the example of the Heisenberg principle to explain that no phenomenon remains unchanged because of measurements performed on it. Social scientists, like my fellow political and cultural ecologists, have eloquently explained the "unintended consequences" of ethnography, of field measurement. Bumper stickers everywhere generically capture this notion as "shit happens."

And so it was with my presence, too, even if I earnestly attempted to minimize my presence as a disruptive force. People knew I was there, taking notes and asking questions. For the time spent in the field and a few years after, my own delusion was that what you read now would be objective in some way, unfiltered by the baggage I carry myself. Internally, I found myself remembering the dry, desolate ranges of the Corbières, a mountainous region in southwestern France. I mentally compared those landscapes of my childhood with the ones I found in Sonora, down to the poplar-lined roads that connected the study region with the capital of Hermosillo. Edward Said has written about European perceptions of the Middle East and East and that most of those texts reflect an "Orientalism" that is difficult to ignore. Perhaps what I have done is reflect the "Occidentalism" in my own mind, comparing European with North American landscapes, but comparative work would be nearly impossible without these built-in biases. Fairly or not, this cultural baggage shaped my initial perceptions and questions, as well as my long-term comparative perspectives on regions that suffered from recent rural depopulation.

Interviews and Observations

Establishing rapport and some sense of personal trust and confidence was the first step during the course of field research. I did this in a variety of ways, but always with a first, informal visit with the owner of a ranch and his or her family. In this meeting, I did not use a tape recorder or take extensive notes, only jotted down some of the more prescient information they were willing to share (size of the ranch, location, kind of animals, etc.). If the ranch was promising and offered some valuable comparison to others in the region, I would then pay a second visit asking them if I could get access to their ranch. Only two ranchers declined at this stage, out of the nineteen involved in the eventual, intensive portion of the field study. One did so because the ranch had only been in her possession for a matter of weeks, and there were still legal issues to clarify with her relatives, as to the ultimate fate of the property. The other declined simply because he did not know me well enough to give me a ranch gate key. Admittedly, some informants and acquaintances in the area never took a shine to me.

List of Interviews and Informants

The second step in the long-term work of profiling the individual ranches of the study was the interview process. I say "process" because some were so simple as to take two to three hours either because of candor, time constraints, or the small size of the property. Others were far more complicated, as they involved interviews with the owner, the vaqueros on the ranch, part-time laborers, spouses of these groups, and the occasional *mescalero* or *chiltepineros* encountered (Perramond 2005). All of these parties had valuable information to convey, whether they knew it or not, and their insight and time made remarkable contributions to my understanding of private ranching. And while personal interviews were largely not as excruciating and demanding as some of the biophysical measurements described later in this appendix, it is truly difficult to convey how challenging a four-hour interview is in 110-degree (Fahrenheit) heat, on a July afternoon. In the full interests of disclosure, I must admit that many of these discussions, although recorded formally and with a response form to fill out, took place over ice-cold cans of Tecate. Toward the end of a particularly hot day in August, after I had taken some time in carefully describing what *ethnography* was and why it was important, one vaquero joked, "Man, you are doing Tecatografía, not anything else!"

The final systematic aspect of the human geographic portions of fieldwork consisted of surveys and forms for labor hours; I conducted all of the surveys and left an example form with the ranch manager or vaquero in charge. The form was designed to be a simple chart on a weekly basis, so that they could fill in their estimated number of hours on any given activity. We discussed what the various categories of work entailed, from "herd management" to "ranch infrastructure," until all possible questions were answered. A small stipend of about $NP30 per week was provided for completing the forms on a weekly basis, even if it took little time to complete. These data were compiled between October 1996 and October 1997, for a full year's activities on the study ranches. Of the 204 forms completed and returned, only 2 were problematic, because of unrecorded tasks. These were excluded from the compiled labor measures reported in chapter 3 (see fig. 3.2).

I conducted follow-up interviews on a monthly basis with every rancher and every vaquero from each case study ranch. These involved more historical details, about the ranch, communities, relations between ranchers, between ranchers and communal smallholders (ejidatarios or comuneros) in their particular municipio. About a third of the ranchers own their property in a municipio outside the one in which they reside, even if they are not considered "absentee" because of frequent travel to the ranch. I conducted additional interviews and questionnaires with other ranchers, not owners of the case study ranches, to complete the regional picture and to ensure some balance of inclusive comparison. In total, 34 ranchers and 17 cowboys were interviewed using the three-tiered system described, even if the labor data come from only 17 ranches. The additional 156 informants were interviewed briefly, then with more depth, at a later date. In addition, the chiltepineros (chile pepper collectors) and women were administered a questionnaire after interviews were completed.

All of the interviews and the detailed oral historical discussions were conducted by the author in Spanish and followed the methodology of Emerson, Frez, and Shaw (1995), from initial jottings to the formal ethnographic field notes that were the end product. The complete notes recorded the gestures and tone of voice, whenever notably different, or when some change of expression was used regarding specific questions. This procedure slowly morphed into ethnography, in the sense that a closer relationship and participation with the author in the daily round of social and work activities usually took place. While anthropologists are quick to point out that ethnography is a way to get "inside the culture" of informants, this is really rather impossible, though a laudable goal to be sure.

Oral history is not a frequently used technique or approach for geographers, although a few studies have used this general term to great effect (Lewis 1992; Stevens 1993; Perramond 2001). In contrast to written, archival documents, the data from oral methods are not commonly quantitative; rather, they reflect current perceptions and memories of the past. These memories are frequently embellished or reconstructed in such a way as to establish the storyteller as the authority on the subject or to erase any political aspects or controversy she or he may have been involved in. I am well aware of the limitations, but given the paucity of good, archival records in Sonora, the richness of the data precludes ignoring the importance of oral history as a source of information. I should specify that I did not use "oral tradition" in the strict sense, since few people in Sonora share the same range of stories, a central body of oral lore easily recounted by many people (cf. Vansina 1984). There are myths, stories, and rumors of course, but the more common types of anything remotely like oral tradition serve as fables or moral lessons for children at bedtime. Oral historical sources, then, deal with reminiscence, hearsay, eyewitness accounts, and memory of facts, events, or sequences as remembered by individuals (Vansina 1984, 11–12). So I have not ventured into oral tradition, and instead depended on the memories of storytellers still alive at the time of fieldwork, rather than any set of inherited stories passed on from an earlier generation.

Oral history was valuable for the twentieth-century details of ranching and how livelihoods and the industry changed. Archival materials that address for ranching, specifically, are notoriously poor; most of the extant materials, even for the colonial period, are unreliable or simply not useful. They will, of course, mention "rich, fine pastures on the hills" of Sonora or simply state that no other province is as well suited to livestock raising as Sonora (Nentvig 1980; Pfefferkorn 1989). The current dominant vegetation species in Sonora are much as they were two centuries ago, yet the spatial arrangement of land cover has certainly changed, as it has in other parts of Mexico (Rzedowski 1994, 57–96). The lack of consistent and explicitly spatial data makes any statements about the timing and sequence of land degradation or overgrazing purely speculative. Of course, the oral testimonies of older Sonorans are valuable in this case, but even their nostalgic reconstruction of landscapes is problematic, as it may reflect a desired memory (Johnson and Lewis 1995). The land-cover summaries and changes referred to in chapter 4 should be taken as working hypotheses, to be tested against the reconstructed memories of the informants consulted here.

Ranch Measurements and Monitoring

Systematic observations were made on the seventeen study ranches during the course of an entire year (more time, in the case of four ranches). These were dedicated to field mapping the individual ranches, with all external and internal pasture boundaries, roads, and rangeland features. Water resources were included in these sketch maps, as well as the kind of water feature. These water storage devices ranged from the humble and makeshift (e.g., giant tractor tires sliced open on one side that served as troughs) to the more permanent (e.g., natural springs bubbling with measurable discharge). I noted and mapped the presence of mineral supplements, such as salt licks, and any changes in infrastructure between visits, such as repaired fences or improved ranch roads or gates. Sketches of ranch biogeography, imperfectly drawn to scale, also helped me ask the right questions about plant types and any noticeable plant geography changes over time, and most vaqueros could remember the time frame of significant change within a five-year window.

Soils were sampled qualitatively, but systematically, along randomly placed transects to note any important changes in organic material, compaction differences, and particle-size variance. Compaction was not measured in the standardized kilogram-to-centimeter fashion, but using a Lang penetrometer that records qualitative resistance to compaction with a long, blunt needle. While difficult to compare with studies using the kilogram-to-centimeter measurements, they did provide me with a better understanding of where soil compaction and the bulk density of surfaces were notably higher or lower. The smaller ranches involved a week's worth of work (5–6 days, 12 hours a day), while some of the largest ranches took several weeks (18–25 days). Access to some areas was easy in a pickup; alternatively, a horse was used to survey some of the more remote locations. Two of the ranches had pastures inaccessible to motorized vehicles and led to many saddle sores.

Coda

One final and important aspect about field and research ethics should be noted. I have attempted, through the use of pseudonyms, to protect the testimonial and personal aspects of the ranchers included in this study. This extends, unfortunately, to some of the cartography in the first chapter as well, since I did not want the statements of private ranchers to be used against them. So it is not by accident that my maps may "lie" to the reader; there is no error by choice of projection: It is very much intentional. Frank discussions would not have been possible without this agreement, and only a few were amused by my precautionary and paranoid tendencies to protect identity. When I brought this agreement up in my first visits to ranches in the summer of 1995, one year after the Zapatista uprisings in the southeastern state of Chiapas, one rancher quipped: "Hey, relax, this is not Chiapas and there are no Zapatistas here." While we had a laugh over this one, all I had to do was respond with "Yeah, but didn't the Mexican Revolution start in Cananea?" Cananea lies approximately one hour north of this study area. Despite my necessary masking of individual identities and cloaking cartography of specific ranch locations, I hope that readers will find that my depiction and portraits were fair and true to the complexities of the region, the society, and the everyday lives of landowners, vaqueros, and their extended families in northern Mexico.

Notes

All translations appearing in English are mine unless otherwise noted. See the glossary for Spanish terms and meanings.

Chapter 1

1. *Political ecology* has been defined, used, and abused in any number of ways. Arguably, Watts (1983) produced the first example of political ecology, even if the term had been coined a decade earlier in anthropology (Wolf 1972). Some early programmatic statements were tendered in Blaikie and Brookfield's (1987) benchmark work, followed by Bryant (1992); more recent works that nicely capture the array of approaches can be found in Robbins (2004), Peet and Watts (2004), and Zimmerer and Bassett (2003). Readers of, even practitioners of, political ecology will find a maddening diversity of approaches, themes, and influences in the literature, even if the subfield has reached near-hegemonic status in certain fields of human-environment research. To be sure, many of us are simply reformed "cultural ecologists" now engaging with a literature burgeoning with the influence of political economists and peasant studies. Others arrived more directly through an engagement of livelihood struggles and continental theory (also known as poststructural theory). Regardless, the field is massive, and any reviewer engaging in a project of synthesis is bound to trample on some empirical or theoretical feet in this subfield. Anthropologists, political scientists, and to some degree, sociologists are all contributing to this growing literature. A good and creative batch of papers from anthropologists can be found in Biersack and Greenberg (2006).

2. While analytically commendable, this study did not follow Sayre's (2001, 13) multiscalar approach to analyzing ranch ecologies with four levels: plant, pasture, ranch, and watershed. The ranch is the spatial and empirical unit of analysis in this study.

3. I refer readers to such works as Craib (2004), a closet geographer, but also Kourí (2004), Amith (2005), and Boyer (2003, esp. chap. 5). An exception in the social sciences is Camp's (2002) splendid analysis of how the largely urban elite in Mexico City has developed, how networks of elites are formed nationally, and how they are shaped internationally through such influences as higher education.

4. PROCEDE is usually translated as the Program for Certification of Ejidal Rights and Titling of Urban Patios. The program, overseen by the Registro Agrario Nacional (National Agrarian Registry), was started as a way to provide federalized ejidos, agrarian nuclei, with title rights to lands and resources. It ended in 2006. While nearly all ejidos participated at some level, many simply certified the outside boundaries of the total communal property without seeking individual rights by household member. See chapter 6 for more on this program and its implications for this region.

Chapter 2

1. "One can assure one's self, that if it is difficult to arrive at an exact statistical database in one of the states in the Mexican Republic, it is undoubtedly Sonora."

2. *Ganado mayor* refers to cattle, horses, and mules. *Ganado menor* refers to goats, pigs, and sheep.

3. It is probable that haciendas were more numerous in the south because of the width of the floodplain; the narrow river bends so common near Arizpe become a wider expanse of fertile, alluvial soils near the town of Banámichi, narrow again to half this size near the town of Aconchi, and then widen closer to Baviácora. The river does not narrow again in expanse until the Río Sonora turns southwestward at the small hamlet of Mazocahui.

4. For a thorough treatment of the historical land-tenure terms, see Aguilar-Robledo (2003). *Hacienda* was typically the largest land estate designation in Mexico, which may have included one or more *estancias* (land areas) that were used for grazing or crop production, depending on regional location. The lowlier *rancho* implied both a smaller land base and a more humble direction in land use, directed at subsistence rather than cash crop generation. An assemblage of ranchos, especially if occupants were related, could also be termed a *ranchería* in both colonial New Spain and in late nineteenth-century Mexico. These informal clumps of separate structures can still be observed today in Mexico, with toponyms hinting at place-based signifiers or the old family name tied to the site.

Chapter 3

1. The cultural importance of ranching versus any economic gains acquired is also strongly argued in Starrs (1998). See chapter 7 for more on this matter.

2. These are aggregate, averaged, summary data. For a fuller discussion of the data, including full graphs and tabular versions, please consult Perramond (1999, 100–109).

3. *Conchudo* roughly means "cheapskate" in English.

Chapter 4

1. "Poncho" is an abbreviated nickname for Francisco. He shares this name with his father, who because of his age and stature in San José de Baviácora, is referred to as Don Francisco.

2. This section, "The Wet and the Dry," is adapted from Patrick Kirch's (1994) work to describe the "wet" irrigated subsidy of feed crops for the "dry" rangeland cattle of Sonora.

3. Mr. Gámez worked in the Sierra Aconchi west of the town of Aconchi during the 1940s, felling pine and oak forest in the high elevations, and making the first cut so the wood could be carted back to town or dragged by teams of mules or horses. A substantial carpentry business still does exist in the town of Aconchi, though the number of people producing these goods—mainly furniture—has declined in the past 50 years. As to his statement, four craft woodworkers, apart from the nearly twenty furniture manufacturers, remain in the town as of 2007.

4. For more specific information on the methodology employed, see appendix B. These are merely quick summaries for the soil erosion, compaction, and land-cover data; for fuller treatment, including graphs and tables, see Perramond (1999, 115–43).

5. By the "three states," I refer to the Mexican federal government, the Sonoran state government, and affiliated international agencies and funding sources (which may include private banks in the Borderlands).

Chapter 5

1. I am fully aware that "who we are" structures many of the questions we can and do ask and the answers we get from any study participant or informant. My gender did matter in getting access to study ranches and in acquiring data from state agencies, yet was also constraining in terms of access to women in the study communities. The situated knowledge evoked by a female colleague would, of course, be highly contingent on their abilities. So while I believe both women and men were forthright and candid about sharing their opinions, I have no illusions that the "what" and the "how" of their stories were quite structured by my questions and presence as well as the context.

Chapter 6

1. *Chingado* is a frequently used expletive, which can express general disappointment or be used as a label for a specific person. The term is a modified noun from the vulgar verb *chingar* (to copulate) and has about a dozen modified forms, some more socially acceptable than others.

2. Like many other natural features named after Geronimo, this one carries the story of a buried treasure in the mountainside, and one of the older neighboring ranchers swears he's seen the reflection of gold on the top. Gold, however, has never been found. Only small veins of copper run through the Cerro Gerónimo. The myth of Geronimo's gold may have more to do with the very small gold-mining operation further east, at higher elevation, named La Cabecita.

3. This quantity was measured in March 1997 by the author, using a simple watch and one-liter nalgene bottle.

4. After an hour-long discussion of the 1982 and 1995 "crises," a ranch owner threw his head at an angle, tongue in cheek, and asked me, "When has Mexico not been in some kind of economic crisis?" I clarified that I understood his point, but as he shook his head more vigorously, he then added, "No, the real issue is that if it's not the economy, it's drought or El Niño, or I guess La Niña, because El Niño is supposed to be good for us here in the summers. And when life is good, and it's rained, and there's no crisis or problem with the peso, we still get screwed because of corruption or bribery or election issues." What he was so clearly and poignantly explaining was the larger concept of *risk* for everyone in the Río Sonora Valley, indeed, for everyone living in rural Mexico. On both sides of the national border, too, this umbrella concept of risk is used increasingly by ranchers troubled with multitasking or ranking the forms of risk that are common (Vásquez-León, West, and Finan 2003).

5. The *poquiteros* treated by Pérez López (1993) and Camou-Healy (1998) were largely small-scale cattle ranchers, mostly ejido members, with some private owners with little access to rangelands but with some landownership in the prized, irrigated areas of the Río Sonora. A term that is frequently used in describing these households with livestock in the backyard is *traspatio*, indicating the intimate link between the household and the livestock, always valued for their constant milk production and their occasional role in providing cash or meat on special occasions when an animal is slaughtered for a wedding, a wake, or a *quinceañera*.

Chapter 7

1. An obvious play on and borrowing of Gerardo Otero's *Farewell to the Peasantry?* (1999).

Glossary

acequia. An irrigation canal.

agrarismo. Agrarian ideology, but most strongly linked to the Mexican Revolution (1910–1917) and peasants who identified with land-based reforms.

aguas (las). The summer rainy season in northwestern Mexico, usually between the months of July and early October.

arroyo. A riverbed or an ephemeral water course.

bacanora. The regional term in Sonora for mescal, named after the town of Bacanora in central Sonora; a drink derived from *Agave* species.

cabecera. The seat of a *misión* district.

cantina. A rustic bar.

Cardenismo. The ideology and movements associated with Lázaro Cárdenas, typically related to land-tenure reforms and the redistribution of private or unoccupied lands.

carne asada. Grilled steak, on its own or in tacos; considered the epitome of local cuisine and a luxurious staple for a Sonoran diet.

chiltepinero. Someone who collects *chiltepines*, the wild hot chili pepper (*Capsicum annuum* var. *aviculare*) on a seasonal basis.

científico/a. A scientist, or conversely, someone who thinks they're smart but is locally hated or deprecated; associated with the period known as the Porfiriato, when dictator Porfirio Díaz ruled Mexico and used this term for his technical aides who helped plan "scientific" development of the country.

comunero. A formal member of a *comunidad*.

comunidad. A community, but used most of the time to label communities that preexisted the Mexican Revolution and the invention of ejidos; a place that claimed or still claims to be indigenous.

condueñazo. A form of property co-ownership distinctive of Mexican land tenure; co-owners are known as *condueños*.

corrida. An annual roundup of cattle, usually in the fall before calves are sold in the live market; also, occasionally, rounding up unbranded cattle.

corrido. A folkloric song, and in many ways, one of the last forms of oral tradition in Mexico's rural communities.

coyote. Generally used today to mean a smuggler of any type, whether referring to human or narcotics trafficking; also a middleman who buys rural products (cattle, chile peppers) for resale elsewhere.

criollo. (1) A person of Spanish (peninsular) background but born in the New World. (2) A cattle breed (*see* ganado criollo).

desmonte. The process of leveling extant desert vegetation, a.k.a. "bulldozer ecology," typically practiced before exotic grasses such as buffelgrass are seeded in a pasture.

ejidatario/a. A member of an ejido. Technically, someone who is registered on the rolls of the ejido or an heir of a member.

ejido. The post-revolutionary communal land institution in Mexico, whereby the landless or land-poor village members could claim possession of arable lands or natural resources. It also served as a rural development institution in many parts of Mexico.

equipatas. The regional name for the gentle winter rains in northwestern Mexico.

estancia. A ranch or a single large parcel of a ranch. In colonial Mexico, several estancias were needed to be properly termed a *hacienda*.

fayuquero. A rural, itinerant merchant.

ganadero/a. A rancher.

ganado corriente. In Sonora, common cattle. These are the original, scrawny but tough, cattle from the colonial period.

ganado criollo. The tough, rangy descendents of the original Spanish cattle; a synonym for *ganado corriente*.

ganado mayor. Large livestock (cattle, horses, and mules).

ganado menor. Smaller livestock (donkeys, goats, and sheep).

gringo/a. A generic, usually derogatory, term used for U.S. citizens.

hacienda. A large, landed estate, typically associated with the colonial period. Very few survived the Mexican Revolution, but some large ranches remain. Sometimes indiscriminately used as a synonym for *latifundio*.

latifundio. A large estate in Mexico; the related term *latifundismo* refers to the survival or rebirth of large estates during the twentieth century.

licenciado/a. A generic title for an attorney, but also intentionally used as a derisive reference to burros and donkeys.

mayordomo. A foreman or designated labor boss.

mescal. The local moonshine, made from distilling agave hearts.

mescalero/a. Someone who harvests, distills, and sells mescal.

mestizo/a. Someone of mixed ethnic heritage; technically refers to someone of both Spanish and indigenous ancestry.

milpa. Irrigated field, found along the floodplain.

milpa de temporal. Rain-fed field, not supplemented by irrigation.

monte. Scrubland or smaller forested areas; also backcountry.

municipio. The local equivalent of a township, a jurisdictional area surrounding the most populated area. For example, the township of Baviácora is centered on the small town of Baviácora.

narco(-traficante). A drug trafficker.

Opatas. The native group present along the Río Sonora at the time of Spanish contact.

paca. A hay bale, typically alfalfa.

pariente(s). Relative(s).

peón. A laborer on a hacienda; the term is considered derogatory and is no longer used.

pinche. Simultaneously an adjective or adverb equivalent to *fucking*; when used to label people, it is highly derogatory.

pinole. A porridge, commonly made from mesquite pods, though now more typically from cornmeal.

Porfiriato. The period during which Porfirio Díaz ruled Mexico.

potrero. A pasture.

PRI (Partido Revolucionario Institucional). The dominant political party in Mexico for some eighty years following the Mexican Revolution.

ranchería. A loose, scattered cluster of homes or a rural estate.

ranchero/a. Someone who owns a small property; can also be used as a derogatory term for someone who is "too country" or "too rustic."

rancho. A ranch, typically private. It can also refer to the main ranch structure itself.

repartimiento. The colonial-period institution involving grants of labor from native villages to local Spanish elites, usually coordinated with a native *cacique* (boss or village elder).

Serrana (La). The region of semi-arid foothills to the west of the Sierra Madre Occidental.

Serrano. Someone from the Sierra or La Serrana region.

sitio. A land grant, usually for livestock-raising purposes.

terrenos baldías. Unoccupied or abandoned land.

vaquero/a. Cowboy or cowgirl.

vecino. In the colonial period, a lay Spanish settler; also used interchangeably with the designation *gente de razón*.

visita. A smaller missionary church site, not permanently staffed with Jesuit or Franciscan personnel but literally visited on a fixed schedule for pastoral services.

zacate. Grass.

Works Cited

Abruzzi, W. S.

    1995   The Social and Ecological Consequences of Early Cattle Ranching in the Little Colorado River Basin. *Human Ecology* 23 (1): 75–98.

Adamson, J.

    2002   Encounter with a Mexican Jaguar: Nature, NAFTA, Militarization, and Ranching in the U.S.–Mexico Borderlands. In *Globalization on the Line: Culture, Capital, and Citizenship at U.S. Borders,* ed. C. Sadowski-Smith, pp. 221–39. New York: Palgrave.

Agrawal, A.

    2005   *Environmentality: Technologies of Government and the Making of Subjects.* Durham, NC: Duke University Press.

Aguayo Quezada, S.

    1998   *Myths and (Mis)Perceptions: Changing U.S. Elite Visions of Mexico.* Boulder, CO: Lynne Rienner.

Aguilar-Robledo, M.

    1998   Ganadería, tenencia de la tierra e impacto ambiental en una región fronteriza de la Nueva España. *Estudios Geográficos* (Madrid) 59:5–35.

    2003   Formation of the Miraflores Hacienda: Lands, Indians, and Livestock in Eastern New Spain at the End of the Sixteenth Century. *Journal of Latin American Geography* 2 (1): 87–110.

Allen, T.F.H.

    1998   The Landscape "Level" is Dead: Persuading the Family to Take It off the Respirator. In *Ecological Scale: Theory and Applications,* ed. D. L. Peterson and V. T. Parker, pp. 35–54. New York: Columbia University Press.

Alonso, A. M.

    1995   *Thread of Blood: Colonialism, Revolution, and Gender on Mexico's Northern Frontier.* Tucson: University of Arizona Press.

Amith, J. D.

    2005   *The Mobius Strip: A Spatial History of Colonial Society in Guerrero, Mexico.* Palo Alto, CA: Stanford University Press.

Anable, M. E., M. P. McClaran, and G. B. Ruyle.

    1992   Spread of Introduced Lehmann Lovegrass (*Eragrostis lehmanniana* Nees.) in Southern Arizona, USA. *Biological Conservation* 61:181–88.

Arnade, C.

1961 Cattle Raising in Spanish Florida, 1513–1763. *Agricultural History* 35 (3): 116–24.

Arriaga, L., A. E. Castellanos V., E. Moreno, and J. Alarcón.

2004 Potential Ecological Distribution of Alien Invasive Species and Risk Assessment: A Case Study of Buffel Grass in Arid Regions of Mexico. *Conservation Biology* 18 (6): 1504–14.

Ascencio Franco, G.

1992 *Los mercaderes de la carne.* Zamora, Mexico: El Colegio de Michoacán.

Astorga, L.

2005 *El siglo de las drogas.* Mexico City: Random House Mondadori.

Baer, M. D.

1997 Dispatch: Misreading Mexico. *Foreign Policy* 108:138–50.

Bahre, C.

1991 *A Legacy of Change: Historic Human Impact on Vegetation in the Arizona Borderlands.* Tucson: University of Arizona Press.

Bantjes, A. A.

1998 *As If Jesus Walked on Earth: Cardenismo, Sonora and the Mexican Revolution.* Wilmington, DE: Scholarly Resources.

Baretta, S.R.D., and J. Markoff.

1978 Civilization and Barbarism: Cattle Frontiers in Latin America. *Comparative Studies in Society and History* 20 (4): 587–620.

Barfield, T.

1993 *The Nomadic Alternative.* Englewood Cliffs, NJ: Prentice Hall.

Baroni, A.

1991 Agricultura, ganadería y sociedad en la Cuenca media del Río Sonora de 1900 a 1950. In *Potreros, Vegas y Mahuechis,* ed. E. Camou Healy, pp. 61–119. Hermosillo: Gobierno del Estado de Sonora.

Bass, J.

2004 Incidental Agroforestry in Honduras: The Jicaro Tree (*Crescentia* spp.) and Pasture Land Use. *Journal of Latin American Geography* 3 (1): 67–80.

Bassett, T.

1988 The Political Ecology of Peasant-Herder Conflicts in the Northern Ivory Coast. *Annals of the Association of American Geographers* 78 (3): 453–72.

Bauer, C. J.

2004 *Siren Song: Chilean Water Law as a Model for International Reform.* Washington, DC: Resources for the Future.

Baxter, J. O.

1987 *Las Carneradas: Sheep Trade in New Mexico, 1700–1860.* Albuquerque: University of New Mexico Press.

Bazant, J. S.

1971   *Alienation of Church Wealth in Mexico: Social and Economics Aspects of the Liberal Revolution, 1856–1875.* Trans. and ed. M. P. Costeloe. Cambridge: Cambridge University Press.

Behnke, R. H., I. Scoones, and C. Kerven, eds.

1993   *Range Ecology at Disequilibrium: New Models of Natural Variability and Pastoral Adaptation in African Savannas.* London: Overseas Development Institute.

Bell, S.

1998   *Campanha Gaucha: A Brazilian Ranching System, 1850–1920.* Stanford, CA: Stanford University Press.

Beneria, L.

1992   The Mexican Debt Crisis: Restructuring the Economy and the Household. In *Unequal Burden, Economic Crises, Persistent Poverty and Women's Work,* ed. L. Beneria and S. Feldman, pp. 83–104. Boulder, CO: Westview Press.

Bennett, J. W.

1969   *Northern Plainsmen: Adaptive Strategy and Agrarian Life.* Chicago: Aldine.

Bensin, B. M.

1935   Agroecological Exploration in the Soto la Marina Region, Mexico. *Geographical Review* 25 (2): 285–97.

Bernus, E.

1974   *Les Illabakan (Niger): Une tribu Toureque Sahelienne et son aire de nomadisation.* Paris: Office de la Recherche Scientifique et Technique d'Outre-Mer.

Berthoff, R.

1986   Celtic Mist over the South. *Journal of Southern History* 52:523–50.

Bestelmeyer, B., J. R. Brown, J. E. Herrick, D. Trujillo, and K. M. Havstad.

2004   Land management in the American Southwest: A State and Transition Approach to Ecosystem Complexity. *Environmental Management* 34 (1): 38–51.

Biersack, A., and J. B. Greenberg, eds.

2006   *Reimagining Political Ecology.* Durham, NC: Duke University Press.

Bishko, C. J.

1952   The Peninsular Background of Latin American Cattle Ranching. *Hispanic American Historical Review* 32 (4): 491–515.

1978   The Andalusian Municipal Mestas in the 14th–16th Centuries: Administrative and Social Aspects. In *Andalucia Medieval* 1:347–74. Córdoba, Spain: Monte de Piedad y Caja de Ahorros de Cordoba.

Blaikie, P., and H. C. Brookfield.

1987   *Land Degradation and Society.* London: Routledge.

Blumler, M. A.

   1995   Invasion and Transformation of California's Valley Grassland, A Medi-
          terranean Analogue Ecosystem. In *Ecological Relations in Historical
          Times: Human Impact and Adaptation*, ed. R. A. Butlin and N. Roberts,
          pp. 308–32. Oxford, UK: Blackwell.

Bobrow-Strain, A.

   2007   *Intimate Enemies: Landowners, Power, and Violence in Chiapas*. Durham,
          NC: Duke University Press.

Borricand, P.

   1948   La nomadisation en Mauritanie. *Travaux de L'Institut de Recherches
          Sahariennes* 5:81–93.

Boserup, E.

   1965   *The Conditions of Agricultural Growth*. Chicago: Aldine.

Boyd-Bowman, P.

   1964, *Índice geobiografico de cuarenta mil pobladores españoles de América en
   1968   el Siglo XVI*. 2 vols. Bogotá: Instituto Caro y Cuervo.

Boyer, C. R.

   2003   *Becoming Campesinos: Politics, Identity, and Agrarian Struggle in Post-
          revolutionary Michoacán, 1920–1935*. Stanford, CA: Stanford University
          Press.

Brading, D. A.

   1971   *Miners and Merchants in Bourbon Mexico, 1763–1810*. Cambridge: Cam-
          bridge University Press.

   1978   *Haciendas and Ranchos in the Mexican Bajío: León, 1700–1860*. Cam-
          bridge: Cambridge University Press.

Brand, D.

   1961   The Early History of the Range Cattle Industry in Northern Mexico. *Agri-
          cultural History* 35:132–39.

Brenner, J. C.

   2009   Structure, Agency, and the Transformation of the Sonoran Desert by
          Buffelgrass (*Pennisetum ciliare*): An Application of Land Change Science.
          PhD diss., Clark University (MA).

Bresciani, F.

   2004   Tenure Security, Land Markets, and Household Income: PROCEDE
          and the Impact of the 1992 Reform in Mexico. PhD diss., University of
          Maryland.

Brown, D. E., ed.

   1982   *Biotic Communities: Southwestern United States and Northwestern Mex-
          ico*. Salt Lake City: University of Utah Press.

Bryant, R. L.

   1992   Political Ecology: An Emerging Research Agenda for Third World Studies.
          Political Geography 11 (1): 12–36.

Burcham, L. T.

1957   *California Range Land: An Historico-Ecological Study of the Range Resources of California.* Sacramento, CA: Division of Forestry, Department of Natural Resources.

1961   Cattle and Range Forage in California, 1770–1880. *Agricultural History* 35 (3): 140–49.

Burckhalter, D. L., G. P. Nabhan, and T. E. Sheridan.

1998   *La vida norteña: Photographs of Sonora, Mexico.* Albuquerque: University of New Mexico Press.

Burgos A., and M. Maass.

2004   Vegetation Change Associated with Land-Use in Tropical Dry Forest Areas of Western Mexico. *Agroecosystems* 19:475–81.

Burwell, T.

1995   Bootlegging on a Desert Mountain: The Political Ecology of Agave (*Agave* spp.) Demographic Change in the Sonora River Valley, Sonora, Mexico. *Human Ecology* 23 (3): 407–32.

Butzer, K. W.

1988   Cattle and Sheep from Old to New Spain: Historical Antecedents. *Annals of the Association of American Geographers* 78:29–56.

1992   Spanish Conquest Society in the New World: Ecological Readaptation and Cultural Transformation. In *Person, Place, Thing,* ed. S. T. Wong, pp. 211–42. Baton Rouge, LA: Geoscience and Man.

Butzer, K. W., and E. K. Butzer.

1993   The Sixteenth-Century Environment of the Central Mexican Bajío: Archival Reconstruction from Colonial Land Grants. In *Culture, Place, and Form,* ed. K. Mathewson, pp. 89–124. Baton Rouge, LA: Geoscience and Man.

1995   Transfer of the Mediterranean Livestock Economy to New Spain: Adaptation and Ecological Consequences. In *Global Land Use Change,* ed. B. L. Turner III, A. Gómez Sal, F. González Bernáldez, and F. di Castri, pp. 151–93. Madrid: Consejo Superior de Investigaciones Científicas.

1997   The "Natural" Vegetation of the Mexican Bajío: Archival Documentation of a 16th Century Savanna Environment. *Quaternary International* (43–44): 161–72.

Cabeza de Vaca, Álvar Núñez.

1962   [1555] *Adventures in the Unknown Interior of America,* ed. C. Covey. Albuquerque: University of New Mexico Press.

Camacho Rueda, E.

1984   *Propiedad y explotación agrarias en el Aljarafe Sevillano: El caso de Pilas, 1760–1925.* Sevilla: Excma. Diputació'n Provincial de Sevilla.

Camou-Healy, E.

1994   Los sistemas de producción bovina en Sonora. PhD diss., El Colegio de Michoacán, Zamora, MX.

Camou-Healy, E.

1998　*De rancheros, poquiteros, orejanos, y criollos.* Zamora, Mexico: El Colegio de Michoacán.

Camp, R. A.

2002　*Mexico's Mandarins: Crafting a Power Elite for the Twenty-First Century.* Berkeley: University of California Press.

Carrier, E. H.

1936　*The Pastoral Heritage of Britain: A Geographical Study.* London: Christophers.

Castree, N.

2006　From Neoliberalism to Neoliberalisation: Consolations, Confusions, and Necessary Illusions. *Environment and Planning A* 38 (1): 1–6.

Chase, J.

2002　Introduction: The Spaces of Neoliberalism in Latin America. In *The Spaces of Neoliberalism: Land, Place and Family in Latin America,* ed. J. Chase, pp. 1–21. Bloomfield, CT: Kumarian Press.

Chauvet, M.

1999　*La ganadería bovina de carne en México: Del auge a la crisis.* Mexico City: Universidad Autónoma de México.

Chavez, O. E.

1999　The 1994–95 Drought, What Did We Learn from It? The Mexican Perspective. *Natural Resources Journal* 39:35–60.

Chevalier, F.

1952　*La formation des grands domaines au Mexique: Terre et société aux XVI–XVII siècles.* Paris: Institut d'Ethnologie.

Chisholm, M.

1979　*Rural Settlement and Land Use: An Essay in Location.* 3rd ed. London: Hutchinson.

Cohen, J. N., and M. A. Centeno.

2006　Neoliberalism and Patterns of Economic Performance, 1980–2000. *Annals of the American Academy of Political and Social Science* 606:32–67.

Cohn, J. P.

2005　A New Breed of Ranchers. *Américas* 57 (March–April): 6–13.

Collier, G., and E. L. Quaratillo.

2005　*Basta! Land and the Zapatista Rebellion in Chiapas.* 3rd ed. Oakland, CA: Food First Press.

Colyer, R. J.

1976　*The Welsh Cattle Drovers: Agriculture in the Welsh Cattle Trade before and during the Nineteenth Century.* Cardiff: University of Wales Press.

Corbitt, D. C.

1939　Mercedes and Realengos: A Survey of the Public Land System in Cuba. *Hispanic American Historical Review* 19:263–85.

Cornelius, W. A., and D. Myrhe, eds.

1998   *The Transformation of Rural Mexico: Reforming the Ejido Sector.* San Diego: Center for U.S.–Mexican Studies. University of California.

Coronado-Quintana, J. A., and M. P. McClaran.

2001   Range Condition, Tenure, Management and Bio-Physical Relationships in Sonora, Mexico. *Journal of Range Management* 54 (1): 31–38.

Cortés y Vásquez, L. L.

1952   Ganadería y pastoreo en Berrocil de Huebra (Salamanca). *Revista de Dialectología y Tradiciones Populares* 8:425–64, 563–95.

Cotter, J. E.

2003   *Troubled Harvest: Agronomy and Revolution in Mexico, 1880–2002.* Westport, CT: Praeger.

Cowan, R. G.

1956   *Ranchos of California: A List of Spanish Concessions, 1775–1822, and Mexican Grants, 1822–1846.* Fresno, CA: Academic Library Guild.

Cox, J. R., H. L. Morton, J. T. Labaume, and K. G. Renard.

1983   Reviving Arizona's Rangelands. *Journal of Soil and Water Conservation* 38:342–45.

Craib, R. B.

2004   *Cartographic Mexico: A History of State Fixations and Fugitive Landscapes.* Durham, NC: Duke University Press.

Crehan, K.

2002   *Gramsci, Culture and Anthropology.* Berkeley: University of California Press.

Crosby, A. W., Jr.

1972   *The Columbian Exchange: Biological and Cultural Consequences of 1492.* Westport, CT: Greenwood.

1986   *Ecological Imperialism: The Biological Expansion of Europe, 900–1900.* Cambridge: Cambridge University Press.

Curtin, C. G., N. F. Sayre, and B. D. Lane.

2002   Transformations of the Chihuahuan Borderlands: Grazing, Fragmentation, and Biodiversity Conservation in Desert Grasslands. *Environmental Science and Policy* 5:55–68.

Dacy, G. H.

1940   *Four Centuries of Florida Ranching.* St. Louis: Britt Print.

Dary, D.

1989   *Cowboy Culture: A Saga of Five Centuries.* Lawrence: University of Kansas Press.

Davies, S.

1996   *Adaptable Livelihoods: Coping with Food Insecurity in the Malian Sahel.* New York: St. Martin's Press.

De Certeau, M.

1984   *The Practice of Everyday Life.* Berkeley: University of California Press.

Deffontaines, P.
    1964   *Contribution a la géographie pastorale de L'Amérique Latine.* Rio de Janeiro: Publicações do Centro de Pesquisas de Geografia do Brasil.

De Janvry, A., G. Gordillo and E. Sadoulet.
    1997   *Mexico's Second Agrarian Reform: Household and Community Responses, 1990–1994.* San Diego: Center for U.S.–Mexican Studies. University of California.

Denevan, W. M.
    1976   *The Native Population of the Americas in 1492.* Madison: University of Wisconsin Press.
    1992   The Pristine Myth: The Landscape of the Americas in 1492. *Annals of the Association of American Geographers* 82 (3): 369–85.

Desmond, M. J., K. E. Young, B. C. Thompson, R. Valdez, and A. L. Terrazas.
    2005   Habitat Associations and Conservation of Grassland Birds in the Chihuahuan Desert Region: Two Case Studies in Chihuahua. In *Biodiversity, Ecosystems, and Conservation in Northern Mexico,* ed. J.L.E. Cartron, G. Ceballos, and R. S. Felger, pp. 439–51. New York: Oxford University Press.

Doolittle, W. E.
    1984   Agricultural Change as an Incremental Process. *Annals of the Association of American Geographers* 74:124–37.
    1987   Las Marismas to Pánuco to Texas: The Transfer of Open Range Cattle Ranching from Iberia through Northeastern Mexico. *Yearbook, Conference of Latin American Geographers* 13:3–11.
    1988   *Pre-Hispanic Occupance in the Valley of Sonora, Mexico: Archaeological Confirmation of Early Spanish Reports.* Anthropological Paper No. 48. Tucson: University of Arizona.
    2003   Channel Changes and Living Fencerows in Eastern Sonora, Mexico: Myopia in Traditional Resource Management? *Geografisker Annaler A* 85 (3–4): 247–61.

Dorner, P.
    1992   *Latin American Land Reforms in Theory and Practice.* Madison: University of Wisconsin Press.

Dunbar, G. S.
    1961   Colonial Carolina Cowpens. *Agricultural History* 35:125–30.

Dunbier, R.
    1968   *The Sonoran Desert: Its Geography, Economy and People.* Tucson: University of Arizona Press.

Durand, J.
    1983   *La ciudad invade al ejido.* Mexico City: Editorial Casa Chata.

Dusenberry, W. H.
    1963   *The Mexican Mesta: The Administration of Ranching in Colonial Mexico.* Urbana: University of Illinois Press.

Edberg, M. C.

2004   *El Narcotraficante: Narcocorridos and the Construction of a Cultural Persona on the U.S.–Mexican Border.* Austin: University of Texas Press.

Emerson, R. M., R. I. Frez, and L. L. Shaw.

1995   *Writing Ethnographic Fieldnotes.* Chicago: University of Chicago Press.

Escobar, A.

1995   *Encountering Development: The Making and Unmaking of the Third World.* Princeton, NJ: Princeton University Press.

Escobar Ohmstede, A., and T. Rojas Rabiela, eds.

2001   Estructuras y formas agrarias en Mexico. Del pasado y del presente. Mexico City: Registro Agrario Nacional y Centro de Investigaciones y Estudios Superiores en Antropología Social.

Evans, E. E.

1942   *Irish Heritage: The Landscape, The People and Their Works.* Dundalk, Ireland: Dundalgan Press.

1957   *Irish Folk Ways.* London: Routledge and Kegan Paul.

1973   *The Personality of Ireland: Habitat, Heritage and History.* Cambridge: Cambridge University Press.

Ewald, U.

1977   The Von Thunen Principle and Agriculatural Zonation in Colonial Mexico. *Journal of Historical Geography* 3:122–33.

FAO (Food and Agriculture Organization of the United Nations).

1993   *La agricultura en Sonora frente as los retos de la modernización, problemas y potencialidades.* Hermosillo: Gobierno del Estado de Sonora.

Fleischner, T.

1994   The Ecological Effects of Cattle Grazing in the Southwestern United States. *Conservation Biology* 8 (3): 639–44.

Flesch, A. D., and R. J. Steidl.

2006   Population Trends and Implications for Monitoring Cactus Ferruginous Pygmy Owls in Northern Mexico. *Journal of Wildlife Management* 70 (3): 867–71.

Fogerty, J. E.

2001   Oral History: A Guide to its Creation and Use. In *The Historical Ecology Handbook: A Restorationists's Guide to Reference Ecosystems,* ed. D. Egan and E. A. Howell, pp. 101–20. Washington, DC: Island Press.

Franklin, K. A., K. Lyons, P. L. Nagler, D. Lampkin, E. P. Glenn, F. Molina-Freaner, T. Markow, and A. R. Huete.

2006   Buffelgrass (*Pennisetum ciliare*) Land Conversion and Productivity in the Plains of Sonora, Mexico. *Biological Conservation* 127 (1): 62–71.

Freyfogle, E. T.

2003   *The Land We Share: Private Property and the Common Good.* Washington, DC: Island Press/Shearwater Books.

Garate, D.
1993   Sonora's Earliest Brand Book. *Pimeria Alta Historical Society Newsletter.* Material found in el Archivo de Hidalgo de Parral, 2017, no. 5, año 1718. Parral, Chihuahua, Mexico.

Gerhard, P.
1972   *A Guide to the Historical Geography of New Spain.* Cambridge: Cambridge University Press.
1982   *The North Frontier of New Spain.* Norman: University of Oklahoma Press.

Gibson, C.
1964   *The Aztecs under Spanish Rule: A History of the Indians of the Valley of Mexico, 1519–1810.* Stanford, CA: Stanford University Press.

Gilbert, D.
2005   Magicians: The Response of Middle-Class Mexican Households to Economic Crisis. *Journal of Latin American Anthropology* 10 (1): 126–50.

Gómez-Ibáñez, D.
1977   Energy, Economics, and the Decline of Transhumance. *Geographical Review* 67 (3): 284–98.

Gongora, M.
1966   Vagabondage et société pastorale en Amérique Latine. *Annales: Economies, Sociétés, Civilisations* 21: 159–77.

González-Montagut, R.
1999   Factors that Contributed to the Expansion of Cattle Ranching in Veracruz, Mexico. *Mexican Studies/Estudios Mexicanos* 15 (1): 101–30.

González-Sánchez, I.
1969   *Haciendas y ranchos de Tlaxcala en 1712.* Mexico City: Instituto Nacional de Antropología e Historia.

Griffith, J.
1995   *A Shared Space: Folklife in the Arizona-Sonora Borderlands.* Logan: Utah State University Press.

Grossman, L.
1984   *Peasants, Subsistence Ecology, and Development in the Highlands of Papua New Guinea.* Princeton, NJ: Princeton University Press.

Gudeman, S., and A. Rivera-Gutiérrez.
2002   Neither Duck Nor Rabbit: Sustainability, Political Economy, and the Dialectics of Economy. In *The Spaces of Neoliberalism: Land, Place and Family in Latin America,* ed. J. Chase, pp. 159–86. Bloomfield, CT: Kumarian Press.

Guttman, M.
1996   *The Meanings of Macho: Being a Man in Mexico City.* Berkeley: University of California Press.

Haenn, N.
2005   *Fields of Power, Forests of Discontent: Culture, Conservation and the State in Mexico.* Tucson: University of Arizona Press.

Haldane, A.R.B.

1952   *The Drove Roads of Scotland.* London: Thomas Nelson and Sons.

Hamilton, S.

2002   Neoliberalism, Gender, and Property Rights in Rural Mexico. *Latin American Research Review* 37 (1): 119–43.

Haraway, D.

1991   *Simians, Cyborgs and Women: The Reinvention of Nature.* New York: Routledge.

Hardin, G.

1968   The Tragedy of the Commons. *Science* 162:1243–48.

Harris, C.

1975   *A Mexican Family Empire: The Latifundio of the Sánchez Navarros, 1765–1867.* Austin: University of Texas Press.

Harris, D., ed.

1980   *Human Ecology in Savanna Environments.* New York: Academic Press.

Harris, R. C.

1977   The Simplification of Europe Overseas. *Annals of the Association of American Geographers* 67:469–83.

Hart, J. M.

2002   *Empire and Revolution: The Americans in Mexico since the Civil War.* Berkeley: University of California Press.

Hartz, L.

1964   *The Founding of New Societies.* New York: Harcourt Brace and World.

Harvey, D.

1981   The Spatial Fix: Hegel, Von Thünen, and Marx. *Antipode* 13 (2): 1–12.

1989   *The Condition of Postmodernity.* Oxford, UK: Blackwell.

2005   *A Brief History of Neoliberalism.* New York: Oxford University Press.

Harvey, N.

1998   *The Chiapas Rebellion: The Struggle for Land and Democracy.* Durham, NC: Duke University Press.

Hecht, S.

1985   Environment, Development and Politics: Capital Accumulation and the Livestock Sector in Eastern Amazonia. *World Development* 13: 663–84.

Henderson, D. A.

1964   *Agriculture and Livestock Raising in the Evolution of the Economy and Culture of the State of Baja California, Mexico.* Ann Arbor: University Microfilms International.

Hernández, L., ed.

2001   *Historia ambiental de la ganadería en México.* Xalapa, Mexico: Institut de Recherche pour le Développement y Instituto de Ecología, A.C.

Hewes, L.
  1935   Huepac: An Agricultural Village of Sonora, Mexico. *Economic Geography* 11:284–92.
  1973   *The Suitcase Farming Frontier: A Study in the Historical Geography of the Central Great Plains.* Lincoln: University of Nebraska Press.
Holden, R. H.
  1994   *Mexico and the Survey of Public Lands.* Dekalb: Northern Illinois University Press.
Holt, E. C.
  1985   Buffelgrass: A Brief History. In *Buffelgrass: Adaptation, Management and Forage Quality Symposium*, ed. E.C.A. Runge and J. L. Schuster, pp. 1–5. College Station, TX: Texas Agricultural Experiment Station MP–1575.
Hornbeck, D.
  1978   Land Tenure and Rancho Expansion in Alta California, 1784–1846. *Journal of Historical Geography* 4:371–90.
Ibarra, F. A., J. R. Cox, M. H. Martin, T. A. Crowl, D. F. Post, R. W. Miller, and A. Rasmussen.
  1995a   Relationships between Buffelgrass Survival, Organic Carbon, and Soil Color in Mexico. *Soil Science Society of America Journal* 59:1120–25.
Ibarra, F. A., J. R. Cox, M. H. Martin-R. T. A. Crowl, and C. A. Call.
  1995b   Predicting Buffelgrass Survival across a Geographical and Environmental Gradient. *Journal of Range Management* 48:53–9.
Iber, Jorge.
  2000   Vaqueros in the Western Cattle Industry. In *The Cowboy Way: An Exploration of History and Culture*, ed. P. H. Carlson, pp. 21–32. Lubbock, TX: Texas Tech University Press.
INEGI.
  1986   III Censo y Agenda Estadística de Sonora. Aguascalientes, Mexico: INEGI.
INEGI.
  1994a   VII Censo Agrícola-Ganadero, Resultado Definitivos. 2 vols. Aguascalientes, Mexico: INEGI.
INEGI.
  1994b   Panorama Agropecuario, Sonora. VII Censo Agropecuario, 1991. Aguascalientes, Mexico: INEGI.
INEGI.
  1999   Núcleos Agrario, Tabulados Básicos por Municipio, PROCEDE, 1992–1999, Sonora. Aguascalientes, Mexico: INEGI.
Ingold, T.
  1980   *Hunters, Pastoralists and Ranchers: Reindeer Economies and Their Transformations.* Cambridge Studies in Social Anthropology No. 28. Cambridge: Cambridge University Press.

Irwin, R. M.

2003   *Mexican Masculinities.* Minneapolis: University of Minnesota Press.

Iverson, P.

1994   *When Indians Became Cowboys: Native Peoples and Cattle Ranching in the American West.* Norman: University of Oklahoma Press.

Jackson, J.

1986   *Los Mesteños: Spanish Ranching in Texas, 1721–1821.* College Station: Texas A&M University Press.

Jackson, R. H.

1997   *Liberals, the Church, and Indian Peasants: Corporate Lands and the Challenge of Reform in Nineteenth-Century Spanish America.* Albuquerque: University of New Mexico Press.

Jarosz, L.

2004   Political Ecology as Ethical Practice. *Political Geography* 23 (7): 917–27.

Jessen, O.

1952   Cosacos, Cowboys, Gauchos, Boers y otros pueblos a caballos propios de las estepas. *Runa* 5 (1–2): 171–86.

Johnson, D. L., and L. A. Lewis.

1995   *Land Degradation.* Cambridge, MA: Blackwell.

Jones, G., and P. M. Ward.

1998   Privatizing the Commons: Reforming the Ejido and Urban Development in Mexico. *International Journal of Urban and Regional Research* 22 (1): 76–93.

Jones, O. L.

1979   *Los Paisanos: Spanish Settlers on the Northern Frontier of New Spain.* Norman: University of Oklahoma Press.

Jordan, T. J.

1981   *Trails to Texas: Southern Roots of Western Cattle Ranching.* Lincoln: University of Nebraska Press.

1989   An Iberian Lowland/Highland Model for Latin American Cattle Ranching. *Journal of Historical Geography* 15 (2): 111–25.

1993   *North American Cattle Ranching Frontiers: Origins, Diffusion and Differentiation.* Albuquerque: University of New Mexico Press.

Kay, C.

2002   Agrarian Reform and the Neoliberal Counter-Reform in Latin America. In *The Spaces of Neoliberalism: Land, Place and Family in Latin America,* ed. J. Chase, pp. 25–52. Bloomfield, CT: Kumarian Press.

Kirch, P. V.

1994   *The Wet and the Dry.* Chicago: University of Chicago Press.

Klein, J.

1920   *The Mesta: A Study in Spanish Economic History, 1273–1836.* Cambridge, MA: Harvard University Press.

Knapp, G.

1991 *Andean Ecology: Adaptive Dynamics in Ecuador.* Boulder, CO: Westview Press.

Knight, R. L., W. C. Gilbert, and E. Marston, eds.

2002 *Ranching West of the 100th Meridian: Culture, Ecology, and Economics.* Washington, DC: Island Press.

Konrad, H. W.

1980 *A Jesuit Hacienda in Colonial Mexico: Santa Lucia, 1576–1767.* Stanford, CA: Stanford University Press.

Kourí, E. H.

2002 Interpreting the Expropriation of Indian Pueblo Lands in Porfirian Mexico: The Unexamined Legacies of Andrés Molina Enríquez. *Hispanic American Historical Review* 82 (1): 69–117.

2004 *A Pueblo Divided: Business, Property and Community in Papantla, Mexico.* Palo Alto, CA: Stanford University Press.

Kull, C. A.

2004 *Isle of Fire.* Chicago: Chicago University Press.

Lehmann, V. W.

1969 *Forgotten Legions: Sheep in the Rio Grande Plain in Texas.* El Paso, TX: Texas Western Press, University of Texas at El Paso.

Lemus García, Raúl.

1987 *Derecho Agrario Mexicano.* 6th ed. Mexico City: Editorial Porrua.

Léonard, E.

1997 *De Vaches et d'Hirondelles.* Paris: Office de la Recherche Scientifique et Technique d'Outre-Mer.

2003 Titularización agraria y apropiación de nuevos espacios económicos por los actores rurales: El PROCEDE en los Tuxtlas, estado de Veracruz. In *Políticas y regulaciones agrarias: Dinámicas de poder y juegos de actores en torno a la tenencia de la tierra,* ed. E. Leonard, A. Quesnel, and E. Velázquez, pp. 297–327. Mexico City: Centro de Investigaciones y Estudios Superiores en Antropología Social and Institut de Recherche pour le Développement.

Lewis, M.

1992 *Wagering the Land: Ritual, Capital, and Environmental Degradation in the Cordillera of Northern Luzon, 1900–1986.* Berkeley: University of California Press.

Liverman, D.

1990 Drought Impacts in Mexico: Climate, Agriculture, Technology, and Land Tenure in Sonora and Puebla. *Annals of the Association of American Geographers* 80 (1): 49–72.

1999 Vulnerability and Adaptation in Mexico. *Natural Resources Journal* 39:99–115.

Lockhart, J.
1969   Encomienda and Hacienda: The Evolution of the Great Estate in the Spanish Indies. *Hispanic American Historical Review* 49:411–29.
Low, S. M.
2000   *On the Plaza: The Politics of Public Space and Culture.* Austin: University of Texas Press.
Machado, M. A.
1981   *The North Mexican Cattle Industry, 1910–1975: Ideology, Conflict and Change.* College Station: Texas A&M University Press.
MacLeod, D.
2004   *Downsizing the State: Privatization and the Limits of Neoliberal Reform in Mexico.* University Park: Pennsylvania State University Press.
Manzanilla-Schaffer, V.
2004   *El drama de la tierra en México del siglo XVI al siglo XXI.* Mexico City: Secretaría de Reforma Agraria.
Marrero, L.
1972–   *Cuba: Economía y sociedad.* 14 vols. Repr., Río Pedras, Puerto Rico: Edi-
1988   torial San Juan and Editorial Playor, 1992.
Marston, S. A.
2000   The Social Construction of Scale. *Progress in Human Geography* 24 (2): 219–42.
Martín, R. M.
1997   Manejo de pastizales. In *20 Años de investigación pecuaria en el CIPES, INIFAP-SARH.* Hermosillo, Mexico: Gobierno del Estado y Unión Ganadera Regional de Sonora.
Marty, P.
1921   *Etudes sur l'Islam et les Tribus Maures, les Brakna.* Paris: Editions Ernest Leroux.
Massey, D.
1994   Space, Place, and Gender. Minneapolis: University of Minnesota Press.
Matesanz, J.
1964   Introducción de la ganadería en Nueva España, 1521–1535. *Historia Mexicana* 14:533–66.
Mattison, R. H.
1946   Early Spanish and Mexican Settlements in Arizona. *New Mexico Historical Review* 21 (4): 273–327.
McCarthy, J.
2005   First World Political Ecology: Directions and Challenges. *Environment and Planning A* 37 (6): 953–58.
McNamee, G.
1996   The Grass That Ate Sonora. *Tucson Weekly,* April 18–24, 1996.

McWhitney, G., and F. McDonald.

    1985   Celtic Origins of Southern Herding Practices. *Journal of Southern History* 51 (2): 165–82.

Meigs, P.

    1935   *The Dominican Mission Frontier of Lower California (Mexico).* Publications in Geography No. 7. Berkeley: University of California.

Melville, E.G.K.

    1990   Environmental and Social Change in the Valle del Mesquital, Mexico, 1521–1600. *Comparative Studies in Society and History* 32:24–53.

    1994   *A Plague of Sheep.* Toronto: York University Press.

Merrill, K. R.

    2002   *Public Lands and Political Meaning: Ranchers, the Government, and the Property between Them.* Berkeley: University of California Press.

Montaño Bermúdez, R.

    1991   Apuntes para una historia de la ganadería en Alamos, Sonora. In *Potreros, Vegas y Mahuechis: Sociedad y ganadería en la Sierra Sonorense,* ed. E. Camou-Healy, pp. 239–86. Hermosillo: Gobierno del Estado de Sonora.

Moore, D. S.

    2005   *Suffering for Territory: Race, Place, and Power in Zimbabwe.* Durham, NC: Duke University Press.

Mora, J.

    1949   *Californios: The Saga of the Hard-Riding Vaqueros, America's First Cowboys.* Garden City, NY: Doubleday.

Morett Sánchez, J. C.

    2003   *Reforma agraria: Del latifundio al neoliberalismo.* Mexico City: Universidad Autónoma Chapingo.

Mörner, M.

    1973   The Spanish American Hacienda: A Survey of Recent Research and Debate. *Hispanic American Historical Review* 53:183–216.

Morrisey, R. J.

    1950   The Early Range Cattle Industry in Arizona. *Agricultural History* 24: 151–56.

    1951   The Northward Expansion of Cattle Ranching in New Spain. *Agricultural History* 25:115–21.

Moynihan, R. B., S. Armitage, and C. F. Dichamp, eds.

    1990   *So Much to Be Done: Women Settlers on the Mining and Ranching Frontier.* Lincoln, NE: University of Nebraska Press.

Murphy, M. E.

    1986   *Irrigation in the Bajio Region of Colonial Mexico.* Boulder, CO: Westview Press.

Myres, S.
1969   *The Ranch in Spanish Texas, 1691–1800*. El Paso, TX: Western Texas Press, University of Texas at El Paso.

Nabhan, G.
1985   *Gathering the Desert*. Tucson: University of Arizona Press.

Nadal, D. M., and H. W. Alberts.
1947   The Early History of Livestock and Pastures in Puerto Rico. *Agricultural History* 21:61–64.

Nash, M. S., E. Jackson, and W. G. Whitford.
2003   Soil Microtopography on Grazing Gradients in Chihuahuan Desert Grasslands. *Journal of Arid Environments* 55:181–192.

Nentvig, J.
1980   *Rudo Ensayo: A Description of Sonora and Arizona in 1764*. Tucson: University of Arizona Press.

Netting, R. McC.
1993   *Smallholders, Householders: Farm Families and the Ecology of Intensive, Sustainable Agriculture*. Stanford, CA: Stanford University Press.

Nostrand, R. L.
1966   The Santa Ynez Valley: Hinterland of Coastal California. *Historical Society of Southern California Quarterly* 48:37–56.

Nuijten, M.
2005   Power in Practice: A Force Field Approach to Natural Resource Management. *Journal of Transdisciplinary Environmental Studies* 4 (2): 1–14.

Olive, R.F.A.
1952–   Pastos y forrajes: Una vista panorámica de su historia en Cuba. *Revista de*
1953   *Agricultura* (Cuba) 36 (1): 89–108.

Olwig, K. R.
1996   Recovering the Substantive Nature of Landscape. *Annals of the Association of American Geographers* 86 (4): 630–53.
2002   *Landscape, Nature and the Body Politic: From Britain's Renaissance to America's New World*. Madison: University of Wisconsin Press.

Orozco, W. L.
1895   Legislación y jurisprudencia sobre terrenos baldíos. Vol. 1. Mexico City: Imprenta de El Tiempo.

Otero, G.
1999   *Farewell to the Peasantry?* Boulder, CO: Westview Press.

Otto, J. S.
1986   The Origins of Cattle Ranching in South Carolina, 1670–1715. *South Carolina Historical Magazine* 87:117–24.
1987   Livestock Raising in Early South Carolina, 1670–1700: Prelude to the Rice Plantation Economy. *Agricultural History* 61:13–24.

Otto, J. S. and N. E. Anderson.

1988   The Origins of Southern Cattle Grazing: A Problem in West Indian History. *Journal of Caribbean History* 21:138–53.

Parry, M. L., and T. R. Slater, eds.

1980   *The Making of the Scottish Countryside.* London: Taylor and Francis.

Parsons, J. J.

1972   Spread of African Pasture Grasses to the American Tropics. *Journal of Range Management* 25 (1): 12–17.

1977   Geography as Exploration and Discovery. *Annals of the Association of American Geographers* 67 (1): 1–16.

Peet, R., and M. Watts.

2004   *Liberation Ecologies: Environment, Development, Social Movements.* 2nd ed. London: Routledge.

Pennington, C. W.

1980   *The Pima Bajo of Central Sonora, Mexico.* Salt Lake City: University of Utah Press.

Pérez Castañeda, J. C.

2002   *El nuevo sistema de propiedad agraria en México.* Mexico City: Palabra en Vuelo.

Pérez López, E. P.

1993   *Ganadería y campesinado en Sonora, los poquiteros de la Sierra Norte.* Mexico City: Consejo Nacional para la Cultura y las Artes.

Perramond, E. P.

1996–1997, 2002, 2003, 2009. Field notes, Sonora, MX.

1996–1997. Interviews, Sonora, MX.

1999   *Desert Meadows: The Cultural, Political, and Ecological Dynamics of Private Cattle Ranching in Sonora, Mexico.* Ann Arbor: University Microfilms International.

2000   A Preliminary Analysis of Soil Erosion and Buffelgrass in Sonora, Mexico. *Yearbook, Conference of Latin Americanist Geographers* 26:131–138.

2001   Oral History and Partial Truths in Mexico. *Geographical Review* 91 (1–2): 151–57.

2002   Grazing the Periphery: The Political Ecology of Private Ranchers in Sonora, Mexico. In *Cultural and Physical Expositions: Geographic Studies in the Southern United States and Latin America*, ed. P. H. Hudson and M. K. Steinberg, pp. 51–57. Baton Rouge, LA: Geoscience Publications.

2005   The Politics of Ecology: Local Knowledge and Wild Chili Collection. *Journal of Latin American Geography* 4 (1): 59–75.

2007   Tactics and Strategies in Political Ecology Research. *Area* 39 (4): 499–507.

2008   The Rise, Fall, and Reconfiguration of the Mexican Ejido. *Geographical Review* 98 (3): 356–371.

Pfefferkorn, I.
    1989   *Sonora: A Description of the Province.* Tucson: University of Arizona Press.
Phillips, J. D.
    1999   *Earth Surface Systems: Complexity, Order and Scale.* Walden, MA: Blackwell.
Polanyi, K.
    1957   *The Great Transformation: The Political and Economic Origins of Our*
    [1944]   *Time.* Boston: Beacon Press.
Poole, B.
    2007   Help Wanted in War against Buffelgrass. *Tucson Citizen,* November 26, 2007.
Prem, H. J.
    1992   Spanish Colonization and Indian Property in Central Mexico, 1521–1620. *Annals of the Association of American Geographers* 82 (3): 444–59.
Purcell, M., and J. C. Brown.
    2005   Against the Local Trap: Scale and the Study of Environment and Development. *Progress in Development Studies* 5 (4): 279–97.
Radding, C.
    1995   *Entre el desierto y la sierra. Las naciones O'odham y Teguima de Sonora, 1530–1840.* Mexico City: Centro de Investigaciones y Estudios Superiores en Antropología Social.
    1997   *Wandering Peoples: Colonialism, Ethnic Spaces, and Ecological Frontiers in Northwestern Mexico, 1700–1850.* Durham, NC: Duke University Press.
    2005   *Landscapes of Power and Identity: Comparative Histories in the Sonoran Desert and the Forests of Amazonia from Colony to Republic.* Durham, NC: Duke University Press.
Randall, L., ed.
    1996   *Reforming Mexico's Agrarian Reform.* Armonk, NY: M. E. Sharpe.
Rap, E.
    2006   The Success of a Policy Model: Irrigation Management Transfer in Mexico. *Journal of Development Studies* 42 (8): 1301–24.
Reed, J. L.
    2004   The Corn King of Mexico in the United States: A South–North Technology Transfer. *Agricultural History* 78 (2): 155–65.
Reff, D. T.
    1991   *Disease, Depopulation, and Culture Change in Northwestern New Spain, 1518–1764.* Salt Lake City: University of Utah Press.
Robbins, P.
    1998   Authority and Environment: Institutional Landscapes in Rajasthan, India. *Annals of the Association of American Geographers* 88 (3): 410–35.
    2004   *Political Ecology: A Critical Introduction.* Oxford, UK: Blackwell.

Robinson, P. S.

1984   *The Plantation of Ulster: British Settlement in an Irish Landscape, 1600–1670.* Dublin: Gill and Macmillan.

Robledo Rincón, E.

2000   El sector agrario en México. In *Reforma agraria y desarrollo rural en el siglo XXI,* ed. E. Robledo Rincon, pp. 463–94. Mexico City: Procuraduría Agraria.

Rojas, A. R.

1964   *The Vaquero.* Charlotte, NC: McNally; Santa Barbara, CA: Loftin.

Romero, S. J.

1995   *De las misiones a los ranchos y haciendas. La privatización de la tenencia de la tierra en Sonora 1740–1860.* Hermosillo: Gobierno del Estado de Sonora.

Rouse, J. E.

1977   *The Criollo: Spanish Cattle in the Americas.* Norman: University of Oklahoma Press.

Ruiz, R. E.

1988   *The People of Sonora and Yankee Capitalists.* Tucson: University of Arizona Press.

Russell, S. A.

1993   *Kill the Cowboy: A Battle of Mythology in the New West.* Reading, MA: Addison-Wesley.

Rzedowski, J.

1994   *Vegetación de México.* Mexico City: Grupo Noriega Editores.

Salzman, P. C.

2004   *Pastoralists: Equality, Hierarchy and the State.* Boulder, CO: Westview Press.

Sanderson, S. E.

1981   *Agrarian Populism and the Mexican State: The Struggle for Land in Sonora.* Berkeley: University of California Press.

1986   *The Transformation of Mexican Agriculture: International Structures and the Politics of Rural Change.* Princeton, NJ: Princeton University Press.

Sauer, C. O.

1966   *The Early Spanish Main.* Berkeley: University of California Press.

Savory, A.

1988   *Holistic Resource Management.* Washington, DC: Island Press.

2002   Re-Creating the West . . . One Decision at a Time. In *Ranching West of the 100th Meridian: Culture, Ecology, and Economics,* ed. R. L. Knight, W. C. Gilbert, and E. Marston, pp. 155–70. Washington, DC: Island Press.

Sayre, N. F.

1999   The Cattle Boom in Southern Arizona: Towards a Critical Political Ecology. *Journal of the Southwest* 41 (2): 239–71.

2001   *The New Ranch Handbook*. Santa Fe, NM: Quivira Coalition.

2002   *Ranching, Endangered Species, and Urbanization in the Southwest: Species of Capital*. Tucson: University of Arizona Press.

2004   The Need for Qualitative Research to Understand Ranch Management. *Journal of Range Management* 57:668–74.

2005a   Ecological and Geographical Scale: Parallels and Potentials for Integration. *Progress in Human Geography* 29 (3): 276–90.

2005b   *Working Wilderness: The Malpai Borderlands Group and the Future of the Western Range*. Tucson: Rio Nuevo Press.

2008   The Genesis, History, and Limits of Carrying Capacity. *Annals of the Association of American Geographers* 98 (1): 120–34.

Schein, R. H.

1997   The Place of Landscape: A Conceptual Framework for Interpreting an American Scene. *Annals of the Association of American Geographers* 87 (4): 660–80.

Secretaria de Economía, Gobierno del Estado de Sonora. Figures on population consulted March 23, 2008 http://www.sonora.gob.mx/portal/Runscript.asp?p=ASP\pg141.asp

Scott, J. C.

1985   *Weapons of the Weak: Everyday Forms of Peasant Resistance*. New Haven, CT: Yale University Press.

Serrano, Jesús Gómez.

2000   *Haciendas y ranchos de Aguascalientes*. Aguascalientes, Mexico: Universidad Autónoma de Aguascalientes.

Serrera Contreras, R. M.

1977   *Guadalajara ganadera: Estudio regional novohispano, 1760–1805*. Sevilla: Escuela de Estudios Hispano-Americanos.

Sharp, P. F.

1955   Three Frontiers: Some Comparative Studies of Canadian, American, and Australian Settlement. *Pacific Historical Review* 24 (4): 369–77.

Sheridan, T. E.

1988   *Where the Dove Calls: The Political Ecology of a Peasant Corporate Community in Northwestern Mexico*. Tucson: University of Arizona Press.

1992   The Limits of Power: The Political Ecology of the Spanish Empire in the Greater Southwest. *Antiquity* 66:153–71.

2001   Cows, Condos and Contested Communities: The Political Ecology of Ranching in the Arizona-Sonora Borderlands. *Human Organization* 60 (2): 141–52.

2007   Embattled Ranchers, Endangered Species, and Urban Sprawl: The Political Ecology of the New American West. *Annual Review of Anthropology* 36:121–38.

Shreve, F.

1937   Lowland Vegetation in Sinaloa. *Bulletin of the Torrey Botanical Club* 64:605–13.

Simpson, L. B.

1952   *Exploitation of Land in Central Mexico.* Berkeley: University of California Press.

1963   Introduction. In *Land and Society in Colonial Mexico by Chevalier.* Berkeley:
[1952]   University of California Press.

1971   *Many Mexicos.* 4th ed. Berkeley: University of California Press.

Slatta, R. W.

1990   *Cowboys of the Americas.* New Haven, CT: Yale University Press.

Sluyter, A.

1996   The Ecological Origins and Consequences in Sixteenth-Century New Spain. *Geographical Review* 86:161–77.

1997   Landscape Change and Livestock in Sixteenth-Century New Spain: The Archival Data Base. *Yearbook, Conference of Latin Americanist Geographers* 23:27–39.

1998   From Archive to Map to Pastoral Landscape: A Spatial Perspective on the Livestock Ecology of Sixteenth-Century New Spain. *Environmental History* 3 (4): 508–28.

2002   *Colonialism and Landscape: Postcolonial Theory and Applications.* Lanham, MD: Rowman and Littlefield.

Snyder, R.

1999   After Neoliberalism: The Politics of Reregulation in Mexico. *World Politics* 51 (2): 173–204.

2001   *Politics after Neoliberalism: Reregulation in Mexico.* Cambridge: Cambridge University Press.

Starrs, P. F.

1989   The Cultural Landscape of California Pastoralism: 200 Years of Changes. In *Landscape Ecology: Study of Mediterranean Grazed Ecosystems,* ed. W. J. Clawson, pp. 49–61. Proceedings of Man and the Biosphere Symposium, 16th International Grasslands Conference, Nice, France.

1998   *Let The Cowboy Ride: Cattle Ranching in the American West.* Baltimore: Johns Hopkins Press.

2002   Ranching: An Old Way of Life in the New West. In *Ranching West of the 100th Meridian: Culture, Ecology, and Economics,* ed. R. L. Knight, W. C. Gilbert, and E. Marston, pp. 2–23. Washington, DC: Island Press.

Steffen, J. O.

1980   *Comparative Frontiers: A Proposal for Studying the American West.* Norman: University of Oklahoma Press.

Stern, S. J.
  1995   *The Secret History of Gender: Women, Men, and Power in Late Colonial Mexico*. Chapel Hill: University of North Carolina Press.

Stevens, S. F.
  1993   *Claiming the High Ground: Sherpas, Subsistence, and Environmental Change in the Highest Himalaya*. Berkeley: University of California Press.

Stewart, M. A.
  1991   Whether Wast, Deodand, or Stray: Cattle, Culture and the Environment in Early Georgia. *Agricultural History* 65 (3): 1–28.

Stoleson, S. H., R. S. Felger, G. Ceballos, C. Raish, M. F. Wilson, and A. Búrquez.
  2005   Recent History of Natural Resource Use and Population Growth in Northern Mexico. In *Biodiversity, Ecosystems, and Conservation in Northern Mexico*, ed. J.L.E. Cartron, G. Ceballos, and R. S. Felger, pp. 52–86. New York: Oxford University Press.

Sullivan, S.
  1996   Towards a Non-Equilibrium Ecology: Perspectives from an Arid Land. *Journal of Biogeography* 23 (1): 1–5.

Taylor, M. J.
  2006   Biomass in the Borderlands: Charcoal and Firewood Production in Sonoran Ejidos. *Journal of the Southwest* 48 (1): 63–90.

Taylor, P. J.
  2005   *Unruly Complexity: Ecology, Interpretation, Engagement*. Chicago: University of Chicago Press.

Teja, Jesús F. de la.
  1995   *San Antonio de Bexar: A Community on New Spain's Northern Frontier*. Albuquerque: University of New Mexico Press.

Tellman, B., ed.
  2002   *Invasive Exotic Species in the Sonoran Desert Region*. Tucson: University of Arizona Press.

Thiesenhusen, W. C.
  1995   *Broken Promises: Agrarian Reform and the Latin American Campesino*. Boulder, CO: Westview Press.

Toledo, V.
  1995   La ley agraria: Un obstáculo para la paz y el desarrollo sustentable. *La Jornada del Campo* 33 (February 28): 1–2.
  1996   The Ecological Consequences of the 1992 Agrarian Law in Mexico. In *Reforming Mexico's Agrarian Reform*, ed. L. Randall, pp. 247–60. Armonk: M. E. Sharpe.

Trens, B. M.
  1992   *Historia de Veracruz*. Veracruz: Secretaría de Educación y Cultura, Gobierno del Estado de Veracruz.

Trow-Smith, R.

1959   *A History of British Livestock Husbandry, 1700–1900.* London: Routledge.

Truett, S.

2006   *Fugitive Landscapes: The Forgotten History of the U.S.–Mexico Border-lands.* New Haven, CT: Yale University Press.

Turner, B. L., II.

1997   Spirals, Bridges and Tunnels: Engaging Human-Environment Perspectives in Geography. *Ecumene* 4 (2): 196–217.

Turner, M. D.

2004   Political Ecology and the Moral Dimensions of "Resource Conflicts": The Case of Farmer-Herder Conflicts in the Sahel. *Political Geography* 23 (7): 863–89.

UGRC.

2007   Unión Ganadera Regional de Chihuahua, accessed January 8, 2008. http://www.ugrch.org/exportacion

Vansina, J.

1984   *Oral Tradition as History.* Madison: University of Wisconsin Press.

VanWey, L. K.

2005   Land Ownership as a Determinant of International and Internal Migration in Mexico and Internal Migration in Thailand. *International Migration Review* 39 (1): 141–72.

Van Young, E.

1981   *Hacienda and Market in Eighteenth-Century Mexico: The Rural Economy of the Guadalajara Region, 1675–1820.* Berkeley: University of California Press.

1983   Mexican Rural History since Chevalier: The Historiography of the Colonial Hacienda. *Latin American Research Review* 18 (3): 5–61.

Vásquez-León, M., and D. Liverman.

2004   The Political Ecology of Land-Use Change: Affluent Ranchers and Destitute Farmers in the Mexican Municipio of Alamos. *Human Organization* 63 (1): 21–33.

Vásquez-León, M., C. Thor West, and T. J. Finan.

2003   A Comparative Assessment of Climate Vulnerability: Agriculture and Ranching on Both Sides of the US–Mexico Border. *Global Environmental Change* 13:159–73.

Vassberg, D. E.

1984   *Land and Society in Golden Age Castile.* New York: Cambridge University Press.

Vayda, A., and B. Walters.

1999   Against Political Ecology. *Human Ecology* 27 (1): 167–79.

Vázquez-Castillo, M. T.

2004   *Land Privatization in Mexico: Urbanization, Formation of Regions, and Globalization in Ejidos.* New York: Routledge.

Velasco, J. F.

1985 [1860–1865] *Noticias estadísticas del Estado de Sonora, 1850.* Hermosillo: Gobernio del Estado de Sonora. (Orig. pub. by the Sociedad Mexicana de Geografía y Estadística, 1860–1865)

Wagoner, J. J.

1952 *History of the Cattle Industry in Southern Arizona, 1540–1940.* Social Science Bulletin No. 20. Tucson: University of Arizona.

Wainwright, J.

2005 The Geographies of Political Ecology: After Edward Said. *Environment and Planning A* 37:1033–43.

Walker, P.

2006 Political Ecology: Where Is the Policy? *Progress in Human Geography* 30 (3): 382–95.

2007 Political Ecology: Where is the Politics? *Progress in Human Geography* 31 (3): 363–69.

Walker, P., and L. Fortmann.

2003 Whose Landscape? A Political Ecology of the "Exurban" Sierra. *Cultural Geographies* 10 (4): 469–91.

Watts, D.

1987 *The West Indies: Patterns of Development, Culture and Environmental Change since 1492.* Cambridge: Cambridge University Press.

Watts, M.

1983 *Silent Violence: Food, Famine and Peasantry in Northern Nigeria.* Berkeley: University of California Press.

Wescoat, J. L., Jr.

1987 The "Practical Range of Choice" in Water Resources Geography. *Progress in Human Geography* 11 (1): 41–59.

West, R. C.

1949 *The Mining Community in Northern New Spain: The Parral Mining District.* Berkeley: University of California Press.

1993 *Sonora: Its Geographical Personality.* Austin: University of Texas Press.

Westoby, M., B. Walker, and I. Noy-Meir.

1989 Opportunistic Management for Rangelands Not at Equilibrium. *Journal of Range Management* 42:266–74.

Whatmore, S.

2002 *Hybrid Geographies: Natures, Cultures, Spaces.* London: Sage.

White, C.

2006 Mugido: Rethinking the Federal Commons. *The Quivira Coalition* 7 (4): 1, 20–27.

Whiteford, S., F. A. Bernal, H. Díaz-Cisneros, and E. Valtierra-Pacheco.

1998 Arid Land Ejidos: Bound by the Past, Marginalized by the Future. In *The Transformation of Rural Mexico: Reforming the Ejido Sector,* ed. W. A.

Cornelius and D. Myrhe, pp. 381–99. San Diego: Center for U.S.–Mexican Studies. University of California.

Wilder, M., and P. R. Lankao.

2006   Paradoxes of Decentralization: Water Reform and Social Implications in Mexico. *World Development* 34 (11): 1977–95.

Wilder, M., and S. Whiteford.

2006   Flowing Uphill toward Money: Groundwater Management and Ejidal Producers in Mexico's Free Trade Environment. In *Changing Structure of Mexico: Political Social and Economic Prospects*, ed. L. Randall, pp. 341–58. New York: M. E. Sharpe.

Wilken, G.

1987   *Good Farmers: Traditional Agricultural Resource Management in Mexico and Central America*. Berkeley: University of California Press.

Wilkinson, C. F.

1992   *Crossing the Next Meridian: Land, Water, and the Future of the West*. Washington, DC: Island Press.

Williams, M.

1994   The Relations of Environmental History and Historical Geography. *Journal of Historical Geography* 20 (1): 3–21.

Willis, K.

2000   No es fácil, pero es posible: The Maintenance of Middle-Class Women-Headed Households in Mexico. *European Review of Latin American and Caribbean Studies* 69:29–45.

Wolf, E.

1972   Ownership and Political Ecology. *Anthropological Quarterly* 45:201–5.

1982   *Europe and the People without History*. Berkeley: University of California Press.

1999   *Envisioning Power*. Berkeley: University of California Press.

Wuerthner, G., and M. Matteson, eds.

2002   *Welfare Ranching: The Subsidized Destruction of the American West*. Washington, DC: Island Press.

Yapa, L.

1996   Innovation Diffusion and Paradigms of Development. In *Concepts in Human Geography*, ed. C. Earle, K. Mathewson, and M. S. Kenzer, pp. 231–70. Lanham, MD: Rowman and Littlefield.

Yetman, D.

1996   *Sonora: An Intimate Geography*. Albuquerque: University of New Mexico Press.

Yetman, D., and A. Búrquez.

1994   Buffelgrass—Sonoran Desert Nightmare. *Arizona Riparian Council Newsletter* 7 (3): 1, 8–9.

1998   Twenty-Seven: A Case Study in Ejido Privatization in Mexico. *Journal of Anthropological Research* 54 (1): 73–95.

Yetman, D., and T. R. Van Devender.

2002   *Mayo Ethnobotany: Land, History and Traditional Knowledge in Northwest Mexico.* Berkeley: University of California Press.

Zimmerer, K.

2000   The Reworking of Conservation Geographies: Nonequilibrium Landscapes and Nature-Society Hybrids. *Annals of the Association of American Geographers* 90 (2): 356–69.

2006   Cultural Ecology: At the Interface with Political Ecology; The New Geographies of Environmental Conservation and Globalization. *Progress in Human Geography* 30 (1): 63–78.

Zimmerer, K., and T. J. Bassett, eds.

2003   *Political Ecology: An Integrative Approach to Geography and Environment-Development Studies.* New York: Guilford Press.

Index

About the Author

Eric Perramond is a geographer and an associate professor of Southwest Studies and Environmental Science at the Colorado College, in Colorado Springs. He previously taught at Stetson University (DeLand, Florida) and during his days as a graduate student at the University of Texas at Austin where he earned his doctorate. He has published numerous journal articles and book chapters on a range of topics including wild chilies, Native American agricultural history, and the impacts of the illicit drug trade in the Southwest. Although strongly motivated by his Southwestern interests, he also pursues comparative research on matters of environmental governance across international borders, including protected areas management in the Pyrenees. His current research projects in Colorado and New Mexico focus on ranch livelihood struggles in light of military expansion and water adjudication efforts, respectively. This is his first book.